THE EDUCATION OF AFRICAN CANADIAN CHILDREN

The Education of African Canadian Children

Critical Perspectives

Edited by
AWAD IBRAHIM AND ALI A. ABDI

McGill-Queen's University Press
Montreal & Kingston • London • Chicago

© McGill-Queen's University Press 2016

ISBN 978-0-7735-4807-7 (cloth)
ISBN 978-0-7735-4808-4 (paper)
ISBN 978-0-7735-4845-9 (ePDF)
ISBN 978-0-7735-4846-6 (ePUB)

Legal deposit third quarter 2016
Bibliothèque nationale du Québec

Printed in Canada on acid-free paper that is 100% ancient forest free (100% post-consumer recycled), processed chlorine free

This book has been published with the help of a grant from the Canadian Federation for the Humanities and Social Sciences, through the Awards to Scholarly Publications Program, using funds provided by the Social Sciences and Humanities Research Council of Canada.

McGill-Queen's University Press acknowledges the support of the Canada Council for the Arts for our publishing program. We also acknowledge the financial support of the Government of Canada through the Canada Book Fund for our publishing activities.

Library and Archives Canada Cataloguing in Publication

The education of African Canadian children : critical perspectives / edited by Awad Ibrahim and Ali A. Abdi.

Includes bibliographical references and index.
Issued in print and electronic formats.
ISBN 978-0-7735-4807-7 (hardback). – ISBN 978-0-7735-4808-4 (paperback). – ISBN 978-0-7735-4845-9 (pdf). – ISBN 978-0-7735-4846-6 (epub)

1. Black Canadian children – Education. 2. Black Canadians – Education. 3. Education – Social aspects – Canada. 4. Black Canadians – Social conditions. I. Ibrahim, Awad, editor II. Abdi, Ali A., 1955–, editor

LC2804.E482 2016   371.829'96071   C2016-903830-0
C2016-903831-9

This book was set by True to Type in 10.5/13 Sabon

*We dedicate this book to all black people in Canada
and to their struggle for education.
Your spirit of hope will guide us forever.*

Contents

Figures

Acknowledgments

This book came about as a labour of love. One anonymous reviewer who fully grasped the intention of the book is worth quoting at length: "A text of this scope is not currently available to researchers. The book focuses on youth and children who are members of the black population in Canada. Specifically, its significance is that it fills a gap in the research literature in Canada and as such has the potential to become a primer book that is sought after and read by scholars, graduate and undergraduate students and community members. Although blacks are the focus of many studies and books in the US, comparable considerations are practically non-existent in Canada." In this spirit, we would like to thank the reviewers for expressing the essence of this book. Their feedback was timely and extremely useful. We would especially like to thank James MacNevin and Ryan Van Huijstee from McGill-Queen's University Press and their editor for their meticulous reading of earlier versions of this book. We also want to thank our authors for their commitment, patience, and hard work. We could not be more blessed by having you in this book! Finally, we would like to thank our families for their patience as we worked on this significant book.

THE EDUCATION OF AFRICAN CANADIAN CHILDREN

The Education of African Canadian Children: An Introduction

Awad Ibrahim and Ali A. Abdi

We, the survivors of the crossing, clung to the beast that had stolen us away. Not a soul among us had wanted to board that ship, but once out on open waters, we held on for dear life. The ship became an extension of our own rotting bodies. Those who were cut from the heaving animal sank quickly to their deaths, and we who remained attached wilted more slowly as poison festered in our bellies and bowels. We stayed with the beast until new lands met our feet, and we stumbled down the long planks just before the poison became fatal. Perhaps here in this land, we would keep living.

Aminata, in *The Book of Negroes* (Lawrence Hill 2007, 94–5)

In addition to desiring "living," perhaps Aminata, the young fictional character in Lawrence Hill's historical novel *The Book of Negroes*, also wanted an education. Even today, Aminata's educational struggle and triumph are still too real, as the essays in this edited volume show. From slave time (Canada did have slavery: see Cooper 2006; James et al. 2010; Mensah 2002; Walker 1980; Winks 1997) to the present moment, education has always been important to African Canadians. They knew, and still know, that education is their bridge to the promised land of mental decolonization and social well-being, their ticket into gaining standing in the larger Canadian society and finding jobs, and their ship carrying them to the land of full citizenship and social and democratic participation.

In its totality, the struggle of African Canadians for education is long and historical. The first black person known to have come to what would later be called Canada was Mathieu da Costa in 1605. He "served" as an interpreter for the Mi'kmaq Nation, which suggests that not only he had been to the "New World" earlier but that he mastered the Mi'kmaq language. It is worth noting that, even though da Costa was a free man, most of the early history of African Canadians was dominated by slavery. The first documented African slave in New France was Olivier Le Jeune in 1628. But Le Jeune was an anomaly, because he was brought directly from Africa (Madagascar or Guinea). Records show that slaves primarily were brought to Canada (the first waves arriving in Nova Scotia) either from the Thirteen Colonies or the West Indies (James et al. 2010; Mensah 2002).

In the country's early days, many Canadian towns and villages did not have public schools, and, as contributor Afua Cooper shows (this volume), towns that did have schools often refused to let black children attend. This was the case especially in Nova Scotia and Ontario, which passed laws to keep black children in separate schools. There, in an Aminata spirit of wanting an education, black communities rallied to create their own educational institutions. Around 1796 in Nova Scotia, for example, with the help of the Church of England, black teachers were able to teach black children either in their homes (Joseph Leonard in Brindley Town) or in log schoolhouses built by black residents (Catherine Abernathy in Preston). Next door in New Brunswick (NB), a school for black children was set up in Fredericton, and in Saint John (NB), the first school for black children, The African School, was established. A few years after this, in the latter part of the 1800s, the Old Bog School was established as a desegregated school in Charlottetown, Prince Edward Island (Hill 1996).

Buxton Mission School in North Buxton, Ontario, however, was a category of its own. Opened in 1850 to serve the black settlement of Elgin, the school was so exceptional in its educational quality that white parents started sending their children there. Indeed, white children outnumbered black children, and, after fifteen years, the school became part of the local school system, in part, also, because many black families left the region and returned to the United States after the American Civil War. As time went on, however, Buxton Mission School's quality became an exception. In fact, black children in Ontario and across Upper and Lower Canada were kept in under-funded, poorly equipped, inadequately staffed and segregated schools. Black parents objected strongly to these conditions, demanding that their children receive educational opportunities equal to everyone else's, and that they be allowed to send their children wherever they saw fit. The struggle for desegregation and equal opportunity continued until 1954 in Nova Scotia and 1964 in Ontario (Hill 1996). Interestingly enough, segregated schools experienced a sense of community, cohesion, and exceptional moral support, which were lost after desegregation (Walker 1980).

The Education of African Canadian Children is a collective tribute to this history. We pay homage to those who struggled before us to make it possible for African Canadian children to receive their rightful education. The journey has been long, arduous, and painful, and we need to remember the struggles of Arthur Richardson and Mary Matilda Winslow, the first two educators to graduate from the University of New Brunswick in 1833 and 1905, respectively. They were both refused teaching jobs in New Brunswick. We need to remember Mary Ann Shadd, who ran a private school for black children in Windsor, Ontario, in the 1850s; her students ranged from ages four to forty-five. Finally, but definitely not least, we must remember Wilson O. Brooks, Toronto's first black teacher and principal (Hill 1996).

This history reminds us that the education as well as the presence of African Canadians in this country have a long history. It also confirms what Milan and Tran (2004) have observed as a statistical trend in this population in Canada: over 54 per cent of African Canadians are born in this country. Except for Japanese Canadians, 65 per cent of whom are Canadian-born, more than half of African Canadians are born in Canada, compared to 29 per cent of South Asians and 25 per cent of the Chinese. Moreover, more than 10 per cent of African Canadians are third-generation Canadians, and in certain parts of Canada that have a longer history of black settlement, more than 84 per cent of blacks are at least third-generation Canadians (James et al. 2010, 35).

IN SEARCH OF A NEW DEMOCRACY OF EDUCATION

Milan and Tran (2004) indicate that, when it comes to age, African Canadians are a young ethnoracial group. This ethnoracial group carries historico-cultural packages constructed via colonial and marginalized minority platforms that make it vulnerable to universalist, mainstreamed learning systems that exclude their history. As such, African Canadian learners face what we may term a democratic education deficit where the rhetoric claims education is for them, but in reality, it is not really of them. That is, while education has been designed to fit their contexts, it depends for its elemental, structural and epistemic contents on the external, detached readings of the lives of these students. African Canadians thus find themselves outside the imaginary of the nation (which assumes itself white), and are turned into an object to be studied and consumed. Therefore, this calls for a new democracy of education, one in which we need to address the theories, practices, and observed problems as well as the prospects of African Canadian children's education, social development needs, and aspirations. Indeed, while almost all African Canadian children attend some form of schooling by virtue of the law of the land that makes schooling mandatory, such simplistically quantifiable, numerical representation hides the deeper and more complicated issue of the qualitative disconnections these learners experience with the instructional intersections that have been constructed for them, and on which they are institutionally located. It is also important to note that, while Canada typically ranks as the most educated country in the world (Organization for Economic Cooperation and Development [OECD] 2013) and although the performance of Canadian children in this year's Program for International Student Assessment (PISA) did not meet previous records, ranking at 13 out of 65 countries (OECD 2013), the situation is more complicated for African Canadian learners. Indeed, while we are not willing to accord too much credence to the fundamentally biased PISA testing schemes, which do not disaggregate population data according to race, such tests nevertheless hide the educational plight of those whom we may call here the externalized categories of Canada's otherwise almost "stellar" learning and pedagogical platforms (Abdi 2014).

There are, of course, a number of reasons for this, of which the most prominent may be the now exhaustively researched and established connection between social class and educational access and achievement (Willis 1981; Dolby, Dimitriadis, and Aronowitz 2004). Here, our reading is as much philosophical (see Abdi and Simmons chapters), historical (Cooper and Nelson), social (Egbo, James, Shizha, and Thésée and Carr), linguistic (Ibrahim), auto-narrative (Diallo) and methodological (Nashon) as it is economic and political (James and Dei). Indeed, the quasi-celebrated characterization of social class that is predicated on the presumably measurable socio-economic status (SES) occasionally gives problematically delineated lines that, as far as we are concerned, provide some narrow but loud exhortations about how social class is a function, indeed, an outcome of one's education and income. With this understanding, the relationship between social class and educational success should not be too complicated to comprehend. That is, those children who have a constructive relationship with the schooling system (read: those from well-educated, middle- to high-income families) should succeed, by and large, in the learning projects in place.

The contributors to this volume are exceptionally mindful of the power of SES, but are not ready to buy into the proliferation of research studies that unproblematically connect low socio-economic status to failure in educational outcomes for students. Indeed, the authors conclude that SES cannot be decoupled from the cultural, historical, and social aspects of students' lives. Taking their cues from Dobbie and Fryer's (2011) recent study, which shows the significance of both SES and the social, cultural, and historical factors in educational success, the authors in this volume also want to commit to community engagement. In fact, as Shizha shows us in his chapter discussing Afrocentric schools, it is the intersection of the social, cultural, historical, and SES that most likely makes possible the success of African Canadian children.

Nevertheless, the role of SES in educational achievement needs further discussion. We agree that the SES, with respect to its impact on educational opportunities, has some pragmatism in it. Such impact, though, almost always functions detrimentally in relation to the education of African Canadian children and others who do not come from middle-class or upper-middle-class families (Willis 1981; Bourdieu and Passeron 1990). Whatever the case, the authors in this volume argue that the situation is certainly more complicated, and that, without a doubt, historico-cultural attachments are as important, if not selectively more important, than the heavily economized normativities of the case. Therefore, we submit that the success of African Canadian children in the country's classrooms will depend on the cultural relationships these children establish with the education system, a system which, thus far, does not sufficiently have their interest at its centre. To be sure, how this volume's contributors locate culture is wider, more inclusive, and more active in the way the construct and its practical possibilities generally have been packaged and distributed. In our critical readings of culture, we prefer to unshelve it from the static, dusty, and epistemically non-liberating bookcases of the old anthropological assumptions that culture is a thetic and static entity (Ibrahim 2014). In the place of such assumptions, we deploy culture and its operational categories as the stuff of life: how we are attached to our present, to our historiographies, and, as well, to our families and communities; how we are attached to the way we read the world and the word (with Freireian analytical fragments), to the way we discern and construct our identities, and certainly to how we learn and/or use our languages to leave meaningful lives that are defined by, and correspond well with, our social and physical environments.

This is where we locate the African Canadian identities. These are socially constructed categories whose centre is "blackness," an umbrella category that subsumes under it ever-shifting, ever-changing, organic, multicultural, and multilingual complexities. African Canadian identities are diasporic identities that come from across the globe: from Nigeria, Somalia, South Africa, Jamaica, Trinidad and Tobago, Brazil, the US, and the UK, to name but a few. As such, African Canadian identities are multinational, rhizomatic (Ibrahim 2014), and diasporic "black" identities, in which (as the authors of this volume show) "blackness" hides a complex array of historical, social, cultural, linguistic, national, gender, sexual, ability, and religious backgrounds (among many other things).

It is with this complex social and historical understanding that we may be developing a mini-thesis that elevates the role of culture as having a greater impact on educational development and achievement than does the much-discussed SES collective, especially as the situation concerns African Canadian learners. Indeed, with culture managing the social constructions of ideas, knowledge, and the inter-subjective discourses that mediate these, we shall be able to see the thick connections between culture, education, and social well-being, which is contrarian to the cultural disconnections with African Canadian learners becoming detached from contemporary schemes of teaching and learning (cf. Dei, Mazzuca, and McIsaac 1997). Needless to add, this detachment is not purely of a cultural nature but is also historically located. As was explicated above, though the historical issues are problematic, we believe these could have been remedied through cultural reconstructive possibilities which, while not denigrating the past experiences of African Canadians, can provide these young students with new epistemic and epistemological connections that affirm their presence and their needs, as well as their expectations and rightful demands.

Perhaps it is appropriate here to forewarn those who may be experiencing a sense of what might be called a "culture of complaint dissonance syndrome" (ccds). Familiar questions arise from this syndrome: What cultural inclusion do African Canadian children want? Why don't they just work as hard as others and achieve like others? Anyone might ask these questions, and, in many cases, they deserve consideration; that is, everyone, especially teachers, educational policy makers, and educational managers, should be taught that the intention of demanding viable historico-cultural connections as a platform of educational achievement is not about irrationally seeking a separate cultural accommodation. More reasonably, it is about achieving cultural redemption not only for those whose histories and achievements are excluded in the educational project but for those whose ontologies and livelihoods are still exposed to falsely demeaning learning and pedagogical dispensations. These dispensations, Abdi (2009) argues, still partially

uphold the de-culturing of African life in Canada, and continue to locate it within a colonial framework, among others. Indeed, as these categories continue to dominate the educational relationship (among
African Canadian learners and others), one needs to fully consider the
alienating and culturally deforming effects current schooling could
have on the lives of young students in terms of their developing identity. This problem is actually complemented by African experiences and
African historical examples that function as an identity-boosting
prospect for other students. This point certainly touches an important
issue that should deserve more descriptive and analytical exposure than
we can afford here, but for now we can propose two questions we ask
in university classes: As human beings, do we perhaps have a psycho-
physiologically attached need to feel superior to at least one group or
one person, and do we thrive on such assumptions of superiority? Interestingly, the questions and their presumptive answers may be more
affirmative than one might have expected, but in their totality, such assumptions contradict the findings of some of the most comprehensive
studies that confirm the genetic falsity both of racism and ethnic superiority (see, inter alia, Gould [1981]1996; Cook 2005).

It is within these complex and contemporaneously non-viable and
unharnassable educational and social well-being realities that we are
behoved to re-read and re-align the needed conjectures of the education
of African Canadian youth. In so doing, we must redefine our histories,
cultures and immediate educational needs, thus liberating ourselves
from the de-meriting and cognitively colonizing subjectivities imposed
on African Canadian learners and their communities. This should, indeed, be an important project of both subjective and epistemic liberations led by the engaged leadership of African Canadian intellectuals,
including both academic and traditional intellectuals (such as artists,
poets, clergy, and common community leaders) who can continuously learn from earlier generations in the North American context. For
example, W.E.B. Du Bois and Malcolm X, via steel-bending academic
writings (see Du Bois [1903]1994) and massively oratorical public space
exhortations, realigned political and social development dispensations
for the relative benefit of the perennially marginalized. As Edward Said
(1996) so cogently noted, the role of the public intellectual should min-
imally include challenging power, modelling for the disempowered the
hope as well as the practice of reclaiming their rights. As we continue
doing this work, therefore, we need to carefully excavate the sites of the
educational problematic so as to seek ways of enfranchising both the
learning as well as the achievement potential of African Canadian learn-

ers, who, as much as anything else, need urgent onto-epistemological rebuilding that affirms their identity and attendant citizenship rights. When this is realized, it will enhance not only the lives of these students, their families, and their specific communities but also the quality of life in the Canadian public space, as well as the future social development of the country.

Hence we present this volume, which brings together some of the major academics and authors whose research and writings have tangible attachments with the educational and social development needs of African Canadians in general and African Canadian children's education in particular. The essays, which were written from either reflective or research positions, cover historical, socio-cultural, social-well-being, and human rights issues that affect the educational contexts of learners. All of these are presented and analyzed in ways that give an inclusive picture of where the education of African Canadian learners has been, where it is now, and where it should be going. Even though some field-based studies have been conducted on African Canadian children's education, we believe this is the first volume that is comprehensively inclusive both in its topical and analytical focus. The subsequent chapters cover topics as diverse as the history of African Canadian children's segregation in schools; citizenship and African diasporic communities in Canada; theories of learning; sports and the representation of the black body; philosophical and personal reflections on African Canadian education; accessing dominant markets; Afrocentricity; and language and symbolic violence.

Clearly, this edited volume comes at an important juncture in the education of African Canadian children, but more work still needs to be done in this crucial area of educational and social development. It is indeed worth noting that one of the essays in this volume is written by someone who was a high school student at the time of the writing (Habiba Cooper Diallo). In it, as in all of the essays, one sees how history has marked us in ways that we are yet to fully understand, but also one sees a pedagogy of hope and resilience that does not wait for others to understand the plight of African Canadian children's education. As the essays show, African Canadians are creating alternative spaces – hopeful and visionary spaces – where we are not captives of our painful history but active, creative historical agents who are already using the past as a compass that guides us to the promised land and our bodies as canvases to draw a new, desired, hopeful and beautiful future. We are guided by the prophecy of the global hero and Africa's native son, Nelson Rolihlahla Mandela (1994), who passed away on 5 December 2013 and was accorded an honorary Canadian citizenship. Technically, therefore, and from an interesting turn of events, Mandela was African Canadian. So as the world celebrates his unique legacy, and as we are still searching for a tangible, epistemically and epistemologically liberating education for African Canadian children, we recall his powerful words in his magisterial work, *Long Walk to Freedom*. Mandela told us that to live free is not merely to cast off one's chains but to live in a way that respects and enhances the freedom of ourselves and others.

ORGANIZATION OF THE BOOK

With these learning realities and pedagogical issues that concern the schooling of African Canadian children in mind, we invited a variety of authors to contribute to this book. What emerges from this compilation are multiple subjective and analytical platforms that represent the multiple, at times convergent and occasionally divergent perspectives of African Canadian scholars' work, with each bringing his or her historical, cultural, and educational experiences that influence the shape as well as the intensity of their observations and analyses. As we asked these scholars to contribute to the volume, we deliberately avoided being too directive. Apart from designating the overall theme of the current condition of the education of African Canadian children, we invited each contributor to formulate their preferred focus and to suggest ways of improving the situation. We could not have been more satisfied with the submissions we received. The topical foci are eclectic, with selectively connecting threads that emanate from, or extend into, the historical, the cultural, the philosophical, and the political, with intentionally fragmentary commentaries that locate the subjective within and outside the communal. Indeed, it was a delight to see these scholars' insistence to implicate the desired liberation of African Canadian education through their own descriptive, epistemic, analytical and empirical work. Clearly, the time for apologia is over, and, with a no-nonsense descriptive and with critical dispositions, contributors to this volume are showing what their transformational lives can create and share for the long overdue liberations that are being sought by African Canadians and others of related, minoritized statutory locations.

After this introductory chapter, the book contains twelve chapters that examine the case from multiple theoretical, practical, and suggestive perspectives that should illuminate not only the problems of the story but also ways of moving forward to alleviate the educational liabilities these youths are exposed to on a daily basis. In chapter 2, Afua

Cooper discusses how, throughout the middle decades of the nineteenth century in Southern Ontario, black parents combatted educational racist discrimination against them and their children by suing school boards and municipalities. She records that, during the 1830s and 1840s, white Ontarians responded negatively to the increasing black migration into the province by opposing the entry of black children to attend state-run schools. In many instances, whites simply used their power to block and prevent black children from attending local schools. The state's response to white hostility was to pass the Separate Schools Act of 1850, which was enshrined in the broader Common School Act. This Act legalized separate (and as it turned out) unequal education for African Canadian children. However, the Act itself had a corollary clause which noted that, if no segregated schools were established to meet the needs of black children, these children then could attend the local common school.

As a result of the Separate Schools Act, writes Cooper, a plethora of black segregated schools was founded. However, not all black communities had the requisite number of students to set up such facilities. According to legislation, these black children should have been able to attend the local white-run schools. But this was not to be. Whites used various methods to prevent black children from gaining access to these schools. As a result, numerous African Canadian students were denied an education. The Separate Schools Act supposedly was designed to aid black children; however, it had the effect of institutionalizing educational discrimination. This chapter looks at three court cases in which black parents sued for the right of their children to attend local common schools dominated by white school supporters. All the black parents who sued paid the school tax, and thus, they were particularly incensed at white aggression against their children. Using documents from Ontario's educational archives, Cooper explores the issue of separate schooling for African Canadian students at mid-century. It foregrounds the voice of black parents in the black community's resistance against white racism and black subordination. It further calls for continued research on black education in Canada.

In chapter 3, "The Education of African Canadian Children: Historical, Philosophical, and Socio-Cultural Analysis," Ali A. Abdi establishes the connecting threads that combine the multiple marginalizations that affect Africa and Africans. He demonstrates how, through colonial and postcolonial constructions, such marginalizations are both epistemically and cognitively extrapolated to the actual world of African Canadian students in the country's public schooling systems. Abdi highlights the need to respond to the legitimate and inclusive learning needs of these youngsters, who, after all, are Canada's citizens and future workers and leaders.

In chapter 4, "Diaspora, Citizenry, Becoming Human, and the Education of African Canadian Youth," Marlon Simmons, staying with the philosophical discussion, seeks to understand the ways in which African Canadian youth come to understand questions of citizenry through ancestral familyhood, belief in common origin, shared histories, and collective consciousness immanent to the African Diaspora. He is concerned with the experiences of African Canadian youth regarding questions of the self, as the self comes to be historically contoured through the social terrain of the mutable cultural configurations of Euro-modernity. He is also interested in how and by what means African Canadian Diasporized bodies come to make meaning of their everyday social interactions. Simmons' hope is to invoke a sense of critical perspicacity on the quotidian moments within Diasporic life in order to understand how the myriad experiences of African Canadian youth might come to be accepted through colonial forms of abjection. The purpose here is to extricate the category of "African Canadian youth" from a homogeneous socialization of Euro-modernity by engaging in what might be called "selective communicative practices" that come to self-determine Canadian citizenship. More specifically, Simmons is concerned with what it means for African Canadian youth to have to engage these spaces through fixed colonial suggestions of ethnicity.

In chapter 5, "Slavery, Childhood, and the Racialized 'Education' of Black Girls," Charmaine A. Nelson begins by questioning the historical Eurocentric definition of childhood and the concomitant exclusion of black children from Childhood Studies. Considering childhood as a unique time of life, defined by the protection, love, and care from parents and society-at-large which allows for experiences such as education, exploration, and play, Nelson examines the lives of black slave mothers and their offspring, and argues that slavery effectively rendered the experience of childhood an impossibility for black children. Nelson's exploration of the visual representation of black girls in western art analyzes portraiture and genre studies across various media to examine the nature of the alternative "educations" to which black girls were normally subjected and to critique the social, cultural, and psychic displacement of black girls, not only as documented but as generated within visual culture.

In chapter 6, "High School and the Black Body in Canada: A Recollection of a Female High School Student," Habiba Cooper Diallo explores the high school experience as a detrimental space for black students. The editors came to know Ms Cooper Diallo through her youth activism. Beyond the general editing and relative formatting of all chapters, she did not receive any specialized or structured analytical training to prepare her contribution, and she was more than willing to prepare her work as a part of the reader. We were equally enthusiastic to include the voice of a young high school student whose perspectives are formed by immediate memories and interpretations that shape the way she interacts with and interprets her quotidian schooling experiences. In her analysis, Cooper Diallo notes how researchers have long shown that systemic institutionalized racism correlates with a high dropout rate among black students. When asking why black students are dropping out, it is important to assess their day-to-day experiences in high school, particularly with respect to representations of their humanity. Indeed, through personal life stories, anecdotes, and thought-provoking arguments, the work provides a comprehensive, first-hand analysis of how negative descriptions of Africa and blackness serve to demoralize black students, effectively complicating, and, in many instances, obstructing their pursuit of education. Through this chapter, Cooper Diallo brings awareness to the impact of racism on the physical bodies and emotional lives of black students. She maintains that the misconceptions and degrading discourses around blackness are ultimately a form of epistemic violence. In highlighting the intrinsic paradoxes of our education system, which purports to offer a "healthy" learning environment while producing a toxic, anti-black space, the chapter makes the case for institutional reform around policy and education to bring about a more holistic and inclusive learning space for all students.

    In chapter 7, "Making Education Count: Critical Educational Practice and the Life Chances of African Canadian Children," Benedicta Egbo contends that compelling research and anecdotal evidence have shown that structural and contextual variables mediate schooling, subsequently leading to different outcomes and life chances for various groups of students. Despite this knowledge, Egbo adds, strategies for increasing educational success among vulnerable groups of students remain elusive. Conceptually grounded in critical race theory, a framework with increasing application in education, Egbo's chapter explores the trajectories of critical educational practice and the life chances of African Canadian children. Taking as a starting point the view that critical practice remains the nexus of transformative schooling which, in turn, contributes to individual and societal success, the chapter discusses current knowledge in the area, and answers the question, What are negotiable and non-negotiable knowledge for engendering school success among African Canadian children? Egbo concludes with a "framework for critical practice" for micro-level educational practitioners.

In chapter 8, "Proposing Methodological Approaches to Elucidating African Canadian Students' Metacognition across Learning Contexts," Samson Nashon notes how, despite the varying definitions of metacognition, synthesis of the existing body of literature highlights its importance in learning. He says that there is convergence on characterizing metacognition as one's awareness and executive control of one's own learning process. Thus, understanding one's own learning process is very empowering and is central in terms of independent learning. Despite this centrality in independent learning, Nashon writes, there is no research on how metacognition manifests among and gets engaged by African Canadian learners during learning discourses. In this chapter, Nashon argues that a study involving African Canadian learners is necessary, as knowledge is, in large part, culturally and contextually constructed. Moreover, learning and metacognition are viewed as processes that manifest cross-contextually. He views learning as an idiosyncratic and a dynamic process developed through experiences that are interpreted in terms of learners' prior knowledge, attitudes, and personal backgrounds. Moreover, he adds, learning occurs at the group (community of learners) and individual levels. Given the importance of metacognition in independent learning coupled with the absence of empirical studies on how African Canadian learners engage metacognition, Nashon argues that understanding the African Canadian learner is important to illuminate manifestations and engagement of metacognition among African Canadian learners cross-contextually.

In chapter 9, "Triple Whammy and a Fragile Minority within a Fragile Majority: School, Family and Society, and the Education of Black, Francophone Youth in Montreal," Gina Thésée and Paul R. Carr point out how the stigmas of street gangs, poor educational achievement, linguistic deficits, over-representation in lower-level and special education classes, under-representation in the sciences, and high school dropout rates are attached to young African Canadians educated within the French-language school system in Quebec. They note how both past and present educational research highlights the plight of those who continue to struggle within the system as well as those who have been disillusioned by the experience. Whether they are of Caribbean or other African origin, whether they are declared anglophone, creolophone or francophone, whether they are first, second or even third generation African Canadians, the youth are obliged to confront severe educational vulnerabilities within francophone Quebec. To analyze these realities and critically address them, Thésée and Carr seek to contextualize and to start a dialogue.

In chapter 10, "'Who Owns My Language?' African Canadian Youth, Postcoloniality, and the Symbolic Violence of Language in a French-Language High School in Ontario," Awad Ibrahim intersects authority-language-and-symbolic power in an attempt to tell the story of a group of continental, francophone African youth who find themselves in an urban French-language high school in southwestern Ontario, Canada. Through their narrative, one is confronted by the trauma of one's own language being declared an illegitimate child, hence becoming a "deceptive fluency" in the "eyes of power," thanks to race and postcoloniality. The students are fully conscious of this situation and their "linguistic return," thus gazing back at the eyes of power and declaring themselves "subjects" capable of love and desire. Ibrahim briefly addresses questions of hospitality and language ownership, and concludes by addressing the need to re-think the connection between race, power, and language.

In chapter 11, "The Alchemy of Sport and the Role of Media in the Education of Black Youth," Carl James uses media representations to explore the role of media in helping to shape the athletic interest and educational trajectory of young, black male students. Three themes that emerge from a review of newspaper reports form the basis of the discussion: a) sport can be a way out of Canada's "tough" neighbourhoods; b) youth with "natural" athletic ability are most likely to do well in sports; and c) youth who apply themselves will ultimately be rewarded with athletic scholarships to US postsecondary institutions. James argues that the values, expectations, and behaviours learned through sports are rooted in the neoliberal assertions of individual choice, personal responsibility, hard work, self-discipline, colour-blindness, and free enterprise. These assertions, promoted through media, educational, athletic and other institutions, help to maintain the dream of making it in society through sports. He concludes by suggesting that, when young people and their parents intensely focus on individual efforts, skills, genetics, interests, and aspirations, they leave unacknowledged the accountability, role, and responsibility of educational institutions, social agencies, athletic bodies, and governments to equitably and justly respond to the needs, interests, and aspirations of black youth.

In chapter 12, "Marginalization of African Canadian Students in Mainstream Schools: Are Afrocentric Schools the Answer?," Edward Shizha says that the foundations of schooling in Canada are based on Eurocentric cultural capital, although Canada is regarded as multicultural and open to cultural differences. However, he notes, when it comes to education and schooling, multiculturalism becomes contentious and questionable, and curriculum in Canadian schools favours dominant Anglo-Canadian cultural ideology while marginalizing minority cultures, such as African Canadian cultures. Shizha discusses how research has documented Afro-Canadian students' struggles in the Canadian mainstream education systems, and one solution to overcome their disengagement has been to open publicly funded Afrocentric schools. While some people argue that the schools are a progressive strategy to promote the academic achievement of Afro-Canadian youths, others see them as regressive. The chapter discusses challenges Afro-Canadians face in mainstream schools, and argues that, while Afrocentric schools might, theoretically, be the best way to promote Afro-Canadian students' academic performance, the schools have unintended consequences and may be regarded as dysfunctional to social integration. In addition, the chapter argues that changes should be made to the Canadian (provincial or territorial) school curriculum and staffing to make them inclusive. Teachers should implement culturally responsive and critical pedagogies that challenge current conventional practices, and schools should apply in their teaching holistic models that promote the total lived experiences of diverse students.

In chapter 13, the concluding chapter of the book, "Reflections on African Canadian Education," George Dei offers broad reflections and revisits some philosophical issues about black/African Canadian schooling in a critical dialogue on educational change in Canada. Starting with an interrogation of certain aspects of Euro-Canadian schooling that is anchored in the liberalism and dictates of a capitalist modernity, to interrogate and make the case for African-centred schooling as a legitimate course of action for the black/African Canadian community, as far as the education of our children is concerned. The chapter asserts the importance of reclaiming history, culture, and language as cornerstones for black/African Canadian education, and calls for understanding educational success, broadly reiterating some key debates on the Afrocentric schooling.

REFERENCES

Abdi, A.A. 2009. "Re-centering the Philosophical Foundations of Knowledge: The Case of Africa with Special Focus on the Global Role of Teachers." *Alberta Journal of Educational Research* 55(3): 269–83.

– 2014. "Difference, Social Justice and Educational Equity in Canada." In *Education in North America*, edited by D.E. Mulcahy, D.G. Mulcahy, and R. Saul, 67–83. London: Bloomsbury Publishing.

Bourdieu, P., and J.-C. Passeron. 1990. *Reproduction in Education, Society and Culture.* 2nd ed. Thousand Oaks: Sage.

Cook, M. 2005. *A Brief History of the Human Race.* New York: W.W. Norton.

Cooper, A. 2006. *The Hanging of Angélique: The Untold Story of Canadian Slavery and the Burning of Old Montreal.* Toronto: HarperCollins.

Dei, G.J.S., J. Mazzuca, E. McIsaac, and J. Zine. 1997. *Reconstructing "Drop-Out": A Critical Ethnography of the Dynamics of Black Students' Disengagement from School.* Toronto: Toronto University Press.

Dobbie, W., and R. Fryer. 2011. "Are High-Quality Schools Enough to Increase Achievement Among the Poor? Evidence from the Harlem Children's Zone." *American Economic Journal: Applied Economics* 3(3): 158–87.

Dolby, N., G. Dimitriadis, and S. Aronowitz, eds. 2004. *Learning to Labor in New Times.* New York: Routledge.

Du Bois, W.E.B. (1903)1994. *The Souls of Black Folk.* New York: Dover Books.

Gould, S.J. (1981)1996. *The Mismeasure of Man.* New York: W.W. Norton.

Hill, L. 1996. *Trials and Triumphs: The Story of African-Canadians.* Toronto: Umbrella Press.

– 2007. *The Book of Negroes.* Toronto: HarperCollins.

Ibrahim, A. 2014. *The Rhizome of Blackness: A Critical Ethnography of Hip-Hop Culture, Language, Identity, and the Politics of Becoming.* New York: Peter Lang.

James, C., D. Este, and W. Thomas Bernard. 2010. *Race & Well-Being: The Lives, Hopes, and Activism in African Canadians.* Halifax: Fernwood.

Mandela, N.R. 1994. *Long Walk to Freedom.* New York: Little, Brown & Company.

Mensah, J. 2002. *Black Canadians: History, Experiences, Social Conditions.* Halifax: Fernwood.

Milan, A., and K. Tran. 2004. "Blacks in Canada: A Long History." *Canadian Social Trends* 72: 2–7.

Organization for Economic Cooperation and Development (OECD). 2012. *PISA 2012 Results.* http://www.oecd.org/pisa/keyfindings/pisa-2012-results.htm.

– 2013. *Education at a Glance 2013.* https://www.oecd.org/edu/eag2013%20(eng)—FINAL%2020%20June%202013.pdf.

Said, E. 1996. *Representations of the Intellectual.* New York: Vintage.

Walker, J. 1980. *History of Blacks in Canada: A Study Guide for Teachers and Students.* Hull, QC: Supply and Services Canada.

Willis, P. 1981. *Learning to Labor: How Working Class Kids Get Working Class Jobs.* New York: Columbia University Press.

Winks, R. 1997. *The Blacks in Canada: A History.* 2nd ed. Montreal: McGill-Queen's University Press

2

Black Canada and the Law:
Black Parents and Children in the Legal
Battle for Education in Canada West:
1851–1864

Afua Cooper

We regard the education of colored people in North America as being one of the most important measures connected with the destiny of our race. By it we can be strengthened and elevated-without it we shall be ignorant, weak, and degraded. By it we shall be clothed with a power which will enable us to arise from degradation and command respect from the whole civilized world; without it, we shall ever be imposed upon, oppressed and enslaved; not that we are more stupid than others would be under the same circumstances, indeed very few races of men have the corporal ability to survive, under the same physical and mental depression that the colored race have to endure, and still retain their manhood.

Henry Bibb, in *The Voice of the Fugitive*, 15 January 1851

The blacks in Canada West faced several obstacles in obtaining an education for their children and themselves.[1] One such obstacle was the practice of white school supporters in denying admission to the black children who wanted access to the local common schools. Blacks fought this practice in several ways, one being to sue the white school supporters in question.

This study on black education in Canada West shall then focus on three court cases that took place between 1851 and 1864. The cases are Hill v. Camden Zone, Washington v. Charlotteville, and Stewart v. Sandwich. Six cases have been found that involved black parents and school supporters, but I have chosen to present only the above three because they illustrate clearly the general picture of black education in Canada West in the nineteenth century.

BLACK AND EDUCATED:
A DANGEROUS COMBINATION

Many blacks who settled in Canada West during the early and middle decades of the nineteenth century were largely illiterate or semi-literate due to the legal constraints placed upon the black education in both the southern and northern states. In eighteenth-century colonial and revolutionary America, an educated slave was viewed as an asset. But with the coming of the nineteenth century, and with it the industrial revolution, a harsher form of slavery was ushered in. In this new period, enlightened slaves were viewed as dangerous and were feared because they had the ability to read "abolitionist" literature.[2] It became the common view among slaveholders that literate slaves would not be contented with their lot and would rebel or incite other slaves to rebel. The slaveholders were not merely speculating; nineteenth-century slave uprisings proved their point. Two of the major slave revolts of the nineteenth century were led by educated slaves – Denmark Vesey and Nat Turner.[3]

Between 1817 and 1864, with the threat of the educated slave in mind, slaveholders in the southern United States attacked the policy of educating slaves, and promulgated statutes after statutes to prevent blacks (both slaves and free) from acquiring an education. In some states, punishment varied from lashes to imprisonment, and even to death. The objective of these proscriptive laws, according to Carter C. Woodson (1915), was "to complete the work of preventing the dissemination of information among the Negroes and their reading abolition Literature. This they endeavoured to do by prohibiting the communication of the slaves with one another, with the better-informed free persons of color, and with the liberal white people; and by closing all the schools theretofore opened to Negroes" (164).

In the northern states, too, blacks faced much opposition in gaining an education. In the 1830s, one Miss Crandall, a white teacher, was imprisoned and lost her school, because she admitted black students to it. In the states of Michigan, Ohio, and Indiana, blacks were either prevented from going to school with whites, or were relegated to substandard segregated schools (Sterling 1997; Tyack 1974).

In spite of these virulent measures against black education, many slaves did learn to read and write. In many instances, it was indulgent masters, mistresses, and white children who taught the slaves, furtively of course, to read and write. Many of the slaves who were taught in that manner were children of the slaveholders. Sometimes it was the slaves who educated themselves. Some studied secretly under private tutors, black and white; some acquired tools of literacy by virtue of the trade they were engaged in. It was also not uncommon for some slaves to advance to higher branches of study. By age thirty-five, Harrison Ellis of Alabama was a good Latin, Hebrew, and Greek scholar (Woodson 1915). Woodson noted that, in many southern communities, the law was openly violated, as many black schools were opened and maintained for blacks. In Savannah, Georgia, a black woman by the name of Deveaux had conducted a school in the city for thirty years (Woodson).

Yet, despite the efforts of educated blacks and liberal-minded whites, teaching slaves to read and write was a crime. Their efforts, then, remained restricted and confined. As a result, only a small percentage of the total black population acquired rudiments of literacy. Because of the restrictions on black education in the United States, the vast majority of blacks who fled to Canada had a great thirst for learning. Many believed that education was the panacea for most of the ills that affected the race. It was "the best fortune that a father could give his son, a treasure that could never be squandered" (Bibb 1851, 2). It was also felt by many blacks that, by acquiring an education, they would command respect and be able to secure a good livelihood. There was also another reason blacks were eager to obtain an education, and that was to demonstrate intellectual parity with whites and thereby to undermine racist allegations of US slaveholders (Silverman 1985). Once in Canada, the black refugees made use of every opportunity to educate themselves and their children.

What prompted blacks to trek northward to Canada? Silverman (1985) suggests that, prompted by the uncertainties of life in the United States, many blacks, slave and free, emigrated to Canada during the decades of the nineteenth century. Many blacks who escaped slavery preferred to go straight to Canada, where they were less fearful of being caught by slave-catchers. Even free blacks who lived in the northern states did not enjoy many civil and legal rights. For example, Indiana blacks were denied the right to inherit property, and were prohibited from testifying in court. In the end, northern blacks feared abduction and enslavement. Silverman (1985) notes that the first major effort made by blacks to establish their own community in Upper Canada occurred as a direct response to legislated discrimination in Ohio. There, several anti-black laws passed between 1804 and 1850 acted as propellants to push blacks into seeking a new life in Canada.

PATTERN OF BLACK SETTLEMENT
IN CANADA WEST

By the middle of the nineteenth century, black communities were firm-
ly rooted in six areas of Canada West: along the Detroit frontier, that is,
at Windsor, Sandwich, Amherstburg, and their environs; in Chatham
and its surrounding area, where the all-black settlements of Dawn and
Elgin were established; in what was then the central section of the
province, particularly London, the Queen's Bush, Brantford, and the
black settlement of Wilberforce (now Lucan); along the Niagara penin-
sula at St Catharines, Niagara Falls, Newark, and Fort Erie; in the larger urban centres on Lake Ontario, that is, Hamilton and Toronto; and
at the northern perimeter of Simcoe and Grey counties, especially Oro,
Collingwood, and Owen Sound.

Besides these centres of black population, small clusters of blacks, as
well as individual black families, were settled throughout Canada West
(Hill 1996). The first major wave of blacks arrived in Canada West or
Upper Canada, as it was then called, between 1817 and 1822. The second major wave began arriving in 1850, when the American Congress
passed the Fugitive Slave Act. This migratory flow ceased in 1861 with
the outbreak of the American Civil War. As a result, the black population of Canada West increased dramatically between 1850 and 1861
(Bibb 1851). The black population of Canada West prior to the American Civil War has never been precisely ascertained. Henry Bibb, editor
of the black newspaper, *Voice of the Fugitive* (1851), figured that the population was around 35,000, while Samuel Gridley Howe (1864), a contemporary of Bibb, placed the size of the black population at 20,000.
Historians Loren Schweninger (1975) and Jason Silverman (1985) place
it at 50,000 and 10,000 respectively.

White Canadians received the blacks with tolerance and ambiva-
lence, but from the very start of American black emigration to Canada,
the blacks were met with prejudice and, in many instances, hostility.
By 1840, Canadians generally viewed Americans negatively. Silverman
(1985) states, "Canadian recipience of the fugitive slaves did not guar-
antee their assimilation into mainstream society, nor did opposition to
slavery necessarily represent pro-black sentiment. Anti-slavery advocates
exploited the legal sanction offered to fugitive slaves, but the influx of
blacks prompted the original forbearance on part of white Canadians
to turn increasingly into intolerance" (44).

Did this prejudice faced by the blacks affect their search for an
education in Canada? If it did, in what ways? What kinds of educa-

tional facilities were available to blacks? The study of black education in Canada West in the nineteenth century is perhaps reflective of the wider black experience. Before discussing whether blacks faced prejudice in their quest for an education, it is worthwhile to delineate the types of schools that were available to the black and fugitive population.

SCHOOLS FOR THE BLACK
AND FUGITIVE POPULATION

Three main types of schools were available to the black community in the period under discussion: (1) private schools run by religious and philanthrophic bodies, (2) schools on all-black settlements, such as the ones in Dawn, Wilberforce, Elgin, and the lands of the Refugee Home Society, and (3) state-funded schools.

Some religious organizations opened schools for black students. Several missionary bodies operated in Canada West; of these, the American Missionary Association was the most active among the black population. By 1848, the AMA was supporting the work of missionary Isaac Rice at Fort Maiden (Amherstburg), where he had a large school for black children. Isaac Rice had started that school about 1838. Support was also given to missionaries Mr and Mrs J.S. Brooks at Mount Hope. Rev. Hiram Wilson was also sponsored by the AMA in his educational and religious works among the blacks at Amherstburg and the Dawn settlement. With the passing of the Fugitive Slave Act in 1850, more fugitives entered Canada West, and the educational demand became even greater. Thus, in 1851, the AMA expanded its educational efforts, placing teachers such as Mary Bibb at Windsor, Mary Ann Shadd at Sandwich, and Rev. E.E. Kirkland and his wife Theodosia Lyon at New Canaan. The British-based Colonial Church and School Society was another body that did work among the fugitive population in Canada West. In 1854, the ccss opened a school for black children in London. The school flourished, and by the end of 1855, there were 450 scholars with 950 more on the waiting list (Haviland 1887; Landon 1924; Cooper 1954).

Organized black settlements also boasted their own schools, which were accessible to blacks whether they lived on or off the settlements. The first of these colonies, Wilberforce, was organized by Ohio blacks around 1817. This settlement had two schools. In 1842, the British-American Institute, under the management of Josiah Henson, opened its doors to pupils at Dawn.

The inhabitants of the Elgin settlement, under the leadership of William King, operated a school which proved to be so superior to the white schools that white parents closed their school and sent their children to the Elgin school. Another settlement school was operated by the Refugee Home Society. Both the RHS and the school itself were founded and organized by Henry Bibb, with assistance from his wife Mary and other fellow helpers. The school was established in the area of Puce, east of Windsor. Opened in 1851, the RHS school employed the missionary Rev. David Hotchkiss among its teachers (Carlesimo 1973; Pease 1957).

The third type of schools available to blacks, and with which this chapter shall deal more extensively, was the state-funded or public schools. Many blacks settled in Canada West during the time when the superintendent of education, Egerton Ryerson, was promoting public education province-wide. Through a series of various schools acts, public education was consolidated throughout the province. Within several of these acts were clauses that allowed for separate schooling. Stamp and Wilson (1970) note that the 1841 Common School Act created separate schools, but only for Catholics and Protestants. The 1843 act reinforced this concept of separate schooling (Wilson, Stamp and Audet 1970). By 1846, when Ryerson was appointed as superintendent, separate schooling was already in practice.

Blacks could legally send their children to the common schools, but by 1846, even though colour was not mentioned in the acts of 1841 and 1843, blacks were requesting and setting up their own schools due to the prejudice they faced in sending their children to the local common school (Drew 2008). In Chatham, as early as 1840, black children were denied entry to the school there, and so their parents set up a separate school. In Hamilton and St Catharines, black children were rejected from the common school, resulting in their having no schooling at all. In 1846, Isaac Rice, missionary at Amherstburg, wrote a letter to Ryerson on behalf of the black parents. In the letter, the blacks quoted the trustees and whites of Amherstburg as saying they would rather "cut their children's heads off ... than have the two races study together" (Silverman 1985, 130). The black parents further explained how the whites had claimed "their" school was private, when, in fact, it was public and receiving public funds, but the black school (Rice was the teacher) was not receiving any public monies. Ryerson apologized to the parents, but nothing was done about the situation (Silverman 1985). One major issue that emerged from this complaint by the blacks was the fact that they were paying the school tax, but not enjoying the fruits of it.

In the towns of Sandwich, Simcoe, and London, the fugitives faced similar discrimination. During all of the 1840s in Sandwich, only one school for blacks existed. In London, black children were prevented from entering the common school until 1949, when a separate school opened for them. In 1850, the black children in Simcoe were turned away from the common school. They protested to Ryerson, who suggested they sue for damages. The black residents, however, declined his advice, but agreed to a segregated school. This school was never constructed due to lack of money. As a result, the black children of Simcoe received no formal schooling at all (Silverman 1985).

The various school acts made between 1840 and 1850 legally endorsed the concept of separate schools, though not in a racial context. However, white Canadians interpreted the law loosely and used it to justify black segregation. Therefore, de facto segregation was in place in Canada West before 1850. Recognizing that black separate schooling was already a fact, and with the rising protests of black parents against this injustice, Ryerson was prompted to include in the school act of 1850 a clause that authorized separate schools "not only for the Protestants and Catholics but also for the Coloured people" (Wilson, Stamp, and Audet 1970). The appropriate section of the clause, as it pertained to the black populace, read, "Upon the application in writing of five or more heads of families resident in a township, city, town or village, being coloured people, the council of the township or the board of public school trustees of the city, town or village shall authorize the establishment therein of one or more separate schools for coloured people" (Carter 1962, 118).

Still, while blacks obtained the right to open separate schools, they nevertheless had to pay local common school rates. A share of the school fund amounting to a government grant toward teachers' salaries was allowed each school (Wilson, Stamp, and Audet 1970). The clause of the act was interpreted by many whites to mean that blacks could be excluded legally from the common schools and forced to set up their own schools, whether they wanted to or not. Howe (1864), commenting on the issue, noted,

> Now, there is a growing feeling among the whites that they made a mistake in giving the blacks their choice; and a strong disposition is manifested in many places to retract it, and to confine colored children to separate or caste schools.
>
> On the other hand there is a growing feeling on the part of the colored people that they made a mistake in asking for separate

schools; and a strong disposition is manifested to give them up;
but the whites will not allow them to do so. (50)

Howe went on to note how white sympathy for the fugitives had been
converted into prejudice as the black population increased. In his concluding remarks on black education, he stated, "Moreover, it would
seem that by permitting the school Trustees to establish separate
schools upon the petition of colored people, the legislature did not
contemplate the establishment of such schools against their will. The
spirit of the law clearly contemplated common schools, not compul-
sory caste schools; and if these can be established in virtue by a by-law,
then verily, the letter killeth the spirit" (Howe 1864, 53–4).

Some of the strategies used by whites to prevent black children from
gaining entry to the common schools included gerrymandering of
school boundaries to produce racially segregated districts, declaring
local common schools to be private institutions, and the withdrawal
of white children from the common schools by their parents. Many
times, the latter action led to the invariable collapse of the school due
to the drop in attendance (Houston and Prentice 1988). For many black
children in the province, these tactics simply led to their not obtaining
an education at all.

Blacks protested their debarment from the common schools by writing letters of protest to superintendent Ryerson. One recurring piece of
advice that he always gave was that the blacks should prosecute. Most
who were given this advice did not prosecute, as they were not familiar with the legal process, and many did not have the financial resources
to do so (Winks 1959). In addition, the legal process was time-con-
suming. However, in the atmosphere of conflict and uncertainty ushered in by the 1850 school act, many blacks who had their children
barred from the common schools found they had no other recourse
but to sue.

THE LEGAL BATTLE

My research has discovered six cases that involved black parents taking
either school trustees or the town corporation to court: Hill v. School
Trustees of Camden and Zone; Washington v. School Trustees of Charlotteville; Simmons v. Chatham; Stewart v. School Trustees of Sandwich
East; Hutchinson v. St Catharines; and Dunn v. the School Trustees of
Windsor (Winks 1959; Carter 1962). The outcomes of these cases influenced the climate within which the black separate schools existed.

For the sake of efficiency, this discussion focuses on three of these cases: Hill v. Camden Zone, Washington v. Charlotteville, and Stewart v. Sandwich East. Each case reflects some of the strategies used by trustees to keep black children out of the classroom, and the outcome of each case is different.

Hill v. Camden Zone

This case involves Dennis Hill of the United Township of Camden and Zone. He settled in the area during the 1840s, and by 1852, owned a three-hundred-acre farm, with about eighty acres under cultivation. Hill was described by black abolitionist and newspaper editor, Samuel Ringgold Ward, as being "one of the best educated yeoman in Canada" (Ripley and Finkenbine, 1985, 233). Despite Hill's financial and educational status, local trustees denied his son admission to the common school in 1852. Hill protested the decision to Ryerson, who advised him to seek legal common redress. The following is the letter Hill sent to Ryerson.

Dawn Mills, Canada West
November 22, 1850

Rev. E. Ryerson, d.d.
You will pardon me for the liberty I have taken in appealing to you for redress for the base treatment I have receiv'd. from the majority of the trustees of School Section No. 3 in the township of Camden, county of Kent. I have used every respectful effort in my power with them, to have my son, eleven years of age, admitted into above name school, but all to no purpose; they say that I am a Black man and that it would be presumption in me to contend for my son to go to school among White children, though I am among the largest taxpayers in the said school section. The amt. of taxes that I am charged with and have paid this year was $17 or less a few pence. Besides 12 days statuted labour. I am the owner of three hundred acres of land of which between 80 and 90 acres under cultivation situated nearly in the centre of the said school section, and to be debarr'd from my Rights of school privilege I or no other crime than that my skin is a few shades darker than some of my neighbours, I do think it unfair and at the same time these same trustees have invited white children, out of the township and they went as far as invite some whites of the adjoining county to

attend the said school and do enjoy the privileges of sending as many scholars as they please, and the whole of that party put together do pay but littler more taxes than I do. The above are facts. Therefore you will be so kind as to instruct me how to proceed and how I shall arrange matters so as to give my children their education, for I cannot let them grow up in ignorance. Be so good, Most Rev. Sir as to let me hear from you by the earliest opportunity. Your most Humble and obedient ser't.,
Dennis Hill
P.S. Address Dawn Mill, Canada West.⁴

The following is Ryerson's response in full.

Education Office
Toronto, 30th November, 1852

Sir, I have the honor to acknowledge the receipt of your letter of 22nd instant, and to state in reply that from the tenor of the printed regulations on the fourth page of this letter you will perceive that I cannot express any opinion upon the case which you submit.

I may remark however that the 13th clause of the 12th section of the school Act makes it the duty of each corporation of school trustees "to permit all residents in their school section between the ages of five and sixteen to attend the school so long as their conduct shall be agreeable to the rules of the schools."

This requirement is not however to "extend to the children of persons in whose behalf a separate school have been established according to the 19th section of the act." Now, if such a separate school had not been established the duty of the trustee is plain and in case they refuse to perform it they are liable to a fine of 5 to be sued for and collected by the minority of the trustee corporation as provided by the 18th section of the school Act.

But if the minority of the Trustee corporation refuse to take this to secure your justice, you can (after having made a formal demand for the admission of your son to the school) prosecute the trustees for damages, or apply for an injunction against them to compel them to do their duty. Coloured children, upon the same terms as other children are admitted to our model school and to the Common Schools of the city; and the citizens of Toronto, of all classes, have too much good sense, and Christian and British feelings, to make the slightest objection. It is mean beyond expression, as well as unjust, for the trustees and other supporters of the school to levy and receive taxes from you for the education of their own children, and then refuse admissions to yours.

I have the honor, (Signed) E. Ryerson[5]

Hill waited until the next year when his second son had reached school age, and formally demanded entry for both his sons. He was again refused. Following Ryerson's advice, he sued. Between this time and February 1854, when judgment was handed down, Ryerson received two letters from Charles Baxter, a newly elected trustee of Camden Zone, and George Eddington, a teacher in the same township. In his letter, Baxter informed Ryerson that there was one separate school in the united township for all the black families. Baxter believed that the black families who did not live close to the separate school intended to claim the privilege of sending their children to the local common school. Being a new trustee, Baxter was unsure if this would be legal. He asked, "Are the trustees bound to accept the children of Coloured persons in the school or, does the separate section under the bylaw [sic] still exist?" He continues, "I have no hesitation in saying that I am not personally averse to the children being admitted, and that should the law authorise it, I will do my duty in that respect as cheerfully as any part of it. I would be sorry to have any share in helping to foster a prejudice which I really believe to be unchristianlike and disgraceful."[6]

George Eddington, writing on the behalf of the trustees, expressed the feeling of the majority of the trustees that if "colored children are admitted, the interests of the school will be seriously injured."[7] He also informed Ryerson that the local school superintendent, Reverend Gunne, stated that black children had no legal claim to attend the common school, as a section within the municipality had been set aside for them, for which they were being taxed.[8]

We glean from the above that there was a separate school in Camden Zone. What is also clear from both letters is the uncertainty about the by-law on separate school. As a result, it was opened to interpretations by the white school supporters that were prejudicial to the blacks.

In February 1854, Judge Beverly Robinson, chief justice of Canada West, delivered judgement on the case. He pronounced that "the separate schools for colored people were authorized, as the defendants have suggested, out of deference to the prejudices to the white population" (Silverman 1985, 135). He continued, "After the establishment of any such separate school in a division, we do not think a choice was intended by the legislature to be left to the coloured people within that division to send their children nevertheless to the general common school, because that would defeat what we take to have been the intention of the provision." He further elaborated "that the legislature did not mean that it should be imperative on school trustees to receive in the general school for the division the children belonging to a class in whose behalf a separate school should have been established, nor do we see in the statutes an indication of a contrary intention" (Carter 1962, 135). Judge Beverley therefore ruled against Hill, insisting and asserting that once a separate school had been established, a black child had no choice but to attend that school regardless of its quality or distance (Silverman 1985).

What did this court ruling mean for the black families who were seeking admission for their children in the local common schools? What messages did it send out to white school supporters? Silverman (1985) states that the decision "sanctioned educational segregation throughout the province. Notwithstanding the intention or spirit of the law, the highest provincial court had ruled that black children could be willfully excluded in virtually any public school district." It is not known what happened to the children of Dennis Hill. Did they make the four-and-a-half-mile trek to the separate school? Did they remain unschooled? Did Hill hire a private tutor for them, or were they sent to the British American Institute at Dawn? (Hill 1996)

Washington v. Charlotteville

The next case involved George Washington and the school trustees of Charlotteville. George Washington appeared in the census rolls of 1852 as a farmer living in district No. 5. He was born in the US and was a Methodist by faith. He was fifty-three years old, and was married to Harriet Washington, who was thirty-three. They had one son, Solomon, who would be fourteen on his next birthday. The Washingtons owned a one-and-a-half-storey log house and held fifty acres of land. By all indications, George Washington was a thriving yeoman, and compared well with his white neighbours.[9] In the fall of 1853, George Washington sued the trustees of Charlotteville for gerrymandering the boundaries to prevent his son from entering the local common school. After three trials, Washington won his case, and obtained an award for damages. In between the time when Washington sued and when judgement was pronounced, Ryerson received the following letter from an irate trustee:

Charlotteville, August 1st, 1854

Sir,
Whereas it pleased you, at the court-house in the town of Simcoe on the 10th of February, 1853, to announce that, a Mr. Washington (an African) could bring a suit against the Trustees of School Union Section No. 14 for not allowing him to send his (wicked) boy to school; And whereas an action was brought against the Trustees in the fall of 1853, resulting in a non-suit in favor of the Trustees -the jury being 10 to 2 when they first went out.

Now I have lately heard that the Toronto judges are going by so (by some process or other) to grant another suit against the Trustees. That the judges are, as yet, quite ignorant of the real merits of the case, I fully believe, and that a very undeserved sympathy, perhaps, has too much influence over them, for unbiased justice seems likely enough from the fact, that his Lordship's address to the jury last spring was something of an anti-slavery address. From another fact it was proved [sic] in court that the African boy had threatened the life of a small boy – threw hard substance at him and knocked a large hole in his forehead, this was at school, and in going from school the darky boy went in a field where the father of the boy that was hurt, was with three other persons, and in the houghtiess [sic] bragging way possible told them, that he had liked to have killed a little boy today – that he had nearly fixed him out, this he said often ...

Now Mr. Washington lives a full half a mile near another schoolhouse ... He is also living quite near to the African school in the town of Simcoe as any other. And there were arrangements made between Mr. Covernton, local superintendent, and the Trustees of Simcoe, for the said African boy to attend the said African school in Simcoe, where at first he made fight on the darky teacher, and was dismissed, but under another teacher goes occasionally.

The following document completely shields the Trustees of school section No. 14 from all injustice in refusing to allow the African boy the privileges [sic] of the school – indeed his conduct was twice too bad to be allowed in my school.[10]

Smith then presented the contents of a letter signed by local superintendent Covernton that discussed in part the fixing of boundaries for school section No. 14. "I have examined the documents relating to the limits of the school sections of this township, and have discovered a proposal emanating from Mr. Burger that future boundaries of school section No. 14 should be of the description given in a certain plan ... and that the 50 acres occupied by George Washington, is excluded from the limits."[11]

Trustee Smith continues,

Now there is a saying, that, the winners in lawsuits, are the loser, or at least, have a hard case of it, which the trustees have found to be the case, on Mr. Washington's part I believe certain and sundry sympathisers, find the mean, Mr. Hanton his attorney declaring to the trustees, that, the suit should be carried to the utmost against them, and that it should not cost Mr. Washington one cent.

Well the trustees, the winners have found law, dear work they have expended some $20 on a part of which, or perhaps all will be a loss to them or the section.

NOW MY OBJECT IN WRITING TO YOU is, to be informed how the trustees are to proceed, so that the cost will be equally divided in the section? Also whether the lands of the residents can be taxed on the occasion?

I also wish you to inform me who it was that informed you against the school section (at the courthouse in Simcoe in Feb. 1853) and what was the nature of that information.

The fact is, the liberties of the section have been invaded, and it is time the section vindicates its own cause. The school section has done nothing amiss.

The real merit of the question at issue, is, shall African barbarism triumph, over Anglo-Saxon civilisation?

Yours
Philip Smith[12]

This letter clearly shows that Smith was an uncompromising racist. From Covernton's letter, it would appear that Washington's charge of gerrymandering against the trustees was true. It seems that Solomon was not dismissed from school merely because of "bad behavior." Smith's letter, on the other hand, reveals the image of black people in his mind and in that of other whites. And by juxtaposing "African barbarism" against "Anglo-Saxon" civilization, the letter also delineates a central current in contemporary race relations: white supremacy over black inferiority. Smith revealed that he was not interested in equal education for black children, and could not understand why black parents would be pushing to educate their children. Employing the scientific racism gaining popularity in Europe and Euro-descended societies like Canada as support, Smith felt that whites were superior to blacks; therefore, as hegemonic leader of society, whites could dictate how a "lesser" group like blacks could and should be treated. Further, his letter makes clear that he felt "savage and polluting" blackness threatened white society and all that was clean and good, civilized and pure. One could assume from Smith's letter that he would make sure that "African barbarism" would not be victorious over "Anglo-Saxon civilization."

Washington was vindicated after a third trial, but he faced a major problem, as the following letter from his attorney indicates.

Simcoe 23 May 1855

Rev. Egerton Ryerson D.D. Chief
Supt. of Ed.,
Toronto

Sir,

At a school meeting held by you in this town some two years ago, you alluded to the case of George Washington a colored man, whose son had been excluded from a certain school section in Charlotteville owing to his colour: and you recommended that an action should be brought against the trustees ... upon this suggestion an action was brought and at the trial the plaintiff was now suited, the court, however in terms held the ruling of the judge at nisi onus ... and set aside the non-suit leaving such party to pay his own cost. The case was again tried at the following assizes and a verdict rendered for the defendant. The court however thought the finding of the jury contrary to the evidence and granted the plaintiff a new trial on payment of costs. On the third trial the plaintiff obtained a verdict for one shilling damages and the court granted a certificate for full costs: On this verdict the judgement was entered and an execution issued against the defendants for the amount of the taxed costs 1.18.9. The execution however was returned by the sheriff and the defendants, but also the costs of the second trial and his own portion of the costs of the first trial in all some 75. In your remarks at the meeting you hinted that in the event of damages being incurred you had it in your power to keep back certain monies until the damages should be paid.

I am the plaintiffs [*sic*] attorney and write you for the purpose of learning what steps are necessary to obtain monies referred to by you.

The plaintiff has a small farm acquired by his industry and sober habits which he will be under the necessity of sacrificing if he cannot get the assistance in the manner pointed out by you.

I have the honour
Sir
Your obedient servant
G. Hanton[13]

In spite of Hanton's pleas to Ryerson, it turned out that Washington had to sell his farm to defray the court costs (Silverman 1985). Washington's victory turned out to be a hollow one. On one hand, it proved that blacks could win in a blatant case of discrimination. Judge Beverly Robinson pointed out that, as there was no separate black school in Charlotteville, "the effects of attempts to run a school-district line that would exclude the plaintiffs land was to deprive him of schooling entirely. Simply because there was no other school, the plaintiff must be given access to the common schools" (Winks 1959, 17). On the other hand, what was the point of winning, if Washington had to lose his farm? In the analysis of Washington's case, what clearly comes to fore is the question of equality before the law, or rather, equality of outcome. Washington was a black man (possibly a fugitive) who had persevered in bringing the trustees of Charlotteville to court. By virtue of his colour, he was at a disadvantage. But he won his case. Yet, despite winning, he had more strikes against him than the trustees; he lost the means of his livelihood in order to pay court fees. It seems it would have been better for him had he not sued. And certainly many poor blacks in Canada West must have seen it that way.

Stewart v. Sandwich East

In 1864, George Stewart of Sandwich East, Section No. 8, in the county of Essex, took the trustees of that township to court on the charge that they had refused to admit his daughter, Lively Frances Stewart, to school. In his affidavit Stewart stated that he

was a resident freeholder and householder of the said school section and a ratepayer therein and had lived in the same place about
eight years: that he had a daughter named Lively Frances, between
eleven and twelve years old: that there was a common school house
in the section, and school was kept therein: that on the 9th of May,
1864, he went to George Little, one of the said trustees, and required of him that he and his co-trustees would permit his daughter to attend the school and be taught therein, and he replied she
could not be admitted ... that deponent and his daughter were colored people, and this was the reason the trustees had or gave for
not admitting the daughter ... that the school in question was a
common school: that there was no separate school for colored people in the part of the township where deponent resided, and his
residence was not within the boundaries of any school section, and
had paid, on demand, the school rates imposed on him for the
support of that school section ... that he was a British subject by
naturalization. (Carter 1962, 150)

In the 1861 census of Sandwich East, George Stewart was listed as a
farmer of the Baptist faith and was sixty-seven since his last birthday. He
was married to Lively Stewart, who was fifty-one on her last birthday.
They had six children, five girls and a boy. The two youngest girls, Purli-
na and Lively Frances, were fifteen and ten, respectively, on their most
recent birthdays. The census stated that they were listed as being in
school. The family lived in a one-storey log house built in 1853.[14] The
mother, Lively Stewart, was born in the Carolinas, while George was
born in Virginia, and all the children were born in Ohio. It follows that,
as George became a naturalized British subject, then his whole family
automatically became subjects of the Crown, also.

The trustees replied to George's charge, admitting that he indeed
was charged the school rate for the said section. They also stated that
there was a separate school in Sandwich East which was established by
the Refugees' Home Society, but that the school was discontinued by
the beginning of 1861, and that there had been no school for the black
children since that time. They also noted that the local common school
was within about a mile and a half of the Stewarts' residence, while the
school kept by the RHS was about five miles away (Carter 1962).

Chief Justice Draper delivered the verdict in George Stewart's favour,
stating, "We must hold that coloured people are not to be excluded
from the ordinary common schools, if there is no separate school established for their use" (Carter 1962, 152). He further elaborated: "We

do not question the sincerity of those who state their apprehension of the consequences of allowing colored children to enter the common schools, but this is an argument against the law itself, if it can have any weight. The law does give such a right, subject to certain defined exceptions. The existence of those exceptions is not proved in this case – we might rather say it is disproved – and the law, therefore, confers on the applicant, George Stewart, the right he claims, to come to this court for a remedy, because that right is denied to his repeated requests. We think we are bound to grant it" (Carter).

The fact that George Stewart had his "right before the law" did not necessarily mean his daughter was any closer to being admitted to the common school, because the law could not force people to overcome their prejudices. The following letter from trustee George Little to Ryerson throws light on the issue.

November 9th 1864
To the Rev'd Egerton Ryerson

Dear Sir,

I wish to inform you that we are much troubled very much with the collard [*sic*] people in this settlement, The Rev. C. C. Foot bought a quantity of land in this settlement, for the colard [*sic*] people he gave them the land by them paying a little to support a school The Rev. Foot sent them a teacher & a minister to preach to them. He paid the teacher and preacher out of his own pocket the(y) were not satisfied with that the(y) set fire to the church & also the school house.[15] Then the(y) applied to the council for a separate school the council granted them a separate school. The Sept. the school opened for one year then the(y) set fire to that house also about a year agow [*sic*] Mr. Foot agreed to send them a teacher free again they would not accept him I have been living in this township for twenty years and we have paid to a school 6 miles from here [*sic*]. About three years ago the township was divided we get a school section in this settlement & commenced a school the children is learning very fast the colard [*sic*] people is jalous [*sic*] that their children is not mixed with the white children the(y) entered a suit against us in Toronto the judges decided in their favour on the ground the(y) had not their separate school in operation the white children will not come to school if the collard [sic] come. Now sir I am one (of) the trustees of the said school I would thank you for information how to act. Can we build a schoolhouse for them & hire a teacher for them and they pay part of the salary if so you will oblege [sic] me by letting me know

I remain your humble servant George Little[16]

Even though George Stewart had gained the right to send his daughter to the common school, trustee George Little was asking Ryerson if the trustees could build a separate school for the blacks. In essence, he was prepared to ignore the ruling of Judge Draper. Did Frances Lively Stewart gain admittance to the common school? Was a separate school opened for black children, or did Lively have to settle for no schooling? What the case of Stewart v. Sandwich East certainly must have done was to alert white school supporters to the fact that the courts would not allow outright discrimination against the black population.

BY WAY OF CONCLUDING: MEN FIGHTING MEN

The three cases presented elucidate the bigotry blacks encountered in their attempt to obtain schooling. Hill, Washington, and Stewart all lived close to a common school, and were paying the school rate, and yet their children were denied entry to the schools by the white school supporters. All three men went through the court system to seek redress, because, like many blacks in Canada West, they believed that "the British lion was color blind and they would be judged on merit rather than race" (Walton 1978, 9). But the outcome of these cases proved, as Silverman observes, that while "British law protected Black rights it did not legislate equality" (Silverman 1985, 117). White Canadian racism proved to be stronger than the law itself.

Litigation was just one strategy blacks used in their quest for equality in education in Canada West. They were determined to gain access to whatever educational facilities were available. They were not always successful, but the mere thought of getting an education for themselves and their children provided them with the impetus to fight for that education.

It would be worthwhile to discuss other court cases that involved supporters of the Roman Catholic schools, both French and English. The question of gender also deserves attention. It was men who sued the trustees. Their actions underscored the prevailing Victorian ideol-

ogy that men were the "heads of households." While these court cases reflected black subordination and white supremacy, they also articulated
a gender dynamic – men fighting men.

All the court cases that involved black parents certainly warrant further study and research in order to depict clearly how they impinged
on the state of black education in Canada West during the decades of
the nineteenth century. Though not every black parent whose child or
children were denied an education sued the trustees or government,
black parents were outraged and bitter at the massive disenfranchise-
ment their children experienced at the hand of the educational state.
A.T. Jones, African Canadian doctor and London resident, expressed
these sentiments to white American abolitionist Samuel Gridley
Howe, who was touring Canada West in 1863 to assess the condition
of life for blacks in the province. Jones was reacting to the news that
the London school trustees were going to set up a segregated school for
black students. Juxtaposing the loyalty of black people to the Crown
against the marginalization and subordination of black students, Jones
declares, "I have eight children, who were all born in this town, –
British subjects, as much as the whitest among you; and they don't believe in anything else but the Queen, you are trying to plant within
them a hatred from the country; and the day may come when you will
hear them saying, 'This is the country that disenfranchises and deprives
us of our rights.'"[17]

Jones's words have echoed down to our day.

NOTES

1 The terms "fugitives" and "refugees" have been used in the general literature on blacks in Canada to describe the blacks themselves. However, it is
   probably not an accurate description. Did they not cease being "fugitive"
   upon their arrival in Canada? At what time did they also cease being a
   "refugee"? Dennis Hill, before his court case, had been living in Canada
   West for about eight years. He certainly could not have been a "refugee."
   Also there were many blacks living in Canada who did not belong to this
   general body of blacks coming from the United States and who could be
   described as "indigenous." For this chapter, I shall be mainly using the term
   "black" and will use the others only if the context demands it. On the segregation of black children in Canada West's education system, see Afua
   Cooper, "Black Teachers in Canada West, 1850–1870: A History" (master's
   thesis, University of Toronto Press, 1991) and Afua Cooper, "Black Women
   and Work in Nineteenth Century Canada West: Black Woman Teacher

Mary Bibb," in *"We're Rooted Here and They Can't Pull Us Up": Essays in African Canadian Women's History*, eds. Peggy Bristow et al. (Toronto: University of Toronto Press, 1994), 143–70. For an exploration of Canada's Black population see Robin Winks, *The Blacks in Canada: A History* (McGill-Queen's University Press, 1997).

2 Carter G. Woodson (1915, 153), speaking on the effects of the industrial revolution on slave-holding societies of the American south with regards to education, noted: "This revolution then had brought it to pass that slaves who were, during the eighteenth century advertised as valuable on account of having been enlightened, were in the nineteenth century considered more dangerous than useful."

3 Of Denmark Vesey, Woodson (1915, 157–64) noted: "He had learned to read and write, had accumulated an estate worth $8000, and had purchased his freedom in 1800." The plot that Vesey led in Charleston in 1822 was believed by officials to be due to the influence of enlightened blacks. Nat Turner led an uprising in Virginia in 1831. He was a preacher by "profession." Nat learned to read before he was five years old, being taught by his parents and his indulgent master. He "developed into a man of considerable mental ability and wide information" (see also Aptheker 1943).

4 Archive of Ontario, "Education: Incoming General Correspondence, RO2, 22 November 1852." See also Hill 1963, 1986; Silverman 1985.

5 Archive of Ontario, "Education: Outgoing General Correspondence, RG2, C-1, 30 November, 1852."

6 For Baxter's letter, see, "Education: Incoming General Correspondence, RG2, 17 January 1853."

7 See Eddington's letter, "Education: Incoming General Correspondence, RG2, 24 January 1852."

8 See Eddington's letter, "Education: Incoming General Correspondence, RG2, 24 January 1852."

9 Census Rolls for the Township of Charlotteville (Agricultural census), 1852.

10 See Archive of Ontario, "Education: Incoming General Correspondence, RO2, 1 August 1854."

11 See Archive of Ontario, "Education: Incoming General Correspondence, RO2, 1 August 1854."

12 See Archive of Ontario, "Education: Incoming General Correspondence, RO2, 1 August 1854."

13 Archive of Ontario, "Education: Incoming General Correspondence, RG2, 23 May 1855."

14 Census Rolls for the Township of Sandwich East, District no. 3, 1861.

15 See George Little's letter already mentioned. George Little claimed that the coloured people set fire to both the school and church house established by

the Refugee Home Society. However, the following quote taken from affidavits filed in answer to Stewart's charges says otherwise. "The building was put up for a church and school house ... This society was established for the assistance of refugees from slavery. The school was discontinued about the beginning of 1861, and no school had been kept among the colored people since, except for about two months in one year, because the colored people could not afford to maintain it. They were so widely scattered in the township, and so poor, that it was almost impossible for them to maintain a separate school. No common school was kept from 1855 to 1861, except the one established by the Refugees' Home Society" (Carter 1962, 151).

16 The issue of integration/segregation within the context of black education in Canada West was a very heated and controversial one. Many white school supporters could not come to a firm agreement as to what was the better way. This issue also divided sectors of the black community. Some blacks felt that integration was the key to black achievement in the society while others felt that blacks had to have, at first, segregated institutions in order to develop positive self-concept and a deep sense of identity. This issue was never resolved in the black community. However, Silverman notes that in regard to education, "both black and white critics of segregated schools ... may have been blinded by their idealism to the reality of prejudice in Canada West. White Canadians controlled the educational system, and, in most cases, tacitly assumed that segregation embodied the only course acceptable to both races. In any event, whites actually needed no justification because, a majority, they easily overruled the desires of the fugitive-slave minority" (Silverman 1985, 145). For a more recent perspective on the issue see, Kristen McLaren, "'We had no desire to be set apart': Forced Segregation of Black Students in Canada West Public Schools and Myths of British Egalitarianism," *Histoire Sociale/Social History* 37 (2004): 27–47.

17 Samuel Gridley Howe, *The Refugees from Slavery in Canada West: Report to the Freedmen's Inquiry Commission* (Boston: Wright and Potter Printers, 1864), 51–2.

REFERENCES

Aptheker, H. 1943. *American Negro Slave Revolts*. New York: Columbia University Press.

Arthurs, H. 1963. "Civil Liberties—Public Schools—Segregation of Negro Students." *Canadian Bar Review* 41:453–57.

Bibb, H. 1851. "Education." *The Voice of the Fugitive*, 15 January.

Carlesimo, P. 1973. "The Refugee Home Society, 1851–1876." MA diss. University of Windsor.

Carter, F. 1962. *Judicial Decisions on Denominational Schools*. Toronto: Ontario Separate School Trustees' Association.

Cooper, A. 1991. "Black Teachers in Canada West, 1850–1870: A History." MA thesis, University of Toronto.

– 1994. "Black Women and Work in Nineteenth Century Canada West: Black Woman Teacher Mary Bibb." In *"We're Rooted Here and They Can't Pull Us Up": Essays in African Canadian Women's History*, edited by Peggy Bristow et al., 143–70. Toronto: University of Toronto Press.

Cooper, J. 1954. "The Mission to the Fugitive Slaves at London." *Ontario History* 46:133–9.

Drew, B. 2008. *The Narratives of Fugitive Slaves in Canada*. Toronto: Dundurn Press.

Haviland, L. 1887. *A Woman's Life-Work: Labors and Experiences of Laura S. Haviland*. Chicago: C.V. Waite & Company.

Hill, D. 1963. "Negroes in Toronto, 1793–1865." *Ontario History* 64:55–6.

– 1996. *The Freedom Seekers: Blacks in Early Canada*. Toronto: Stoddart Publishing.

Houston, S., and A. Prentice. 1988. *Schooling and Scholars in Nineteenth-Century Ontario*. Toronto: University of Toronto Press.

Howe, S. 1864. *The Refugees from Slavery in Canada West: Report to the Freedom's Inquiry Commission*. Boston: Wright & Potter.

Knight, C. "Black Parents Speak: Education on Mid-Nineteenth-Century Canada West." *Ontario History* 89:269–84.

Landon, F. 1924. "The Work of the American Missionary Association among the Negro Refugees in Canada West." *Ontario Historical Society Papers and Records* 21:198–205.

McLaren, K. 2004. "'We had no desire to be set apart': Forced Segregation of Black Students in Canada West Public Schools and Myths of British Egalitarianism." *Histoire Sociale/Social History* 37:27–49.

Pease, W. 1957. "Opposition to the Founding of the Elgin Settlement." *Canadian Historical Review* 38:203–18.

Ripley, P., and R. Finkenbine, eds. 1985. *The Black Abolitionist Papers, Volume II, Canada, 1830–1865*. Charlotte: University of North Carolina Press.

Schweninger, L. 1975. "A Fugitive Negro in the Promised Land: James Rapier in Canada, 1856–1864." *Ontario History* 67:91–104.

Silverman, J. 1985. *Unwelcome Guests: Canada West's Response to American Fugitive Slaves, 1800–1865*. New York: Associated Faculty Press.

Sterling, D. 1997. *We Are Your Sisters: Black Women in the Nineteenth Century*. New York: W.W. Norton.

Tyack, D. 1974. *The One Best System: A History of American Urban Education*. Cambridge, MA: Harvard University Press.

Walton, J. 1978. "Haven or a Dream Deferred for American Blacks: Chatham, Ontario, 1830–1880." Paper presented at the Canadian Historical Association Meeting, Toronto, Ontario.

Wilson, D., R. Stamp, and P. Audet, eds. 1970. *Canadian Education: A History*. Toronto: Prentice-Hall.

Winks, R. 1959. "Negro School Segregation in Ontario and Nova Scotia." *Canadian Historical Review* 50:165–91.

Woodson, C. 1915. *The Education of the Negro Prior to 1861*. New York and London: G.P. Putnam's Sons.

3

The Education of African Canadian Children: Historical, Philosophical, and Socio-cultural Analyses

Ali A. Abdi

In speaking about the philosophical and epistemological intersections of the education of African Canadian children in the country's public schools, one needs to pay special attention to the thick historical, cultural, and cognitive attachments that would not be necessarily limited to actual locations, relationships, and outcomes of the learning process. As I understand it, the colonial and neo-colonial constructions of Africa and Africans directly affect the new learning relationships these youths are establishing with Canada's teachers and education managers. I will develop this in the coming paragraphs, but let me now very briefly talk about the philosophical and epistemological foundations of schooling, which should clarify, early and as much as possible in this writing, the complex, historic-actual constructions of the multi-trajectory story I intend to narrate in this chapter.

For my purpose here, philosophy is about our select, reflective inquiry with our world and in relation to the overall universe to which we belong, and thus accords us multiple claims and possible applications with almost all life locations that one could say, with some situational certainty, are lived philosophically. Some debates should be instigated regarding the problematic claims of who invented philosophy and who owns it. This may sound like an unexpected question, but as far as the people of African descent are concerned, the question actually joins the larger questions of philosophy. I will return to this issue, but let me quickly introduce the branch of philosophy that concerns us the most here: philosophy of education. If philosophy, the love of wisdom, is the general or systematic inquiry about our world, then philosophy of education focuses on the critical reflections and analysis of the nature as well as the procedures of past or contemporary learning and teaching. As Ozmon and Craver (2002) noted, philosophy of education tends to deal with what we may term the main questions of education: What type of education do we need? How should we do this education? Why should we do one type and not another type of education, in the first place? By extension, philosophy of education is about the select ways we design and achieve learning and pedagogical contexts that are viable in our instructional and social development structures and relationships.

With this preliminary reading regarding the philosophy of education, and then with respect to the history of the African people, the issues return, not to the sub-question of what philosophy of education is, but to the general inquiries about philosophy and education. Indeed, this is where the important historical connections and constructions that still affect the lives of African learners (whether in Canada or elsewhere) are so important to ascertain, analyze, and critique. The learning and social development importance of this point can only be fully appreciated when one realizes that the way blacks were depicted within European philosophical, literary, and related historical writings is, more or less, still intact and even informative with respect to young learners in Edmonton, Toronto, and Vancouver. So how did this happen? What presumptive philosophical and epistemological platforms have established such enduring cognitive deformations that are negatively impacting the educational lives of *caruurta Afrikaanka ah oo hadda Kanada wax ku baranaya* (African children now learning in Canada). To understand this as comprehensively as possible for these discussions, we cannot ignore (either for epistemic failure, for political correctness, or even for writing convenience) the thick historical threads that expansively colour the learner's location vis-à-vis the overall realities of the situation.

The arbitrary, European philosophical and epistemological constructions of the persona Africana that happened even before the full-fledged onslaught of colonialism are not only interesting but are highly presumptive, essentially racist, and of *longue durée*. Some of us are familiar with the psycho-physical outcomes of colonialism, explored mainly through the works of such brilliant thinkers as Frantz Fanon (1967, 1968), Chinua Achebe ([1958] 2000, 2009), Edward Said (1978, 1993), and Hamidou Kane ([1963] 2012). Yet, we also need to engage a pre-colonial reading of how Europeans were prepared, by the so called luminaries of philosophy and literature, including Hegel, Montesquieu,

Voltaire, and Hobbes, to demean, indeed, deny Africa's philosophical, epistemological, educational and, by extension, developmental achievements (Abdi 2008). This should not be difficult to understand; for in order to subjugate people, the oppressor would understandably attribute to them presumed deficiencies that prevented their recognition as beings of agency who are endowed with intellectual capacities that are as good as those of others in the wider society. Such recognition can aid the self-esteem of these learners, which also assures them a higher self-efficacy to manage their lives and chart their futures on their own.

Indeed, what was termed *la mission civilisatrice*, or the civilizing mission (Said 1993), was not primarily invented by colonial administrators and soldiers but by big-name European thinkers who affirmed for their populations the widespread "barbarity" of an Africa and its people they had never studied, were not familiar with, and had never visited even out of the usual exotic curiosity (Abdi 2008). For some deranged but clearly impractical epistemological reasons, therefore, these thinkers paved the way for much of the writings that are still being extrapolated as representative of vita Africana, whether in Africa proper or in the Diaspora. Basically, this philosophic-epistemological onslaught involved, as much as anything else, locating the continent as ahistorical, aphilosophical, and, by extension, aepistemological. By assuming these sweeping and false generalizations about Africa, which were later affirmed by the organized conquest of the people and their lands, the case represented a total denial of African educational and indigenous capacities for progress.

The absurdity of such denials goes against the grain of both natural and social courses of human life. It is natural for all peoples anywhere in the world to live by learning. The point doesn't need too much elaboration, for we cannot exist over millennia unless we develop effective educational systems that define our lives, clarify our needs, and facilitate our chances and capacities to make the changes we require to continue surviving. What was happening, and to some extent still may be happening, was more or less a devaluation of people's life systems, so that, in the eyes of their colonizer societies, the processes of subjugation and exploitations would become epistemically and epistemologically justified. Of course, the reality on the ground was totally different from the colonial de-educationalizations of Africa. In what are now recognized as definitive studies in the case, the works of Julius Nyerere (1968) and Walter Rodney (1982) among others, it has been revealed that precolonial traditional education was not only effective in its learning and pedagogical platforms, it was also relevant and well-designed for its recipients. Again, colonialism and its practical outcomes were not concerned with examining any facts on the ground but with destroying African educational and development contexts (Nyerere 1968) so as to comprehensively establish the epistemic and, by extension, mental colonizations of colonized populations (wa Thiong'o 1986, 2009). From there, the deck was to be cleared (and was cleared) to cement the benighted, colonizer/colonized cultural and epistemological relationships that, even after the fall of formal colonialism, are still intact. These realities also cross into the lives of Africans in Western countries, including Canada, and affect the learning contexts of African Canadian children.

In prefacing my analysis with these enduring global perspectives, I am aware of the possible misunderstanding that would instruct me to simply get to the point and talk about the condition of African Canadian kids' education in today's classrooms, rather than to engage in "sweeping historical generalizations." I will address the former in the following paragraphs, but I deliberately understood my task as adding these important socio-historical trajectories to the story of this book. I also submit that those who do not appreciate the historical realities and, by extension, their philosophical and related learning connections, do not know what they are talking about. In refusing to foreword my analysis with historical vacuity, I believe that critical historical insertions are not only essential but acutely important to comprehensively read and understand the context of the issues faced by today's African Canadian learners. These learners are faced with disconnecting systems of education (Dei, Mazzuca, and McIsaac 1997), and are factually attached to triple learning tragedies that are colonial, postcolonial in Africa proper, and diasporic in Western countries such as Canada. As should be immediately discerned, the first tragedy was experienced by the forefathers of these learners, the second mostly by their own parents, and the current learning tragedy is now faced by themselves. So how are the three phases of the learning tragedy connected? Let me answer this important concern by connecting it to some of the main points already mentioned here, and bring it to the current classroom situation.

For starters, the philosophical and epistemological pre-colonial constructions of Africa/Africans via the falsely concocted epistemic vanguardism and racist activism of European thinkers and the subsequent counter-development, counter-self-esteem, and counter-self-efficacy systems of colonial education imposed upon the continent and its peoples have created extensive deformations in both the psyche as well as the bodies of colonized Africans (wa Thiong'o 1993, 2009; Abdi 1999). This psycho-culturally demeaning and economically destabilizing education was not actually limited to those being subjugated in Africa proper, but was, more or less, of similar qualitative liabilities as that im- posed on those whose forefathers and foremothers were transported to the area mischievously called the "new world." As the African American writer Carter G. Woodson discussed in his classic, *The Mis-education of the Negro* ([1933] 2010), any provision of education to African Ameri- cans (and, by extension, African Canadians, as well) in the postbellum era was laced with the same epistemic and learning deformations that characterized the educational lives of any colonized and/or previously colonized populations. A self-taught man who became a formidable thinker in anti-colonial education campaigns, Woodson wrote that the education of forcefully diasporized Africans was tantamount to their psychosomatic depreciations, and it taught them not to be free but to be affirmatively recruited into their oppression and into demeaning psycho-cultural locations. Basically, therefore, the mis-education of Africans, irrespective of their location, was designed to control their thinking and to eventually turn them into cultural automatons, una- gentic quasi-subjectivities who voluntarily oppress themselves on be- half of the oppressing entity. In describing these general outcomes of mis-education that results in the deconstructive de-patterning of peo- ple's mental dispositions, and that always leads to heavy and enduring clusters of mental colonization, Woodson ([1933] 2010) wrote, "When you control a man's thinking you do not have to worry about his ac- tions. You do not have to tell him not to stand here or go yonder. He will find his 'proper place' and will stay in it. You do not need to send him to the back door. He will go without being told. In fact, if there is no back door, he will cut one for his special benefit. His education makes it necessary" (21).

Indeed, this is not that different from the seminal findings in Albert Memmi's classic work, *The Colonizer and the Colonized* ([1957] 1991). Memmi, one of the most important analysts on the discursive, cultur- al, and practical outcomes of colonial relationships, clearly saw the neg- ative and multi-directionally destructive dialectic that is gradually formed among the colonizer and the colonized: Via the combination of forceful physical subjugations, deliberate mental confinements, and post-traditional formal and even informal colonial education, those who are colonized slowly but eventually internalize heavy doses of onto-epistemological inferiority complexes that force them to collabo- rate with their oppressors for the continuation of their oppression. Con- temporary with Memmi's writings, the even more piercing and more onto-subjectively located analysis of the brilliant Martiniquan psychi-

atrist and psychoanalyst of colonial projects and relationships, Frantz
Fanon (1967, 1968), achieved what is perhaps for me the most important disquisition on the deeply problematic deformations and re-
constructions of colonized minds that actually goes beyond the
collaborative efforts Memmi talks about. Fanon's penetrating and no-
nonsense analyses (especially in his magisterial work, *Black Skin, White
Masks* 1967) critically locates how the combination of perforce cognitive colonizations of the mind and corps induce in their recipients a
desire to abandon their subjectivities and seek refuge in unattainable
selves that belong to the designers and perpetrators of the destructive
program in the first place.

Indeed, as Fanon's compatriot and teacher, the poet Aimé Césaire
([1972] 2001) showed that, as people are collectively labelled inferior
over time and space, and are accordingly oppressed, they develop and
normatively live with precarious subjectivities that become slowly dis-
tilled of primordial self-confidence and, thus, of the important project
of self-efficacy. The latter (see Bandura 2006) is, of course, the sine qua
non of achieving personal and social tasks effectively and contextually.
When this is the case, these deformed subjectivities become quasi-per-
manently injected with irrational and rational fear of the oppressor,
which assures their collective trepidations in their daily lives, and, by extension, the lives of their successive generations. Clearly, these regimes
of collective ontological oppressions do not disappear as people are
born, grow old, or die. These realities of life become culturally ingrained; they become both tempo-spatially and subjectively reflective
of the people, and their life-based endurance is surely realized through
the bitter inheritance of intergenerational exchanges that are now common in many parts of the world. The point about successive generations is very important in that cognitive colonization is, ipso facto,
intergenerational; today's African diasporic children (whether in Canada or elsewhere) still directly deal with the psycho-physical experiences
of their forefathers. These children's parents and grandparents come
from generations of Africans who, even with some resistance, saw the
world more or less the way colonialism and racism created it.

In referencing the work of the anti-racist scholar David Theo Goldberg (2002), we have metaphorically referred to the continuing insti-
tutionalization of the house that "race" has built in educational and
other public contexts in Canada. This should lead us to the spirit, as
well as the possible practices, of critical multicultural education rather
than to symbolic multicultural education that stays with the superfi-

cialities of life, with the former potentially safeguarding the "real" learning rights of all learners (see Ghosh and Abdi 2013). By the real learning of all learners, we are talking about educational contexts and relationships that enfranchise not just the physical presence of the student but, as well and equally, the historic-social, philosophic-cultural, and, certainly, the onto-epistemological locations of so-called "ethnic" pupils in particular, who come from the African Canadian community and from other groups, such as Aboriginal peoples, who have been previously cognitively colonized. As Marie Battiste (1998) so effectively discussed, the exposure of what she termed cognitive imperialism is one of the biggest obstacles to the educational and social development of Aboriginal peoples in Canada. The same also applies to all contexts where local knowledges were suppressed, traditional systems of learning were rescinded, and people's achievements and overall life systems were derided as primitive and not worthy of critical inquiry, effective learning, and active socio-economic progress.

So how do these previous negations of the historical, the philosophical, and the epistemological, all culminating in oppressed subjectivities that partially lose their capacities to define and act on their world, affect the education of African Canadian children in today's classrooms? This important question has been already partially answered in the preceding paragraphs; indeed, the all-too-important philosophical and epistemological critiques, complemented by the thick constructions of cognitive colonization, as discussed above, should suffice to give us a reliable historical grounding for the complicated and marginalizing learning situations with which these children are dealing. It is worth remembering that people are products of their historical circumstances, but they are also agentically or unagentically endowed or not endowed by their current circumstances. By and large, to what extent one is educationally endowed should depend on both the historical package I have analyzed above, and, as a sort of counter-weighing mechanism, by the level of liberating praxes (Mayo 2008) they can harness to succeed in the prevailing learning and social development realities/challenges they encounter. As such, we can talk about two historically interconnected but thematically separate contexts of life and learning that inform the educational opportunities and/or obstacles that African Canadian children may encounter. With the first context of depreciating inherited philosophical and epistemological realities already discussed in this short chapter, we now turn to the new locations of learning that inform the lives of these children.

ACTUALITIES OF CANADIAN CLASSROOMS
AND AFRICAN CANADIAN CHILDREN

In speaking about collective cognitive colonizations that are still affecting the lives of African Canadian children, I have not indicated and
will not indicate a case for the permanent unagentification of the concerned populations. I naturally subscribe to the presence of some
agency, some human dignity, and certainly some expandable threads of
human capacity in all the subjectivities of my foci. But as I have written elsewhere (Abdi in press), for human agency and dignity to thrive,
they should not be either contextually or culturally alienating; that is,
the learning possibilities that are accorded to African Canadian children, born here or elsewhere, must be re-cultured and re-contextualized so a constructive relationship is created between learners and
learning situations. This is important in many ways. Indeed, prominent
pragmatic philosophers of education, including Julius Nyerere (1968),
John Dewey ([1938] 1997), and Paulo Freire ([1970] 2000), have all spoken in favour of educational contextualization and pedagogical relevance. As mentioned above, Nyerere was adamant about establishing
postcolonial learning possibilities that not only rescind the racist structures and contents of colonial schooling but also re-align the new educational programs that should fit the contemporary needs of those
concerned, which include the cultural, social, and economic needs of
the people.

The point about cultural relevance is exceptionally important for my
analysis here, not so much in the manner of shallow, multicultural education exhortations that do not really challenge the now habitual hegemony of the mono-epistemic world, but in the way Dewey intended it
many decades ago. In his short, excellent book, *Experience and Education*
([1938] 1997), Dewey rightly appreciated schooling based on its relationship with the world of the learner, that is, all learners including those
who are coming to the school for the first time. Indeed, in this book
and in related works, Dewey refused to miss the pedagogical importance
of the transitional, that is, the capacity of the schooling system to know
the context the student is coming from, the socio-cultural and personal spaces he or she crosses to reach the new spaces of education, and how
he or she can actively see the connection between their own background
and schooling.

Nyerere and Dewey's philosophical writings represent strong threads
of educational and social development pragmatism wherein, even before the quality of its itemizable contents, the learning project must be

of social and subjective relevance that enhances the personal as well as the collective well-being of all learners and especially of those who need it the most; this includes so many African Canadian children. Indeed, such pragmatic thinking is not detached from other foundational traditions of the philosophy of education, including the idealist threads that are not necessarily detached from this thinking. I would even suggest it may be good to start with some idealist desires, for we are also always tied to the best teachers we could be for learners and to how effectively we relate to the lived realities of our students (not just what we teach them in specific school periods and time zones). As the late African American intellectual W.E.B. Du Bois proposed, it is not what you teach children but what you are to them that will constructively or otherwise affect their educational subjectivities, their zone of learning comfort, and certainly their love of schooling, as well as the after-school possibilities that would either endow or depreciate their life possibilities and well-being.

From Paulo Freire's perspective, there is a thin dividing line in the capacity of education to either liberate or oppress people. Again, the issue here is not necessarily what the curriculum says but what educators do with it. As such, the education of African Canadian children involves, as far as I am concerned, a relational practice that locates these children in detached inter-subjective realities vis-à-vis teachers and school administrators, complemented by problematic contexts of knowledge exclusions and, by extension, depressed self-esteem and self-efficacy intersections that together assign their overall beings to the dustbin of the schooling project. In a number of books, including *Pedagogy of Hope* (2004), Freire refuses to abandon the living reality of hope where the right inter-subjective/inter-human engagements can instil in learners the capacity to critically relate to their surroundings and achieve their best in different and changing socio-cultural and political circumstances. In examining the project of hope in the context of African Canadian children, one need not and cannot escape the counter-hegemonic historical and philosophical constructions that can re-establish the contents and, indeed, the endowments of such possibility. While the intention here is not to abandon hope in hope itself – for that is a dangerous cliff that no one should be seeking – it may be fair to repeat that, as things are now, the overall situation is heavily stacked against these youngsters. With that being as it is, we still need to accentuate the relational subjectivities that should be harnessed to achieve otherwise. As such, for African Canadian students who come from backgrounds that are dotted with multiple liabilities, the powerful learning and pedagogical perspectives of the pragmatist philosophers are as cogent as ever, and the possibilities of educational achievement cannot be forever unattainable. However we do it, though, it is not what we give them as itemized particles of knowledge but how we humanistically understand their lives, needs, and aspirations that signifies.

More often than otherwise, one main pedagogical liability for the well-intentioned Canadian pedagogue could be the way he or she perceives, locates, and practices difference. As I have witnessed in my own collaborative research in the area (see Abdi et al. 2013), the a priori, detached labelling of some learners as being different – and this almost always includes African Canadians – is quite problematic. While being different is arguably the most fundamental socio-physical trait of all persons, and actually directly enhances our unique existence and co-existence with others, the idea and its practice have at least two school-based sides that can be differentiated in their relational intentions and outcomes. A child who is from a socially privileged background, with all the attendant linguistic and material attachments, would be different, but in a way that, ipso facto, actually builds his or her self-esteem and related capacities. Above all else, such a child will reap the massive relational benefits he or she accrues vis-à-vis teachers and other school personnel, who, through the "natural" display of their appreciation for this child's context, actually continually build his or her educational well-being and, by extension, his or her developing self-efficacy to excel, now and into the future. This is not difficult to understand or to see. The school system itself and its attached policy priorities are not necessarily intended to uplift those learners who need such support the most, but rather are meant to affirm the learning subjectivities of those who fit its linguistic, cultural, and socio-economic categorizations. While we should be familiar with some early writings on children's socio-cultural capital, we may not give adequate consideration to the ongoing constitution of the school itself as a cultural and social location that selectively represents some in such capacities, while rescinding the being of others via the same realities. Hence, we see the differentiated constructions of difference as an asset, and from a different angle, a liability.

On the liable platforms of the case, the child from the socially non-endowed side of the tracks encounters difference as something that is manufactured and deployed in ways that are textured by a cluster of historical, cultural, and learning-wise demeriting presumptions about his or her nature, learning, and potential achievement. These assumptions usually depart from the self-fulfilling perspective about these children as being different and as having previously assumed but unsubstantiated educational, behavioural, and developmental deficiencies. Basically, this is the essence of difference: not as natural to all, not as an asset, and surely not as dignity, but as a type of an inherent shortcoming that is specific to African Canadian learners and others who are, in one way or another, marginalized in the country's classrooms. This is not done with hostile intentions, nor is it the outcome of deliberately programmed, irresponsible acts of the school personnel. Rather, my point is that we have not overcome the falsely concocted historical attachments that define and stereotype the lives of those who are different from both the socially constructed norm or from the system-privileged few for whom the school, in its physical, policy, linguistic, and overall pedagogical parcels, is designed and constructed. Needless to add, there are thick philosophical and epistemological threads that are also at work, which interactively establish the relationship between the schooling system and the negatively different African Canadian student.

Dewey's focus on the necessary instructional realignments between the learner, the locus, and the practices of schooling is not monological but dialogical; young learners are not just waiting for what happens, but are interactively seeking spaces of connectively constructive possibilities that respond to their cultural and subjective relationships. That is, the African Canadian child can immediately and critically understand the way their difference is being perceived, constructed, and epistemically relayed to them. That reality will, indeed, make more sense to all of us when we not only shatter, both descriptively and analytically, the false de-philosophications and de-epistemologizations of people in Africa proper and in the African Diaspora, but, as well, and with humanist and inclusive social development intentions, when we eradicate the epistemic marginalization of young learners, who, as I always say to the students I teach, know so much more than we are willing to credit them with.

SOME WAYS FORWARD

It is the case, therefore, that, with the intergenerational cognitive and current familial packages these children carry, someone in the Canadian education system, which is provincially designed, funded, and dispensed, should re-culture and re-contextualize these learning systems for these unique learners. To some a priori oppositional minds, this might seem like asking for irrational interventions on behalf of select populations, interventions that do not make rational sense. I deliberately use the words "rational" and "irrational" to make a wider point. In the planned processes of de-philosophizing and de-epistemologizing African educational and social development possibilities, one of the claims was that these systems were irrational. That is, they were outside the domain of any quasi-measurable epistemic clusters that should have been emanating from the Enlightenment-driven rationalizations of scientism, and they were, therefore, pre-modern, developmentally primitive, and socially backward. As we have entered the debates of post-modern epistemologies and post-structuralist knowledge and textual critiques, we may have quasi-successfully dissipated some of these counter-humanist assumptions of scientism, but when it comes to pre-tertiary education classrooms, not much that enfranchises diverse epistemic possibilities has taken place. This is so much the case that, in current actualities, one can walk into, or electronically connect to, the library systems of some schools in multicultural Canada, and literally encounter subjectively colonizing literatures that are being prescribed as useful knowledge categories. Such realities make clear that we need to extend our epistemic concerns to the decommissioning of the false exhortations masquerading as real knowledge about Africa and Africans that are still with us.

Indeed, in dealing with the problematic learning and teaching intersections that are being described and analyzed here, what we need, as much as anything else, is to establish cogent epistemic and pedagogical counter-points and possibilities that can remedy the situation for the sake of these young learners, who are an important component of Canada's future. That philosophico-praxical intention will help us avoid being overwhelmed by the magnitude of the problems and their attendant complexities and opportunity-blocking outcomes. To be sure, in Canada's factually multicultural, multi-ethnic realities, when African Canadian children are actively and effectively educated along with other Canadians, they procure for themselves, their families, their communities, and their country an important socio-economic well-being perspective and practice that add so much good to the country's public space livelihood possibilities. With this understanding and with Canada's voluntarily globalized location, where the realities of knowledge-based, open-border, and continually competing societies is becoming the norm, all Canadians must see any uniquely useful and epistemically decolonizing opportunities pragmatically constructed through the prevailing educational policies and programmatically implemented viable schooling projects rightfully accorded to these children as bright achievements for their country. As such, it is high time to try to convince Canadian educators to open their minds and to design their pedagogical aims and practices in ways that enfranchise the learning lives of African Canadian students. It bears repeating that the advice we offer here is not about impractically privileging some over others; it is rather about selectively privileging the previously unprivileged in the schooling system with new, inclusive ways of thinking, teaching, and learning that deliberately enfranchise the educational locations and cognitive subjectivities of African Canadian children, as it has been doing for others for so many years.

CONCLUSION

In this chapter, I have engaged a descriptive and an analytical perspective on the historical and related attachments that problematically affect the learning realities of African Canadian children in the country's schooling contexts. The observations contained here may sound critical of current schooling systems, but as far as I am concerned, they are critical in the original constructions of the essence of criticism. That is, they constructively point out that there are tangible weaknesses in the way the learning needs of these children are addressed by the system, and as such, these critical suggestions for improvement must be presented by those like myself whose *devoir intellectuel actif* falls vertically on understanding and analyzing the role of education in the well-being of individuals and societies. Needless to add, the issue actually goes beyond the lives of these specific learners and their specific attachments, extending to their communities or to other socio-geographically identifiable structures. It also has a lot to do with the overall development of the country itself, as these youngsters are tomorrow's productive thinkers, workers, and leaders who should assure that Canada remains an inclusive, globally connected and selectively competitive nation that achieves the best for all its citizens. Without the "right" platforms of education, these personal and national aspirations would not be realized as needed and expected; indeed, they could only be realized in the best possible ways, with so many more resources and better focus. In my reading, therefore, it is imperative that Canadian education policy makers, schools managers, and teachers clearly see this major, essential, and nationally binding need, and respond to it with learning and pedagogical equities that enfranchise the historical, cultural, epistemological, and other cognitively attached needs of African Canadian children, so they may join the ranks of the already privileged in the country's schooling structures and outcomes.

REFERENCES

Abdi, A.A. 1999. "Identity Formations and Deformations in South Africa: A Historical and Contemporary Overview." *Journal of Black Studies* 30(2): 147–63.

– 2008. "Europe and African Thought Systems and Philosophies of Education: 'Re-culturing' the Trans-temporal Discourses." *Cultural Studies* 22(2): 309–27.

– 2014. "Difference, Social Justice and Educational Equity in Canada." In *Education in North America*, edited by D.E. Mulcahy, D.G. Mulcahy and R. Saul, 67–83. London: Bloomsbury Publishing.

Abdi, A.A., L. Shultz, R.A. Van Beers, and S. Wittes. 2013. "Dignity of Difference: Who Is Different in Our Classrooms?" Paper presented at the Central-East Alberta Teachers Association Conference, Edmonton, Alberta.

Achebe, Chinua. 2000. *Home and Exile*. New York: Oxford University Press.

– [1958] 2009. *Things Fall Apart*. Reprint, Toronto: Anchor Canada.

Bandura, A. 2006. "Toward a Psychology of Human Agency." *Perspectives on Psychological Sciences* 1(2): 164–80.

Battiste, M. 1998. "Enabling the Autumn Seed: Toward a Decolonized Approach to Aboriginal Knowledge, Language and Education." *Canadian Journal of Native Education* 22(1): 16–27.

Césaire, A. [1972] 2001. *Discourse on Colonialism*. Trenton, NJ: Monthly Review Press.

Dei, G.J.S., J. Mazzuca, and E. McIsaac. 1997. *Reconstructing "Dropout": A Critical Ethnography of the Dynamics of Black Students' Disengagement from School*. Toronto: University of Toronto Press.

Dewey, J. [1938] 1997. *Experience and Education*. New York: Free Press.

Fanon, F. 1967. *Black Skin, White Masks*. New York: Grove Press.

– 1968. *The Wretched of the Earth*. New York: Gove Press.

Freire, P. [1970] 2000. *Pedagogy of the Oppressed*. Reprint, New York: Continuum.

– 2004. *Pedagogy of Hope*. London: Bloomsbury.

Ghosh, R., and A.A. Abdi. 2013. *Education and the Politics of Difference: Select Canadian Perspectives*. Toronto: Canadian Scholars' Press.

Goldberg, D.T. 2002. *The Racial State*. Malden, MA: Blackwell.

Kane, H. [1963] 2012. *Ambiguous Adventure*. Brooklyn, NY: Melville House.

Mayo, P. 2008. *Liberating Praxis: Paulo Freire's Legacy for Radical Education and Politics*. Rotterdam, Netherlands: Sense Publishers.

Memmi, A. [1957] 1991. *The Colonizer and the Colonized*. Reprint, Boston, MA: Beacon Press.

Nyerere, J. 1968. *Freedom and Socialism: A Selection from Writing and Speeches, 1965–1967*. London: Oxford University Press.

Ozmon, H., and S. Craver. 2002. *Philosophical Foundations of Education*. Upper Saddle River, NJ: Prentice Hall.

Rodney, W. 1982. *How Europe Underdeveloped Africa*. Washington, DC: Howard University Press.

wa Thiong'o, N. 1986. *Decolonising the Mind: The Politics of Language in African Literature*. London: Heinemann.

– 1993. *Moving the Centre: The Struggle for Cultural Freedoms*. London: Heinemann.

– 2009. *Re-membering Africa*. Nairobi: East Africa Educational Publishers.

Said, E. 1978. *Orientalism*. New York: Vintage.

– 1993. *Culture and Imperialism*. New York: Vintage.

Woodson, C.G. [1933] 2010. *The Mis-Education of the Negro*. Reprint, Seattle: Create Space Books.

4

Diaspora, Citizenry, Becoming Human, and the Education of African Canadian Youth

Marlon Simmons

The unceasing emergence of transnational and multicultural identities to Canada has raised important questions with regard to how the politics of race, citizenry, and Diaspora play out in schooling and education. This chapter works to interrupt colonial epistemological configurations of citizenry as historically institutionalized through the conduits of schooling and education. In doing so, I query the ways in which African Canadian youth come to understand questions of citizenry and what it means to be human through ancestral familyhood, belief in common origin, shared histories, and collective consciousness immanent to the African Diaspora. I am concerned with the lived experiences of African Canadian youth regarding questions of the self, as the self comes to be historically contoured through the social terrain of the immutable cultural constellations of Euro-modernity. I am interested in how and by what means African Canadian Diasporized bodies come to make meaning of their everyday social interactions. By way of critical social theory, the pedagogical hope is to invoke a sense of critical perspicacity on the quotidian moments within Diasporic life in order to understand how the myriad experiences of African Canadian youth might come to be accepted through colonial forms of abjection. Moreover, it is important to understand how abjection as immanent to colonialism embodies the ethical and moral conditions of Diasporic "truths" for African Canadian youth to come to make meaning of their experiences within the governing socio-cultural environments in which they reside. Through this interpretive framework, I write to make sense of the way in which terms of citizenry, belonging, and race necessitate and constitute each other. In particular, I wish to explore how citizenry and belonging are spatiotemporally shifting concepts, contested and historically implicating how African Canadian youth experience civic participation in the globalized context of the nation-state. The purpose here is to extricate the category of "African Canadian youth" from a homogeneous socialization of historical, hegemonic Eurocentric cultural practices of modernity by engaging in what I understand to be "selective communicative practices" that come to self-determine civic participation of African Canadian youth within the Canadian public sphere. In other words, I am concerned here with how African Canadian youth come to make intelligible belonging to place through a range of cultural practices and attachments involving local histories within the globalized nation-state context of Canada. In particular, the discussion is interested with the myriad historical orientations of belonging for African Canadian youth as belonging becomes socially constructed and discursively produced within contemporary Canadian societies.

CITIZENRY, COLONIALITY, AND THE EMERGENCE OF THE HUMAN

Historically, citizenry in the context of Canada emerged from colonial settler nation-state relations. Yet, in coming to understand this question of citizenry as immanent to African Canadian youth, we ought to spatiotemporally locate the discursive of citizenry through particular geohistoric specificities as embodied through difference. In so doing, we allow for the variant possibilities of coming to know how questions of belonging and situatedness by way of cultural attachments come to be contextually ascribed through place to particular African Canadian bodies. Indeed, how citizenry comes to be located in the West in relation to Africa has quite distinct moments. For the most part in the West, in particular Canada, citizenry as legitimized by the nation-state reveals itself through particular civic tropes, in which citizenry becomes imbued through universalized classification of morals and principles of equality and character, culminating in human rights and state-endowed rituals of governance (see Chatterjee 1993; Rose 2007; Breton 2005; Montgomery 2005). Often enough, these said rituals of citizenry present themselves as de-raced or de-ethnicized, neutral and objective, as internalized within the imaginary of the public sphere, and as being natural to the lived experiences of what it means to be human. Yet, these naturalized rituals of citizenry have been fashioned through a constellation of historical socio-cultural elements as constituted through colonial epistemologies, which, through time and space, have concretized into an arrangement of edifices that come to be interpreted as always already permanent (Guba and Lincoln 1994). However, concerning the human in the context of African Canadian peoples, we ought to consider how citizenry reveals itself through the myriad lived contingencies of the African Diaspora as augured through colonization, oral histories, cultural ways of knowing, Indigenous knowledge, local languages, religions, land, ancestral lineage, and spirituality (wa Thiong'o 1993,1986). We ought to consider how these African contingencies, when colonially uprooted by way of transatlantic enslavement, become integrated or alienated within the globalized transnational epoch of Canada, tacitly producing the conditions of possibility for African Canadian humanness.

Notable and central to the performative practices of citizenry in the context of Canada are the agentizing acts of being human as cryptically scripted through Enlightenment narratives of Euro-modernity, which have historically been made possible through particular historical exigencies, such as hypermilitarized forms of violence, expropriation of Indigenous lands, and indentureship and enslavement of African peoples. The utopian objective has been the formation of the liberal democratic state, in which, historically, citizenry, for the preferred subject, has been represented through the cultural logic of the colonial settler (see also Jameson 2005). Ultimately, this historical cultural logic of the colonial settler gave rise to a particular citizenry as formed through a cultural homogeneity immanent to the Eurocentric West. This cultural logic was supposedly objective, and universalized as ontological, as some natural process. At the same time, citizenry as emerging from the African Diaspora through anti-colonial practices by way of transatlantic movement becomes immersed within a host of hegemonic cultural exchanges of Western modernity. These cultural exchanges, through the advent of time and myriad configurations of globalization, become spatially located onto bodies, simultaneously ascribing political articulations of citizenry and agency onto African Canadian youth. Within the contemporary epoch of late modernity, these political articulations of African Canadian citizenry diverge and converge through discontinuities and continuities of primordial encryptions of belonging to a particular place, that of Africa, as well as being contiguous with the governing cultural edicts of what it means to belong within the nation-state of Canada. For citizenry of the "Other" – historicized as being less than human, inferior to Western culture, and abject (Fanon 1963, 1967)

– to come into the human condition involves taking up practices, attitudes, expressions, dispositions of Western culture as one's own (Bourdieu 1991). This simultaneously promotes the understanding and the acceptance of the local culture of the "Other" as inferior, hence strategically distancing the self in ways in which one has to de-race, de-ethnicize, and de-culturalize the self to come into the freedoms of what it means to be human.

Of interest is the relationship with these different forms of citizenry as they come to coalesce within the Western sphere, and as they shape and reshape the historical contours of the Western subject. What are the challenges of invoking a sum secured identity onto African Canadian youth, as this sense of being secured comes to be troubled through complex Diasporized histories? What are the limits and possibilities of being human by way of coming to belong to a particular Diasporized nationalist identity through protean yet immutable classificatory edifices, such as race, sexuality, gender, language, religion, ethnicity, nationalism, ableism, and culture? How might we understand variant African Canadian youth subjectivities as experienced through situational boundaries, contingent events within the interstices of nation-state Canada and cultural practices immanent to the African Diaspora? How do we make sense of the ways in which African Canadian youth come to be situated? At the same time, how do African Canadian youth stabilize different political identities through particular historical paradigms?

Admittedly, this involves some arduous work. It involves thinking about what it means to have an invested interest in African Canadian youth, about the social science research methods we utilize within the educational context of African Canadian youth to engage this arduous work, and in doing so, what particular political identities are challenged, secured, made privileged, and empowered. I imagine it involves historically charting the colonial project of education and implicating the role of archetype expert texts in fragmenting the world into "us," "them," and "Other" schisms, and hence the constructing of particular privileged and simultaneous disenfranchised geographies. It involves questions of collective responsibility for pedagogues with the aim of social change, social justice, and lifelong learning. This is an invitation to understand the citizenry of African Canadian as an embodied discursive material space, which comes to be constituted through particular historical practices. It is a material space which becomes shaped through the continuities and discontinuities of the primordial (Geertz 1983) and simultaneously through socio-cultural contingent discourses.

The challenge, as Gramsci (1971) reminds us, is to come to know sub-jectivity through the historically specific procedures that have tacitly sedimented limitless traits within the self (324). How then do we un-derstand African Canadianness through ancestral familyhood, belief in common origin, shared histories, and collective consciousness as transatlantically relocated, spatiotemporally reconfigured, and socio-culturally constituted practices? We ask this, keeping in mind that Di-asporized bodies who historically have embodied social spaces since the colonization of time (Smith 1999) have provided alternative possi-bilities for different African subjects to come to de-centre the colonial unified subject (Hall 1997, 2000, 2005).

BELONGING, BEING HUMAN, AND QUESTIONS OF THE PRIMORDIAL

With the African Diaspora procuring different geo-locations for African Canadian peoples, belonging then becomes experienced through mem-ory of the colonial past and present, and through an embodiment of knowledge as ontologically embedded within cultural artifacts, prac-tices, and variant attachments to the African Diaspora. It is about mem-ory of the past and present. Belonging for African Canadian youth becomes contingent on a multiplicity of factors productive of modes of inclusion and exclusion. We need to think about the means of inclusion and exclusion that govern the lived, socio-cultural public sphere of African Canadian youth. We need to dialectically place the communi-ties of African Canadian youth in relation to colonialism, settler na-tion-state, Eurocentric immigration policies, and anti-colonial practices to historically trace the socio-cultural regulation of African Canadian communities as inscribed through the colonial forays embedded with-in imperial immigration policies. Importantly, African Canadian youth, through the historical contours of capitalism, Diaspora, Civil Rights, and anti-colonial interventions, have come to diverge and converge in ways that are multi-ethnic, multilingual, and multifaith. Heteroge-neous, to say the least, African Canadian youth are transhistorically but-tressed in the present neo-liberal nation-state that is deployed as multicultural. What I am primarily concerned with now regarding African Canadian youth are contemporary questions of governance by way of particular socio-cultural practices that come to inform everyday communicative exchanges. What are the ways in which the lived, socio-cultural practices of African Canadian youth become governed through primordial routes as historically imbued through shared collective consciousness of the African Diaspora? Notably, primordial intersubjectivities of African Canadian youth are protean, existing within the present through historical epistemes, unremittingly transformed through intergenerations of culture (see also Allahar 1994), and continuously informing African Canadian lived experiences through inexpressible ways of coming to know and to understand their everyday, socio-cultural environment. Further, I am suggesting that primordial intersubjectivities, as constituted through the African Diaspora, in and of itself, are immanent within subversive pedagogies. This lends to different forms of agency that speak to the necessity for self-determination for African Canadian youth, insofar as self-determination has become a principled factor in the quest for African peoples with historical proximities to colonial encumbering of what it means to be human.

But how do we understand belonging and becoming human through shared histories, common origins, and collective consciousness immanent to the African Diaspora for African Canadian youth in the present context of globalization and transnationalism within the deployed multicultural nation-state? And how do these understandings of belonging and being human come to help with providing an interpretive framework for the education of African Canadian youth? I suggest this would involve a series of transhistorical loci of questions that dialogue with historical artifacts such as colonization, migration, religion, language, and culture as these historical artifacts become spatiotemporally governed through histories of the past and present alike. The learning objective is to recognize certain instants, germane to the education of African Canadian youth, that surfaced through historic, specific interstices as cryptically codified through the different socio-cultural practices buttressed within the African Diaspora. It involves understanding the historical procedures that come to govern illiberal nomenclatures within the liberal multicultural nation-state. We ought to also understand how these different moments of African Canadian history are interconnected through shared spaces of resistance, alienation, and solidarity, and through cogent ways of integrating within contemporary society. Consequently, our epistemological challenge is to come into ways of knowing and understanding the said preconditions of African Canadian youth in which these shared transatlantic spaces of resistance, solidarity, and cogent integrative practices come to be constituted and govern the self within the present epoch. Importantly, these cultural, transatlantic lacunae of the African Diaspora, as constituted between the primordial and the present, the material and the immaterial, ought to be reified to hence understand transformative possibilities for the education of African Canadian youth.

With the education of African Canadian youth, it is important to note African Canadian subjectivities as shaped through cultural Diasporized sensibilities, and how and what self-determining communicative practices become governed through embodied transatlantic temporalities. Yet, these transatlantic cultural subjectivities of African Canadian youth, as spatially located through the primordial and the present, invariably parlay themselves through mutually exclusive cultural practices within the governing public sphere, and, at times, are dependent on each other coexisting harmoniously. On occasion, these transatlantic subjectivities of African Canadian youth articulate themselves in varied tendencies without unevenness; yet simultaneously they operationalize tangentially or even counter to the hegemonic cultural politics immanent to nation-state citizenry. This hermeneutic task, in and of itself, becomes an exercise in decolonization as it accords decentring hegemonic ways of knowing. However, decolonization for purposes of self-determination of African Canadian youth involves dialoguing with local knowledge (Geertz 1983), local knowledge as imbued through Diasporized polities and cultural sensibilities. Also, self-determination for African Canadian youth, as transhistorically augured, comes into the human through particular terms and conditions of the governing neo-liberal public sphere. Hence, within the racialized particularities of the present, self-determination of African Canadian youth becomes reified through subjectivities, which dialectically interact with its quotidian socio-cultural environment through variable modes of desire and affect to come into some sense of self-actualization for African Canadian youth.

With archives of colonial citizenry as the archetypal referential cartography, African Canadian peoples become charted and mapped in tacit ways that locate the present self simultaneously within the historical simulacra of the preferred Euro-Enlightenment subject. What emerges for African Canadian peoples from these instantaneous corporeal referencings of colonial Enlightenment modernity are a series of cultural relations that cross-sectionally embed embodied modalities of what it means to belong and become human for African Canadian youth as Diasporized within the present. One of the ongoing challenges for the education of African Canadian youth is with understanding how belonging and being human are spatiotemporally governed by primordial means, and how the primordial becomes discursively produced and delimited heuristically through embodied ways of knowing, yet discursively figured through capitalist enterprise.

CITIZENSHIP, MULTICULTURALISM, DIASPORIZED SENSIBILITIES, AND BELONGING IN THE NATION-STATE: CONSTRAINTS, REGULARITIES, AND POSSIBILITIES FOR BECOMING HUMAN

What, then, does it mean for African Canadian youth to come to know the self through geo-histories, through their corporeality that has been historically situated as abject, as materially ontological to plantation geographies, and as dehumanized through colonial epistemologies? How do we make sense of this posthuman immanent to this heterogeneous spatiality of African Canadian youth? Seemingly, these different geographies speak to the phenomenological modalities of Euro-modernity (Foucault 2007; Bauman 2004; Wynter 1995a, 1995b, 2001; Habermas 1998; Gilroy 1993; Giddens 1990, 1991; Appadurai 1996; Goldberg 2002; Scott 1995). Through these geographies we are left to make sense of how African Canadian youth and nation-state simultaneously come to recognize each other. Put another way, we are left to make sense about how African Canadian youth come into the material through protean-like desires and performatives, as well as how African Canadian youth endow particular dualisms immanent to nation-state imbued citizenry, such as permanence and the temporary, finitude and infinitude, and the mutable and immutable forays of being human. To come into this humanism through citizenship would entail embodying particular values, expressions, desires, attitudes, and articulations as parlayed through the historical dispositions of Euro-modernity. These performative moments of the African subject all come to be circumscribed by the state through this classification of ethnicity. Sylvia Wynter's argument is important here, when she notes, "[T]he struggle of our new millennium will be one between the ongoing imperative of securing the well-being of our present ethnoclass (i.e., Western bourgeois) conception of the human" (Wynter 2003, 260). Given the nation-state's historical gripe to secure homogeneity of citizenry and the African Diaspora syncretizing transhistorically through contemporaneous cultural variants, what we have through these tensions, then, are different articulations of the human becoming ontologically embodied by African Canadian youth.

James (1993) argues for the need for a nation-state to produce the integrative citizen, keeping in mind this integration has been, and continues to be, produced in and through a racialized gendering as governed through the capitalist mode of production, one that includes and simultaneously excludes racialized bodies of the Diaspora. Furthermore, my concern with belonging and being human is that it seems to be always already discursively positioned within spaces of the West, replete with a desire to consume the colonial harvest of globalization, and eagerly willing to be immersed within the techno-capitalist sphere of our contemporary social environment (Ahmad 2008: Jameson 2005; Mclaren and Farahmandpur 2005). If we are speaking about the variegated forms of citizenry of African Canadian youth as contextualized through particular historical precedents, we ought then to note the implications and the intricacies with ethnoracial histories of African Canadian youth, and the relationship with the state. This complex imperial relationship speaks to the spatiality of race. Space then becomes racialized/territorialized through particular historical readings on the body (McDermott and Simmons 2013). Legitimized and naturalized belongings become located to spaces in ways in which citizenry becomes engendered through Eurocentric forms of habitus. Indeed, the materialization of space consists of certain procedural arrangements. Citizenry as historically imbued through the "historical racial schema" (Fanon 1967) positions African Canadian youth in ways that de-settle colonial geographies while at the same time stabilizing the national subject (Scott 1995; McKittrick 2006; Ahmed 2000; Thobani, 2007; Simmons 2010, 2014). Althusser's "interpellation" is important here, particularly the thinking about how the material is engaged and the suggestion that "an ideology always exists in an apparatus, and its practice or practices, that this existence is material" (Althusser 2001, 112). With interpellation in mind, my interest concerns the variegated ways in which the African Canadian youth becomes interpellated into the human. It concerns place/space of transnational bodies, that is, bodies as identifying with the archival procedures of the state, as ritualized into the normatized, and as governing the material choices and practices of African Canadian youth. In effect, and as Thobani (2007) notes, African Canadian youth come to be "exalted" into being, into this accepted subject of the state. Yet, these processes of exaltation are embodied through the legal classification of "immigrant," insofar as the "immigrant" has come to be represented through historical polities of racialization. Coming to know the human through this mitigated place of "immigrant" means speaking about the different bodies across time and space, understanding how particular geographies come to count, to be "preferred" and to be accepted, and also understanding the particular relationships with North–South geographies. Ultimately, these capillary-like relations are deeply embedded within a colonial-capitalist agenda, materializing through the auspices of globalization. North–South movements of peoples have historically been, and continue to be, ushered imperially through socio-economic relations. Being/becoming the nation-state subject of this place discursively legitimized as Canada involves the expropriation of Indigenous lands (Zinn 1997; Churchill 2009). It involves movement from geographies that have been impoverished. It involves the centering of particular Euro-cultures and bodies. It involves African Canadian bodies of the Diaspora installing onto itself nation-state practices and policies that accord privilege, privilege that concomitantly articulates complicity with the colonial governmentality of the state.

Doing citizenry for African Canadian youth involves having relationships with the land and the state; it involves Pierre Trudeau's policy of multiculturalism, which supposedly allowed for a legal turn from the colonial perception of white Canada to an inclusive Canada, and concomitantly welcomed bodies of Southern geographies. What, then, does this nation-state deployed discursive of multiculturalism mean for African Canadian youth within present day forms of citizenry in the context of post-Trudeau Canada? Although promising, multiculturalism as a legal policy represented many limitations concerning questions addressing the historical socio-cultural context about citizenry, difference, and Diasporized bodies, systemic racism, power, and privilege. Multiculturalism, however, has given the Canadian state the agency to re-inscribe the nation through bodies of difference, primarily through the organization of racial and linguistic differences as these differences come to be articulated through the celebratory trope of culture (Simmons 2011; Thobani 2007; Walcott 2003; Brand 2001; Ahmed 2000; Ibrahim 2000). Hence, the material tensions immanent within the coloniality of nation-state come to be masked through the normatizing of Diasporic silence. Multiculturalism, then, allows for an African Canadian youth to legally perform her or his citizenry through his or her subjectivity by way of accepting these standardized social practices as engendered through the nation-state. At the same time, the question of authentication always remains suspect regarding the citizenry of African Canadian youth. Belonging to a nation involves a particular discursive material production of bodies. It involves social relations of production. It involves the act of African Canadian youth recognizing the ritualized dispositions of citizenry, an interpellating act that concomitantly continues to produce what it means to be human by way of centring this variegated articulation of the Euro-Enlightenment subject in relation to the abject, tangentialized subject of difference. Perhaps we also need to remind ourselves that this discursive material production of citizenry is underscored by the expropriation of Indigenous lands, the extermination of Indigenous peoples, and the colonial conquest of Indigenousness in which the axiological, the ontological, and the epistemological ways of coming to know across time and space have been deemed universally inferior in their totality (Abdi 2011; Dei and Simmons 2009, 2012). What multiculturalism has yet to do is own up to how these different cultures, as located through histories of conquest, come to be re-located within the imperial West, and, at the same time, how this re-location becomes constituted through the exploitation of local peoples and the underdevelopment of racialized geographies (McLaren and Farahmandpur 2005; Rodney 1982). If we are thinking of belonging and being human as governed through the discursivities of multiculturalism, then I am suggesting we ought to disentangle the politics of movement embedded within the congeries of the nation-state, globalization, and the Diaspora, inasmuch as this politics of movement is about the material as constituted through race.

CONCLUSION

With this discussion, I addressed particular modes of belonging and becoming human for African Canadian youth as engendered through cultural practices, attachments, and Diasporic situatedness. I am suggesting the education of African Canadian youth must consider how citizenry, as a historical variant concomitant to colonial modernity, come to imperially encumber African Canadian youth as essentialized ontological artifacts to particular geo-spaces of the African Diaspora. I am suggesting the governing culture of schooling and education ensues a particular type of citizenry, one in which the determinants have been buttressed through historical trajectories to colonization that works to produce disenfranchising humanisms for African Canadian youth, simultaneously enabling some hegemonic sense of sovereign citizenry through a host of cultural practices and attachments. Citizenry in our contemporaneous moment, as discursively formed through schooling and education, and as embedded within the governing culture of colonial modernity, unevenly organizes African Canadian youth within their socio-cultural public sphere through certain reactionary programs entitled by means of the nomenclatures of "diversity" and "equity." If we are thinking about the education of African Canadian youth, we ought to consider the ways in which African Canadian histories come to be displaced from schooling and education, in that we must think of education through Diasporized bodies alike and that knowledge resides within the experience of all peoples. If our collective goal speaks to questions of social change and justice, it seems to me one of the challenges for educational delivery, especially when it comes to understanding what it means *to be* African Canadian youth in our contemporary historical moment, lies with coming to understand differently what it means *to be human*.

REFERENCES

Abdi, A. 2011. "African Philosophies of Education: Deconstructing the Colonial and Reconstructing the Indigenous." In *Indigenous Philosophies and Critical Education: A Reader*, edited by G. Dei, 80–91. New York: Peter Lang.

Ahmad, A. 2008. *In Theory: Classes, Nations, Literatures*. New York: Verso.

Ahmed, S. 2000. "Multiculturalism and the Proximity of Strangers." In *Strange Encounters: Embodied Others in Post-coloniality*, edited by S. Ahmed, 95–113. New York: Routledge.

Allahar, A.L. 1994. "More Than an Oxymoron: Ethnicity and the Social Construction of Primordial Attachment." *Canadian Ethnic Studies* 26(3): 18–33.

Althusser, L. 2001. *Lenin and Philosophy and Other Essays*. New York: Monthly Review Press.

Appadurai, A. 1996. *Modernity at Large: Cultural Dimensions of Globalization*. Minneapolis: University of Minnesota Press.

Bauman, Z. 2004. *Wasted Lives: Modernity and Its Outcasts*. Oxford: Polity.

Bourdieu, P. 1991. *Language and Symbolic Power*. Cambridge, MA: Harvard University Press.

Brand, D. 2001. *A Map to the Door of No Return: Notes to Belonging*. Toronto: Random House.

Breton, R. 2005. "Ethnicity and Change in Canada." In *Ethnic Relations in Canada: Institutional Dynamics*, edited by R. Breton, 289–324. Montreal & Kingston: McGill-Queen's University Press.

Chatterjee, P. 1993. "Nationalism as a Problem in the History of Political Ideas." In *Nationalist Thought and the Colonial World: A Derivative Discourse*, edited by P. Chatterjee, 1–35. London: Zed Books.

Churchill, W. 2009. "The Indigenous World: Struggles for Traditional Lands and Ways of Life." In *The White Supremacist State: Eurocentrism, Imperialism, Colonialism, Racism*, edited by A.H. Itwaru, 1–24. Toronto: Other Eye.

Dei, G.J.S., and M. Simmons. 2009. "The Indigenous as a Site of Decolonizing Knowledge about Conventional Development and the Link with Edu-
cation: The African Case." In *Indigenous Knowledges, Development and
Education*, edited by J. Langdon, 15–36. Rotterdam: Sense Publishers.
– 2012. "Writing Diasporic Indigeneity through Critical Research and Social
Method." In *Critical Qualitative Research Reader*, edited by S. Steinberg and
G. Cannella, 296–306. New York: Peter Lang.
Fanon, F. 1963. *The Wretched of the Earth*. New York: Grove Press.
– 1967. *Black Skin, White Masks*. New York: Grove Press.
Foucault, M. 2007. *The Politics of Truth*. Los Angeles: Semiotext(e).
Geertz, C. 1983. *Local Knowledge: Further Essays in Interpretive Anthropology*.
New York: Basic Books.
Giddens, A. 1990. *The Consequences of Modernity*. California: Stanford Univer-
sity Press.
– 1991. *Modernity and Self-Identity: Self and Society in the Late Modern Age*.
California: Stanford University Press.
Gilroy, P. 1993. *The Black Atlantic: Modernity and Double Consciousness*. Cam-
bridge, MA: Harvard University Press.
Goldberg, D. T. 2002. *The Racial State*. Oxford: Blackwell Publishing.
Gramsci, A. 1971. *Selections from the Prison Notebooks*. New York: Internation-
al Publishers.
Guba, E.G., and Y.S. Lincoln. 1994. "Competing Paradigms in Qualitative
Research." In *Handbook of Qualitative Research*, edited by N.K. Denzin and
Y.S. Lincoln, 105–17. Thousand Oaks, CA: Sage.
Habermas, J. 1998. "Modernity—An Incomplete Project." In *The Anti-aesthetic:
Essays on Postmodern Culture*, edited by H. Foster, 1–15. New York: The
New Press.
Hall, S. 1997. "Subjects in History: Making Diasporic Identities." In *The
House That Race Built: Black Americans, U.S. Terrain*, edited by W. Lubiano,
280–99. New York: Pantheon Books.
– 2000. "Cultural Identity and Diaspora." In *Diaspora and Visual Culture:
Representing Africans and Jews*, edited by N. Mirzoeff, 21–33. London:
Routledge.
– 2005. "New Ethnicities." In *Stuart Hall: Critical Dialogues in Cultural
Studies*, edited by D. Morley and K. Chen, 441–9. New York: Routledge.
Ibrahim, A.E.K.M. 2000. "'Hey, ain't I black too?' The Politics of Becoming
Black." In *Rude: Contemporary Black Canadian Cultural Criticism*, edited by
R. Walcott, 109–36. Toronto: Insomniac Press.
James, C.L.R. 1993. *American Civilization*. Cambridge, MA: Blackwell
Publishers.

Jameson, F. 2005. *Postmodernism or the Cultural Logic of Late Capitalism.* Durham: Duke University Press.

McDermott, M., and M. Simmons. 2013. "Embodiment and the Spatialization of Race." In *Contemporary Issues in the Sociology of Race and Ethnicity: A Critical Reader,* edited by G.J.S. Dei and M. Lordan, 153–68. New York: Peter Lang.

McKittrick, K. 2006. *Demonic Grounds: Black Women and the Cartographies of Struggle.* Minneapolis: University of Minnesota Press.

Mclaren, P., and R. Farahmandpur. 2005. *Teaching against Global Capitalism and the New Imperialism.* New York: Rowman and Littlefield Publishers.

Montgomery, K. 2005. "Banal Race-Thinking: Ties of Blood. Canadian History Textbooks and Ethnic Nationalism." *Paedagogica Historica* 41(3): 313–36.

Rodney, W. 1982. *How Europe Underdeveloped Africa.* Washington, DC: Howard University Press.

Rose, N. 2007. *Powers of Freedom: Reframing Political Thought.* New York: Cambridge University Press.

Scott, D. 1995. "Colonial Governmentality." *Social Text* 43:191–220.

Simmons, M. 2010. "Concerning Modernity, the Caribbean Diaspora and Embodied Alienation: Dialoguing with Fanon to Approach an Anti-colonial Politic." In *Fanon and Education: Thinking through Pedagogical Possibilities,* edited by G.J.S. Dei and M. Simmons, 171–89. New York: Peter Lang.

– 2011. "The Race to Modernity: Understanding Culture through the Diasporic-Self." In *The Politics of Cultural Knowledge,* edited by N. Wane, A. Kempf, and M. Simmons, 37–50. Rotterdam: Sense Publishers.

– 2014. "Politics of Urban-Diasporized Youth and Possibilities for Belonging." In *Critical Youth Studies Reader,* edited by A. Ibrahim and S. Steinberg, 195–204. New York: Peter Lang.

Smith, L.T. 1999. *Decolonizing Methodologies: Research and Indigenous Peoples.* London: Zed Books and University of Otago Press.

Thobani, S. 2007. *Exalted Subject: Studies in the Making of Race and Nation in Canada.* Toronto: University of Toronto Press.

Walcott, R. 2003. *Black Like Who? Writing Black Canada.* Toronto: Insomniac Press.

wa Thiong'o, N. 1986. *Decolonising the Mind: The Politics of Language in African Literature.* Oxford: James Currey. Nairobi: EAEP. Portsmouth, NH: Heinemann.

– 1993. *Moving the Centre: The Struggle for Cultural Freedoms.* Oxford: James Currey. Nairobi: EAEP. Portsmouth, NH: Heinemann.

Wynter, S. 1995a. "1492: A New World View." In *Race, Discourse, and the Origin of the Americas,* edited by V.L. Hyatt and R. Nettleford, 1–57. Washington, DC: Smithsonian Institute.

– 1995b. "The Pope Must Have Been Drunk, the King of Castile a Madman: Culture as Actuality, and the Caribbean Rethinking Modernity." In *The Reordering of Culture: Latin America, the Caribbean and Canada (in the Hood),* edited by A. Rupercht and C. Taiana, 1–41. Ottawa: Carleton University Press.

– 2001. "Towards the Sociogenic Principle: Fanon, Identity, the Puzzle of Conscious Experience, and What It Is Like to Be 'Black.'" In *National Identities and Socio-political Changes in Latin America,* edited by M.F. Duran-Cogan and A. Gomez-Moriana, 30–66. New York: Routledge.

– 2003. "Unsettling the Coloniality of Being/power/truth/freedom: Towards the Human, after Man, Its Overrepresentation – An Argument." *The New Centennial Review* 3(3): 257–337.

Zinn, H. 1997. *A People's History of the United States.* New York: New Press.

5

Slavery, Childhood, and the Racialized "Education" of Black Girls

Charmaine A. Nelson

Few colored girls reach the age of sixteen without receiving advances from them – maybe from a young "upstart," and often from a man old enough to be their father, a white haired veteran of sin.

A Southern Colored Woman 1904, 587, 589

As we went out in the morning, I observed several women, who carried their young children in their arms to the field ... One young woman did not, like the others, leave her child at the end of the row, but had contrived a sort of rude knapsack ... in which she fastened her child, which was very young, upon her back; and in this way carried it all day, and performed her task at the hoe with the other people.

J.W. Shugert 1836, 150–1

The term "childhood" marks a specific temporal and social designation of assumed human development, which conjures images of attention, love, play, and learning, and being protected by one's parents and sheltered from social contamination (Ross 1993; Duncan 1982). However, childhood is not a universal category, not an automatic benefit of one's age, but rather it is the product of a discursive structure that both empowers and marginalizes on the basis of identity.

Originating in the thought of eighteenth-century philosophers, our current ideals about childhood were forged through the repeated alienation of subjects who were not white and upper class. To examine race and childhood is to call for a postcolonial reading capable of scrutinizing the ways that Childhood Studies has neglected the bodies and subjectivities of black children. To examine race, class, sex, and gender simultaneously is to acknowledge the necessity of black/postcolonial feminist practice and to account for distinctions between male and female subjects. For the purpose of this chapter, I am considering childhood to include the time from infancy into the early to middle teen years, in part because of the socialization and developmental processes that every human must undergo, and also because of the standard age of the start of menarche (globally seen as a girl's rite of passage) in enslaved black girls, which Trussell and Steckel (1978) have calculated as age fifteen (see also White 1999).

It is my contention that historical representations of black children in Canada and in other locations of Diaspora demand an understanding of the erasure of black childhood within transatlantic slavery. Slavery is the very foundational ground upon which notions of personhood and childhood became racialized, and black children were effectively marked off from white children in biology, appearance, behaviour, and experience. Although this chapter attempts to recuperate the social, cultural, and psychic contexts of black girls' lives in Canadian history by examining the ways that they were represented in Canadian art, the task requires an examination of relevant information about, and artworks representing, slave populations and free black subjects in other diasporic contexts.

Slavery was a profoundly conflicted and grotesque institution of mind-boggling events and practices, which seem today to make impossible bedfellows. It necessitated the constant physical, sexual, and biological coerced intimacy between whites and blacks. This *perverse intimacy* – wherein black bodies were a necessity of white power, society, sexuality, economy, and family – did not lead to the liberation of black subjects but to their further marginalization and abuse. Enslaved black children inhabited this world, and their production through visual representation is the necessary foundation for an understanding of their access to, and strategic exclusion from, Western mainstream education. This exploration also sheds light on the nature of the alternative "educations" to which black children were normally subjected.

BLACK FEMALE SLAVES, REPRODUCTION, AND LABOUR

The racial abuses of slavery confounded traditional Western notions of gender, sex, and age. It is clear that the health of all slaves was generally compromised. From most critical accounts, malnutrition and overwork were commonplace and had immediate and long-lasting detrimental impacts on generations of Africans, starting in the womb. Kiple and Kiple (cited in Steckel, 1986) have argued that, although in the prenatal period a fetus will draw from a mother's skeletal stores to satisfy its mineral requirements, the maternal deficiencies of enslaved women, combined with multiple pregnancies, made for a progressive "bankruptcy" of those stores.

Steckel (1986) has compiled significant data on slavery nutrition, health, growth, and mortality in the context of the United States. Commenting on the small stature of black slave children, Steckel has argued, "The origins of poor health can be traced to difficult periods of fetal and infant growth" (732). And these slave children were the "lucky" ones, in that they were able to survive at all. The ability of the enslaved to reproduce themselves, or what slave owners called "natural increase," had much to do with their overall and reproductive health and labour practices, and this differed across location. In most tropical locations of Diaspora, commercial interests were dominated by mono-crop agricultural production fuelled by the labour of black male *and* female slaves. Mair's (2000) scholarship on Jamaica has revealed that "[i]n 1832, sugar employed 49.5 per cent of the slave work force. The majority of those workers were women, the ratio being 920 males to 1,000 females" (390). Black slave women performed hard labour, in gruelling physical, environmental, and climactic conditions, mostly with crude technology and substandard provision of nutrition, access to medicine or other health and welfare care. In the Canadian context, too, the needs of the white owners overrode any normative, upper class gender ideals when it came to black female slaves and labour. In a Halifax slave sale advertisement of January 1779, a Negro woman of twenty-one years was described as "capable of performing both town and country work and an exceedingly good cook" (Riddell 1920, 363). While the reference to town work referenced domestic labour, the country work most likely indicated that this woman knew her way around a farm, and was skilled at various agricultural and field tasks. Due to the consistent absence of the slave mother, and, as a consequence, the absence of the black baby's only or main source of nourishment, slave children were *socialized into deprivation* at a very early stage.

This deprivation was not only about the inability of their mothers to provide sufficient nutrition (Treckel 1989) through the quantity and quality of their milk or through the amount of feedings (Steckel 1986). Absence and inconsistency must be seen as key modalities of the black mother–child relationship within slavery, modalities with profound psychic as well as physical repercussions for mothers and children alike. A chilling recollection that points out the psychic and psychological dimension of this trauma comes from William Wells Brown, who, as a slave child, recalled being the "cause of his mother's whippings" (cited in White 1999, 113). It is hard to fathom the psychic and emotional burden that black slave children would have felt when they reached an age at which they connected their mother's loving attention to her violent abuse.

SLAVERY, "BREEDING," AND SEXUALIZATION OF ENSLAVED BLACK GIRLS

The practice of "breeding" female slaves to reproduce labour became commonplace in the USA by the mid-eighteenth century. As a result, all aspects of a female slave's life, including her marital status, workload, and diet, came under invasive scrutiny (White 1999). The exposed breast of the enslaved black female in the Canadian François Malépart de Beaucourt's *Portrait of a Negro Slave* (1786) [fig. 5.1] indexes her sexual labour and "breeding" potential as active considerations in her value and exchange (Nelson 2010). White has argued that a pregnant slave woman's lowered standard of care, at the discretion of the slave owners, was a strategy of animalization often resulting in illness and death (White 1999).

Black female slaves performed a tandem maternal duty, raising their owners' children and their own. The psychic burden of this coerced responsibility cannot be underestimated for several reasons. First, in various locations of Diaspora, the rearing of the white master's children, which sometimes included the responsibilities of wet nurse, was largely done at the expense of their own offspring (Treckel 1989). How long a slave woman nursed her child was dictated by the economic motivations and whims of her owner. Second, the rearing of white children was literally tantamount to the rearing of a slave's future owner/oppressor. And third, many children born to slave women were mixed race, the product of coerced sexual relations (rape and manipulation). The mental damage suffered by these black mothers who were forced to carry, birth, and care for the interracial children of their enslavers/rapists is difficult to quantify, but must be considered another catastrophic dimension of the trauma of slavery.

There are many nineteenth-century photographs of black women caregivers or nurses with white children. *Mrs Wilson's Nurse* (c. 1890s),

Fig. 5.1: François Malépart de Beaucourt, *Portrait of a Haitian Woman*, 1786.

created by an unknown American photographer, is a compelling example for the ways that it celebrates and seeks to naturalize these problematic cross-racial and cross-class relationships. A stout, middle-aged black woman is depicted lifting a hefty (and well-fed) white infant. The woman's face reflects pride and devotion, the gaze of motherly love. However, the white child does not return the black nurse's gaze. Instead, the baby looks off to the right, indicating another presence in the room. The photograph thereby encodes the likely presence of the white biological mother, whose signalling or noise-making has drawn the white child's attention away from the black mother/nurse, an ominous indication of things to come.

In a Canadian example, William H. Buckley's *Nanny with the Children in Her Care, Guysborough* (c. 1900) depicts a black female as the primary caregiver to the two white children, one standing at her left and the other being pushed by her in a carriage. The group's position evokes the idea of a "Sunday stroll." The black nanny is standing with her hand perched on the handle of the baby carriage as she stares into the camera. Her vision is likely not in her control as she has most likely been summoned to walk, to pose, and to look at the camera by command of William Buckley. The two children also look dutifully at the camera. The black woman's polished clothing, consisting of long skirt, pleated blouse, and decorated hat, mark her as being in the employ of an upper class family. As such, it is very likely that she was a live-in nanny, and that her service came at a very high price for her own family, if she was able to create and sustain one.

A slave girl's "education" into the racialized economy of sexual expectation and abuse would come early in her life. A part of this initiation would be through her contact with her older female family members, especially her mother, grandmother, and aunts, who would have tried to guard her against the unwanted sexual advances. It also would have come from the many moments when these girls were themselves witness to the sexual aggression of males towards other slave women. But slave owners seemed to have been just as quick to use manipulation as outright aggression in their bid for "natural increase."

White has argued that slave owners made it a point to sexually initiate adolescent female slaves by practicing "a passive, but insidious kind of breeding," through which they encouraged young slaves to create relationships by granting black males access to their young female slaves (White 1999, 98–9). In this way, White explains, slavers "educated" black girls about their expected future role as "breeders." "Breeders" were also rewarded with "pay-offs" by their happy masters (99–100). However, biological data of female slaves demonstrates that they clearly resisted, drawing out the time between menarche (mean age of 15) and their first birth (mean age of 20.6) (Trussel and Steckel 1978). However, due to the extreme social and economic value of reproductively healthy female slaves, for a female slave, to be "barren" was to at once experience a reprieve from potential sexual abuse motivated by "natural increase" and to suffer potential public humiliation linked to infertility (White 1999, 101).

BLACK MOTHERHOOD AND BLACK CHILDREN
IN WESTERN ART

The Western visual archive of black children is quite large but unusual. How and when black children appear in portraits and genre act as a disturbing reminder of Western colonial histories. Strategically deployed for their ability to cite exotic locations and mobilize references to the white bodies' colonial reach, wealth, and privilege, black children were often present as slaves or servants within white family portraits in the West. A black child's subservient status was generally noted both compositionally and directly on their bodies. In placement and activity, they were often shown as being "below" the white family in terms of what they were doing (which was labour) and in terms of how they were dressed and positioned (usually on a lower compositional register and at the outskirts of the central action). Due to their "exotic" potential, slaves were often dressed up in exoticizing garb or livery to further convey their foreignness (Tobin 1999). Equally, though, slave children were pictured in tattered, worn, and substandard clothing. As for the use of exoticizing dress, of course black slave children were not always foreign. Rather, many were born in the West and others had a white parent (usually father). However, such portraits allowed whites to erase the ever-increasing "European-ness" of their black slaves.

Black girls were likely to have serious illnesses, to suffer from malnutrition, to be the victim of sexual and racial abuse, and to bear the weight of consistent manipulation at the hands of whites. All this, however horrific, was simply normal. Given the histories of slave labour, sexuality, and motherhood across various locations of Diaspora, certain trends in the historical representation of black subjects are not surprising. One such trend is that there is a general absence of representations of black mothers with *their own* black children, and especially, an absence of works whose focus is the romanticized view of a mother-child bond. Canadian Henrietta Shore's *Negro Woman and Two Children* (c. 1916) [fig. 5.2] is a rare example of a black woman in a maternal role in reference to black children. The woman gazes directly and warily out at the viewers, her arms draped protectively down around the seated children. Her body language connotes an awareness of white antagonism to the black family and the various abuses that this implies. Although not explicitly named as a mother, her body language marks her as a protector. The infant's dress, along with the rattle that she absently grips, seem further to indicate the attentiveness, love, and care of her black "mother." The little girl seated in the im-

Fig. 5.2: Henrietta Shore, *Negro Woman and Two Children*, c. 1916.

mediate left foreground meets the viewers' gaze directly with her own,
a bright smile indicating that her childhood innocence might not yet
have been stolen.

Black subjects have been a frequent presence in the portraits of aris-
tocratic and bourgeois white families, and on rare occasions when the
black subject was the sole sitter, the works were often problematically
commissioned by the subject's white owner or employer, and the
women have remained unnamed, as in Canadian William Notman's
Mrs Cowan's Nursemaid (1871) [fig. 5.3]. *Mrs Cowan's Nursemaid* (1871),
Mrs Wilson's Nurse (c.1890s), and *Nanny with the Children in Her Care,
Guysborough* (c. 1900) all remind us that black women continued to
raise white children and care for white adults well after the end of

Fig. 5.3: William Notman, *Mrs Cowan's Nursemaid*, 1871.

slavery. This domestic servitude was, in part, due to the lack of educational opportunity fostered by racial segregation that ensured a lack of access to other employment. Although, in William Notman's *Mrs Cowan's Nursemaid* (1871), the young black female's white charge is absent, white power and authority is mapped onto the image through the process of naming, which displaced the black nurse's name, replacing it with that of the white employer. As such, even though a century removed from Beaucourt's *Portrait of a Negro Slave* (1786), these images are similarly structured.

REPRESENTING BLACK CHILDREN IN SLAVERY

European slavers did not spare children when purchasing their human cargo (Eltis and Richardson 2003). Children could be sold into slavery, or, due to its matrilineal organization, born into it, if their mothers were enslaved. But slavery in the Canadian context was largely not agriculturally driven, since the climate, which made for harsh winters, was not conducive to a mono-crop plantation culture. Instead, slaves in Canada, panis (Native) and black, worked in industries such as mining, fisheries, and lumber, or worked as domestics. Although as yet there are few known publicly owned artworks that represent black slave girls in Canada, enslaved black girls are represented in significant numbers in another archive. Slave sale and fugitive slave advertisements were posted in newspapers and produced as broadsheets. Slave sales were also documented in the legislation of Upper and Lower Canada and the Maritimes, and were witnessed by notaries or colonial administrators.

While some advertisements included a typecast or woodcut image, many others relied solely on the textual description of the slave's supposed physical characteristic and behaviours. But we must be cautious in using such advertisements and documents as authoritative descriptions of what a slave "really looked like" or how a slave "really acted." Instead, this archive is best used to study what white slave owners and the whites who conspired with them to preserve the status quo of the slave system *thought* about enslaved blacks; the archive reveals the corporeal and behavioural codes, mainly visual, that they constituted and circulated in order to reinforce and protect their power. These representations are about the power of white vision to script black bodies as property. Slavery in Canada was not only about whites needing or desiring labour; it was also about the profits that could be made in the exchange of human beings. As advertised in *The Halifax Gazette* on 15 May 1752, a group of six Negro slaves were "just imported and to be sold" at Major Lockman's store in Halifax (Riddell 1920, 360). The rapid turnaround implied by the word "just" signalled that the owner, Joshua Mauger, was intent on the quick disposal of his "property" for profit.

Canadian slave advertisements, whether regarding sales or runaways, have enormous commonalities with other locations in the Americas. The bulk of any such description then was corporeal, and hinged upon the anatomical and physiognomic specificity of the slave, detailing specific or extraordinary facial or bodily features. Not surprisingly, many of these descriptions, especially in slave sale advertisements, were devised to convey an idea of the good health and strength of a slave's body; for who would want to buy a slave that was sickly or infirm? In the case of the group sale in Halifax mentioned above, the two younger Negro boys (aged twelve and thirteen) were described as "likely, healthy, and well-shaped," an indication, most probably, of their muscle tone that would be read as a sign of their physical strength and endurance. Meanwhile, the eighteen-year-olds were described as being "healthy" and as possessing "agreeable tempers" (Riddell 1920, 360). Another sale at Halifax in 1769 was advertised as "two hogsheads of rum, three of sugar and two *well-grown* negro girls aged 14 and 12" to be sold to the highest bidder, clearly, noted Riddell, "a consignment from the West Indies" (362, italics added). "Well-grown" here likely indicated both their physical strength and, tragically, their future reproductive capacity as "breeders."

Canadian advertisements frequently described the race of the slave, a facet of identification that was extremely important given that both blacks and Natives (panis/panise) were both enslaved. A case in point was the sale in Halifax by Charles Proctor of a "Mulatta girl" to Mary Wood of Annapolis (Riddell 1920, 361–2). As regards black female slaves, these texts also reveal other disturbing information about the standard treatment of enslaved girls in Canada. First, enslaved black girls were regularly sold separately and apart from their parents or any older relatives. In two such cases in 1802, a three-year-old boy named Simon and a five-year-old girl named Catherine, both named as mulatto, were sold in Prince Edward Island (Riddell 1920). Second, there is evidence that enslaved black girls experienced an accelerated "childhood," being considered women in their mid to late teens, whereas comparably aged black male slaves were still listed as boys. Of course, these two issues were related, since it was, in part, the forced separation of slave girls from their mothers that would have accelerated their development into womanhood, if not biologically, then at least socially.

Louison and Isabella were two black slave girls who were very likely in just such a position, and each was sold alone. Louison was described as "a negro woman" of about seventeen years and Isabella or Bell as a "mulatto slave" of about fifteen years (Riddell 1923, 323–4). Both were sold to male buyers, Louison to a captain in the navy in the Montreal garrison on 6 June 1749, and Isabella to the lieutenant governor of Québec, Hectore-Théophile de Cramahé, on 14 November 1778 (Riddell). Isabella's case also highlights the normality of upheaval in a slave girl's life. In the course of several years, she was sold at least four times (Riddell). The prospect of having four different male owners was extraordinarily destabilizing for any slave in terms of relocation, separation from loved ones and familiar environment, climate, food sources, etc., and potentially dramatic changes in lifestyle. But it was especially dangerous for female slaves for whom sexual exploitation and abuse was a daily reality. That danger would have been heightened for the girl of eleven who was advertised for sale along with a boy of the same age by public auction at Halifax on 3 November 1760. The blasé nature of the attitude towards Negro slavery in Canada was expressed in the fact that the two were listed for sale along with "a puncheon of choice cherry brandy with sundry other articles," merely two commodities amongst others; this is much the same as the two negro girls discussed above, who were sold with puncheons of rum and sugar (Riddell 1920).

As mentioned briefly above, black slave girls seemed to be codified differently than their black male counterparts of the same age; girls were constituted as women in their teens when many males of the same ages were identified as boys. In three such cases of the sale of black males in Lower Canada, a fifteen-year-old Negro named Kitts, a sixteen-year-old Negro named Tanno, and a sixteen-year-old mulatto named Pierre were all described as boys, not men (Riddell 1923). But this categorizing practice also existed in other parts of the country. On 27 March 1775, the *Nova Scotia Gazette and Weekly Chronicle* advertised the sale of a "negro boy about 16 year [*sic*] old" (Riddell 1920, 363). In contrast, a black female slave, like Louison discussed above, was described as a woman, although just seventeen years old. The issue of the categorization of childhood is also racialized, of course, since the practice of whites referring to grown black men as "boys" was institutionalized through slavery as a form of public humiliation and psychic castration (Foster 2011).

The frequent international movement of slaves into Lower Canada and other parts of the country also indexes the extraordinary diversity of black Canadian slave populations (Riddell 1920, 1923). Obviously, then, in our discussion of enslaved black girls in Canada (and of enslaved blacks in general), we are dealing with African, African Canadian, African American, African Caribbean, and possibly even other (African South/Central American, etc.) slaves. And indeed, this heterogeneity *within* blackness may actually be one key mark of the distinctiveness of black slaves and the practice of transatlantic slavery in Canada when compared to other locations of the Black Diaspora. As such, and given the dominant trade in black slaves between the islands of the Caribbean and Canada's internationally networked port settlements like Halifax and Montreal, I would like to propose that it would be both a worthy historical and theoretical endeavour to conceptualize a *second Middle Passage between the shores of the Caribbean (and other parts of the Black Diaspora) and Canada*; the passage was secondary only in historical context, but was no less tumultuous a journey across perilous waters. Only this time, it was a journey between two "New World" ports.

BLACK GIRLS IN CANADIAN ART

The legacy of vulnerability of black children to racialized poverty and abuse is evident in the works of Canadian painters Prudence Heward and Louis Muhlstock, both based at Montreal. Although Heward's *Clytie* (1938) shows a little black girl in her "Sunday best," her frozen pose and inscrutable expression seem at odds with twentieth-century ideals of childhood. Clytie stands erect in her pretty pink dress with a blue bow tied above her waist, her hair neatly coiled and held in place by a pink accessory. Her white-gloved hands, white stockings, and clean white shoes also signal that she is "dressed up" for a special occasion. Behind her, a high stone wall only partially conceals a large pinkish house in the distance, as plants peak out from the edges of the painting and purple flowers frame her left shoulder. But the questions of where, why, and for whom the portrait was made haunt its deliberate prettiness. Precisely who is Clytie? Why is she alone in this street, and for whom does she pose? Prudence Heward's own identity as a white female artist provides one layer of initial viewership that allows us to recall the actual act of her creating the portrait. If, indeed, Clytie was a friend of the Heward family cook, then a racial and age power imbalance are both at play in the painting of the work (Jacques 1995, 9).

Meanwhile, the pensive and sorrowful expression of the black girl in Muhlstock's *Evelyn Pleasant, St Famille Street* (1937) marks a convergence of his interest in black subjects, poverty, and social oppression. The young Evelyn stands alone, peering through the dirty window of what we may assume is her home. The interior behind her is impenetrable, an ominous darkness enveloping her like a heavy gloom that we are not allowed to penetrate. The painting, then, does not allow us to enter Evelyn's world, which, unlike that of the representations of her white contemporaries, does not appear too child-like. The imprint of her right hand on the window pane has taken on the distinctive outline of her four small fingers and thumb; she has been pressing her hand against the window, evocative of her bid to escape or, at least, to see beyond her gloomy room.

Fig. 5.4: Dorothy Stevens, *Amy*, c. 1930.

Canadian Dorothy Stevens's painting *Amy* (c. 1930) [fig. 5.4] represents a little black girl who is as stoic and melancholy as the afore-
mentioned pair. Pictured in a circumscribed interior space, her hold on
the white doll that she cradles in her lap is disturbing on at least two
levels: firstly, it evokes the infamous American psychological study of
the preferences of black children for black and white dolls. Conducted
by Mamie Clark and Kenneth Clark (1939, 1947), the study revealed
the process of play as racial socialization and the early stages at which
black children were brainwashed into racial self-loathing and Du-
Boisian double consciousness (Belgrave and Allison 2014). And secondly, it prophesied this girl's likely later station in life as yet another
caregiver to white children.[1] The representation of black women moth-
ering white children helped to produce a hierarchy of family, parental
duty, childhood, and care in which the black family and black children
were forever at the bottom; the preciousness of the white child enabled

the abuse and neglect of the black. This configuration was also emasculating for black male slaves who were effectively barred access to the patriarchal authority and legitimacy that would have enabled them to protect and provide for their loved ones, wives, and children.[2]

As with Clytie above, and perhaps even more so, Amy has been posed. The awkwardness of the chair, turned to the child's right, and the child's body in that chair (also facing her right as her head is turned back to her left, towards the viewer/artist) convey a staged look. Perhaps unconsciously, then, all three of these white Canadian artists have produced paintings in which black girls are decidedly un-childlike in demeanour. It is odd that none of the three girls, even Amy with her doll in hand, is actually in the act of play. Rather, each portrait in its own way is melancholy, again perhaps unconsciously capturing the malaise of childhood for black girls in the first half of the twentieth century.

CONCLUSION

As I have discussed in detail above, black girls were particularly vulnerable to all manner of abuse and exploitation throughout transatlantic slavery and beyond. Disadvantaged from the womb, black girls were violently subjected to an abject "education" by whites who sought to accelerate their sexualization in order to exploit their fertility as "breeders." Due to the prolific nature of black female exploitation and the cross-generational trauma of slavery, we must interrogate not only the artwork and who and what they represent but also pose questions about *how* such representations of black girls came into being. To ask how is to be attentive to the processes of education and cultural production and to the extreme differentials in power between white adult artists and their young, black, vulnerable female sitters/subjects.

The history of the representation of black children and girls in Western art is, in many ways, a parallel trajectory to that of black adults and women. However, in other ways, the roles and function of the black girl have prophesied the racialized and gendered identifications and status of the black female adult subject. While there are examples of black children experiencing the modern ideals of a protected, beloved Western childhood, many artworks represent the exact opposite, that is, the social, cultural, and psychic displacement of black girls as "other" to the paradigmatic ideal of white girls. The colonial discourses that enabled transatlantic slavery to flourish for 400 years are crucial to an understanding of the disparate educations, experiences, and representations of childhood that are always racialized. I hope that I have demonstrated that our attention to race in the field of Childhood Studies should not be an after-thought, but a primary and urgent consideration.

NOTES

1 The normalcy in Canada of racist language to describe black people is evidenced in the fact that this painting was exhibited under the title of *Piccaninny* throughout Ontario in the Exhibition of Pictures by Canadian Artists, under the auspices of The Art Association of Canadian Service Clubs and The Ontario Society of Artists, Winter 1930–31.

2 I do not wish to glamorize or glorify patriarchal authority; however, we must honestly consider the ramifications of the fact that this historical means of supporting, protecting, and providing for one's family was denied to enslaved black males.

REFERENCES

Belgrave, F.Z., and K.W. Allison, eds. 2014. *African American Psychology: From Africa to America*. 3rd ed. Thousand Oaks, CA: Sage Publications, Inc.

Duncan, C. 1982. "Happy Mothers and Other New Ideas in Eighteenth-Century French Art." In *Feminism and Art History: Questioning the Litany*, edited by N. Broude and M. Garrard, 12–23. New York: Harper and Row.

Eltis, D., and D. Richardson. 2003. "West Africa and the Trans Atlantic Slave Trade." In *The Slavery Reader*, edited by G. Heuman and J. Walvin, 49–63. London: Routledge.

Foster, T.A. 2011. "The Sexual Abuse of Black Men under American Slavery." *The Journal of the History of Sexuality* 20(3): 445–64.

Jacques, M. 1995. "A Reassessment of Prudence Heward's Black Nudes." MA diss., York University.

Mair, L. 2000. "Women Field Workers in Jamaica During Slavery." In *Caribbean Slavery in the Atlantic World: A Student Reader*, edited by V. Shepherd and H. Beckles, 387–96. Kingston, Jamaica: Ian Randle.

Nelson, C.A. 2010. *Representing the Black Female Subject in Western Art*. New York: Routledge.

Riddell, W. 1920. "Slavery in the Maritime Provinces." *The Journal of Negro History* 5(3): 360–71.

– 1923. "Notes on the Slave in Nouvelle-France." *The Journal of Negro History* 8(3): 320–31.

Ross, E. 1993. *Love and Toil: Motherhood in Outcast London, 1870–1918*. New York: Oxford University Press.

Shugert, J.W. 1836. *Charles Ball Slavery in the United States: A Narrative of the Life and Adventures of Charles Ball, a Black Man*. New York: John S. Taylor.

"A Southern Colored Woman – The Race Problem – An Autobiography."
  1904. *The Independent* 56 (2885): 587, 589. In *Black Women in White America: A Documentary History,* edited by G. Lerner, 158. (1992). New York:
  Vintage Books, a Division of Random House.

Steckel, R. 1986. "A Peculiar Population: The Nutrition, Health and Mortality
  of American Slaves, from Childhood to Maturity." *The Journal of Economic
  History* 46(3): 722–3.

Tobin, B. 1999. "Bringing the Empire Home: The Black Servant in Domestic
  Portraiture." In *Picturing Imperial Power: Colonial Subjects in Eighteenth-
  Century British Painting,* 13–28. Durham: Duke University Press.

Treckel, P. 1989. "Breastfeeding and Maternal Sexuality in Colonial America."
  Journal of Interdisciplinary History 20(1): 30–42.

Trussell, J., and R. Steckel. 1978. "The Age of Slaves at Menarche and First
  Birth." *Journal of Interdisciplinary History* 8(3): 492–501.

White, D. 1999. *Ar'n't I a woman? Female Slaves in the Plantation South.* New
  York: W.W. Norton.

6

High School and the Black Body in Canada: A Recollection of a Female High School Student

Habiba Cooper Diallo

I am becoming increasingly aware of the impact of school on the bodies of black children in Canada.[1]

Two years ago, in the ninth grade, when I was walking down a hallway to attend a school newspaper meeting, I was struck by what I consider to be an extremely disturbing image of black bodies. As part of an assignment, students had posted a photograph from the 1984 Ethiopian famine. The bodies depicted were naked, dark, gaunt, and crawling. I was horrified, humiliated, and indignant all together.

I quickly went to the administration to express my discontent with the photograph; it was removed from the wall the next day.

Still, I ask myself, why was I the one to bring the image to the attention of the administration? Had the students who worked on the assignment not been able to analyze the derogatoriness of the image, and assess the impact it would have on Ethiopian children in the school, and on other blacks and Africans, for that matter? Going beyond the students, why had the teachers not analyzed the image? Finally, and it is shameful that I must even consider this point, but as passers-by, why hadn't other staff found the image problematic? Assuming that they had indeed found it problematic, why had they neglected to express that sentiment?

Building on my own experience, I would say that such experiences are commonplace for black students (see also Ibrahim, this volume). They are incessant – occurring from elementary through high school and beyond, if, that is, we are not too discouraged to pursue higher education.

Our humanity, it seems, is continually eroded. We experience this through Kony 2012 assemblies, in which we are shown videos of slaughtered black bodies – decapitated and severed. As an audience in general, but particularly as a black audience with particular bodily experience, knowledge, and history, we experience this in the classroom when all the presentations pertaining to Africa harp on the gothic features of the continent – the perpetual "tribal" warfare, famine, and disease – or when entering school in the morning and being assaulted by a student's voice: "The worst countries to live in are Uganda, Sudan, and Congo; if you walk into one of those places you'll just die."

How is it that such a one-sided story of blackness and Africa always takes precedence? What does this do to one's spirit when her humanity is constantly under attack? When the academy, intentionally or not, perpetuates the idea of her "sub-humanity"? When the continent of her origin is trivialized to a mere two, or three, "high-conflict" countries? And when the leaders of those countries are belittled? Most importantly, what does this do to this young African Canadian body?

High school hurts the black body two-fold. All students – regardless of race – must cope with the physical stress of school: commuting there and back home, carrying heavy text books while climbing three flights of stairs, harsh weather conditions, etc. In addition to this, however, black students must also deal with the racial stresses involved in going to school.

During the lunch hour, a student quite often remarks, and I have heard it so many times that it is sickening, "Don't waste your food, because there are starving children in Africa who would be grateful for it," or "There are places in the world – like Africa – where children cannot go to school, so be thankful that you're getting an education." "Africa" has become a kind of punctuation in our sentences, inserted wherever conscience and empathy are concerned. Can the impetus for these catch phrases about Africa really be empathy when students who self-identify as continental African contradict the notions of an impoverished, needy Africa?

Eventually, these statements take on the form of violence – epistemic violence, rendering the acquisition of knowledge difficult for the black student. How is one to concentrate on a chemistry lesson or a biology assignment after being told that Africans like herself cannot go to school?

High school stigmatizes the black body. At my school, I recently witnessed the arrest of a black student. Prior to the incident, two officers were interrogating him and his non-black companions/"friends" on school property. The latter were escorted back inside the school, while the former remained outside for further interrogation. I continued to watch through the window. The officer soon began to search the black student, clearly unable to find anything worthy of arrest. She persisted nonetheless, and in doing so, provoked him, for he became frantic, kicking off his shoes and waving his arms as he proclaimed his innocence. The officer was unrelenting. Within seconds, his chest was pressed against the side of the car, his back to me, and his hands cuffed. Adding insult to injury, a student adjacent to me, having also witnessed the arrest, remarked, "He knows the drill." I could feel my heart sink, and soon the tears began to flow – a physical manifestation of the impact of high school on the black body – as he was driven away, coerced away, away from school, away from an education.

Still, the notion that school is the most essential component of a student's success in the future is perpetually impressed upon us. Students are also made to believe that school is a "safe" and "healthy" place. Given that school is the most fundamental element in our journey to success, and that it also affords us an ostensibly safe and healthy learning environment, how can it coexist with legal, police-authorized coercion from learning?

High school hinders the black body. The bell rang exactly nine minutes following the arrest. Shattered and demoralized as I was, I still had to report to my fourth-period biology class. I had to fulfill my academic responsibility.

High school nullifies the black body. In spite of the major contributions blacks have made, and continue to make, to Canadian society, and more obviously, in spite of our sheer presence in the country, school can erase the histories and contemporary experiences of blacks in Canada. During Remembrance Day ceremonies, why don't we remember the black veterans of World War I from the No. 2 Construction Battalion? I often peruse my textbooks – history, chemistry, and biology, just to name a few – for the sake of a comparative study of the persons depicted as inventors, prominent political figures, and theoreticians relative to those who are portrayed as victims of war, inadequate health care, famine, and political instability. The former are usually images of white bodies, while the latter are people of colour – typically blacks. How do the erasure of the black experience and, ultimately, the suppression of black students nullify the black body? The first strike is psychological dejection – black students' consciousness of the lack of recognition for the black experience is followed by an emotional response – and apathy towards school, as there is no relevance to the experience of black students as human beings. Finally, the black student goes into a state of corporeal shock, questioning the significance of her skin, her features, and, fundamentally, her body in a system that suppresses the expression of her humanity.

I am a black female student in Canada. I write this chapter at the age of seventeen, eleven years of which I have spent in school. Boldly stated, my time in school has been enlightening and intellectually stimulating. For literary assignments, I have had the pleasure of reading Shakespeare's *Romeo and Juliet* and Michael Ondaatje's *In the Skin of a Lion*. I have had the opportunity to listen to Alexandre Trudeau and Michael Ignatieff at school assemblies. I have written about the accomplishments of French microbiologist Louis Pasteur and the military expeditions of Napoleon Bonaparte. However, my experience in school continues to be an emotional and spiritual struggle. My mother can attest to this, for she is the one who is often made to absorb the consequences of this struggle: my tears of indignation upon returning home from an assembly at which a representative from an NGO working in "high-conflict" regions labels black children as "poverty-stricken" and "needy," and my frequent articulation of my dampened morale, my psychic apathy, and corporeal fatigue. Every night upon returning home from school, I turn to my diary – an outlet for the release of negative sentiments which lodge themselves in my body throughout the day – or I immerse myself in reggae and *Wassoulou* dance as a way of recharging my spirit by connecting with one of the most intimate aspects of my personhood, my culture, something which is abrogated and denied me and the masses of other black students in high school.

My black peers share the same sentiments: high school is a collective struggle for black students. When we convene at each other's homes, at the mall, at the movies, or while attending conferences on black students' education, we discuss the challenges we face in school, and offer one another words of moral support and encouragement. Such creative outlets, meetings, and discussions constitute our forms of individual and collective catharsis. They are imperative for the sustenance of the black body in high school, yet they are time-intensive as well. In the case of conferences, they detract from hours and days that could go towards fulfilling important academic responsibilities such as completing homework, studying for tests, or doing research projects.

In November 2012, I attended a three-day conference for black students that was geared towards providing us with tools on coping with racism in school and informing us about career pathways and scholarships of which we would be otherwise unaware. Unsurprisingly, we all had stories to share about our encounters with white supremacy and racism in school. It was a transformative experience, indeed; however, it is saddening to think that, for three days, we had to divorce ourselves from the "mainstream," or in other words, "white" high school experience, in order to be given a platform for such discourse. Notwithstanding the inextricable commonalities between the day-to-day lives of black and white students, our lives as blacks are still marginalized. Today, although the majority of black students in Canadian high schools are Canadian-born, and hence experience a span of existence in the Canadian educational system equal to that of our white peers, we nevertheless are "othered."

My two older siblings have also been through high school, marking a combined eighteen-year discrepancy between the time when my older brother attended high school and now. Their struggles have not been any different from my own or, using my own gaze, those of my black peers.

How do we then put an end to this cycle, so that the bodies of the future generations of black students will not be hurt, stigmatized, hindered, and nullified in high school? It is critical that educators, administrators, curriculum consultants, and policy makers design a program that is reflective of the experiences of blacks in Canada. This could mean integrating into the curriculum texts such as Sharon G. Flake's *The Skin I'm In* and *Unbowed: A Memoir* by Nobel Laureate Wangari Maathai, having students listen to bell hooks at school assemblies (not limited to Black History Month), and assigning work on Imhotep's contributions to philosophy, medicine, and mathematics and Hatshepsut's various expeditions to Punt and Byblos. The experiences of blacks should be normalized to the same extent as those of whites. A solely white and Eurocentric approach to education can no longer be sustained if we are to ensure the success and academic excellence of black students. The aforesaid approach to education reinforces ideas of white supremacy and promotes the marginalization of the black body.

Is there such a thing as academic responsibility when one's human rights are violated? Several articles of the Universal Declaration of Human Rights are relevant to the analysis of the impact of high school on the black body. Articles 1 and 3 affirm the equality[2] and the security of person[3] that is granted all human beings. However, in high school, equality and security of person is rescinded for black students. Section 7 of the Canadian Charter of Rights and Freedoms extends Article 3 of the declaration to protect "both the physical and psychological integrity of the individual."[4] Article 22[5] of the declaration defends every individual's "right to social security," and his or her entitlement to the realization of "social and cultural rights indispensable for his [or her] dignity and the free development of his [or her] personality." Finally, clause 3 of Article 26 maintains that "[p]arents have a prior right to choose the kind of education that shall be given to their children."[6] Hence, there is a need for parents of black students to exercise their political power and to agitate for the realization of these rights in the educational system. In what other ways can we exercise these rights in light of the multifaceted erosion of the humanity of black students and the repression of our bodies? The answer might lie in the filing of a class action lawsuit to disclose and generate concern for the injustices to black students on a national and legal level.

Malcolm X once said, "We declare our right on this earth ... to be a human being, to be respected as a human being, to be given the rights of a human being in this society, on this earth, in this day, which we intend to bring into existence by any means necessary." Besides saying AMEN, we need to remember that, for far too long, high school has hurt the black body. It is high time not only to struggle against this phenomenon but also to abolish it once and for all. This is no wishful thinking. This is wilful thinking.

> For she who hope,
> Tell the journey has begun! [7]

NOTES

1 Disclaimer: Anything written in the feminine shall include the masculine.
2 United Nations General Assembly, Resolution 217A, "The Universal Declaration of Human Rights," Article no. 1, 10 December 1948, http://www.un.org/en/documents/udhr/index.shtml.
3 Ibid., Article no. 3.
4 Graham Garton, "Section 7 – Life, liberty and security of person." In *The Canadian Charter of Rights Decisions Digest.* Justice Canada (2004): http://canlii.ca/en/commentary/charterDigest/s-7.html.
5 United Nations General Assembly, Resolution 217A, "The Universal Declaration of Human Rights," Article no. 22, 10 December 1948, http://www.un.org/en/documents/udhr/index.shtml.
6 Ibid., Article no. 26, clause 3.
7 Cara Rautins and A. Ibrahim, "Wide-Awakeness: Toward a Critical Pedagogy of Imagination, Humanism and Becoming," *International Journal of Critical Pedagogy* 3, no. 2 (2011): 24–36.

7

Making Education Count: Critical Educational Practice and the Life Chances of African Canadian Children

Benedicta Egbo

INTRODUCTION

Compelling anecdotal and research evidence have established the fact that structural and contextual factors mediate schooling experiences, subsequently leading to differential outcomes for various groups of students. However, despite this knowledge, strategies for increasing educational success among vulnerable groups of students remain elusive. Paradoxically, regardless of background, most students (and their families) hold the reasonable expectation that, all things being equal, the outcome of their educational experiences will be life-changing. However, this is not always the case, especially for students who are from diverse backgrounds, as are African Canadian children.

Conceptually grounded in critical race theory – a framework with increasing application in education – this chapter explores the trajectories of critical educational practices and the life chances of African Canadian children. The discussions in the chapter are premised on the view that critical practice is at the nexus of transformative schooling. Furthermore, the chapter argues that improving the life chances of African Canadian children depends on the architecture of the knowledge schools disseminate through the official (explicit) and unofficial (implicit) curricula. To explicate the point, I distinguish between two types of knowledge: non-negotiable and negotiable knowledge. A look at a framework for critical micro-level practice for improving the life chances of African Canadian children concludes the discussions in the chapter.

LIFE CHANCES: THE CONCEPT

With growing visibility in educational discourse, the concept of life chances has to do with the opportunities that are available in a given society as a function of the prevailing social conditions. Such opportunities increase the probability that an individual will live a "successful" life, understood in terms of the particular indices through which success is measured in his or her society. Life chances have two dimensions: options and ligatures (Dahrendorf 1979). Options provide more (and, arguably, better) future choices to the individual, while ligatures are bonds and linkages that people develop with others through co-immersion in a given social milieu such as schools.

Universally, access to education is associated with a greater range of life options (e.g., more career choices and job opportunities) as a function of the knowledge and training acquired. Besides offering more life options, education is also associated with ligatures, which are affinities that individuals develop with others as a result of their shared educational experience. These ties contribute significantly to whether or not an individual or social group feels connected to or alienated from their particular educational environments. Unfortunately, the preponderance of evidence suggests that much of the education that minority students such as those of African Canadian descent receive may not necessarily improve their life chances (see for example, Dei et al. 1997; Egbo 2011; Ghosh 2008), and it may, in some instances, lead to resistance and the development of oppositional sub-cultures, both in school and wider society (Ibrahim 2014).

Peter McLaren's (2007) *Life in Schools* provides a well-known example of life-chance-depreciating education that black children sometimes receive. The book chronicles McLaren's experiences teaching in an inner-city school in Toronto. While the learning environment had some undesirable impact on the minority students in general, McLaren notes that the West Indian female students in his class were particularly disengaged. Not only did they have to deal with family-related challenges, they also had to face the problem of everyday racism at school. To inoculate themselves against public scrutiny, the girls presented a "tough girl" façade, an ostensibly defiant attitude that was, in reality, a defacto defence mechanism and symbolic response to societal constraints, structural inequalities, and their experiences of difference in school, which contrasted sharply with those of their middle-class teachers and peers. McLaren's account underscores the importance of dissecting and understanding the complex interactions of race, ethnicity, and education in any analysis that is geared towards making education count for African Canadian children. Equally important is a critical understanding of the gender dimension of this complex relationship. Annette Henry (2009) emphasizes this point in her exploration of the interdependence of race and gender in education (see also Ibrahim 2014 for the intersection of identity, culture, and race in educational experience).

THEORETICAL FRAMEWORK

Critical race theory (CRT) has its origins in critical legal studies. However, its application to education increased significantly following the publication of Gloria Ladson-Billings and William Tate's (1995) influential article "Toward a Critical Race Theory of Education." As an emergent paradigm for conceptualizing the relationship between race and education, CRT acknowledges the centrality of race, and focuses on how elements of racism and prejudice are embedded in society and social institutions such as schools. The major argument advanced by proponents of CRT is that analyses of discrimination and inequality in society must underscore how race is implicated. Because of its emphasis on how race as a social construct is grossly under-theorized in analyses that purport to deconstruct the workings of society, CRT is committed to social justice and to the elimination of all forms of inequalities, especially those that are racially motivated (Egbo 2011).

With particular reference to education, adherents of CRT argue that, while race is commonly used to sustain inequality in schools and subsequently in society, the concept has not been used in any systematic way to understand how race is implicated in the inequities that exist in education (Ladson-Billings and Tate 1995; Zamudio, Rios and Bridgeman 2011). Solórzano and Yosso (2001, 472–3) have identified five principles of CRT when applied to education that make it an attractive framework for analyzing issues of marginality, exclusion, and *otherness* within the educational arena. These are (although, arguably, not limited to) the centrality of race and racism and their intersectionality with other forms of subordination; the challenge to dominant ideology; the commitment to social justice; and the centrality of experiential knowledge and its transdisciplinary perspective. A similar view is articulated by Zamudio et al. (2011), who argue that CRT "provides ... an alternative theoretical lens and pedagogical orientation that ... help address the problems that students of color confront.

[It] offers educators analytical concepts to better understand educational inequality ... CRT also provides a conceptual lens for looking at educational policies" (161, 162).

Why is CRT relevant in Canadian educational discourse? It is relevant because there is a general perception that Canada is an inclusive society where racism is either non-existent or has little or no impact on one's access to the advantages society has to offer, including access to the right kind of education. Additionally, racism in Canada is often perceived as the anti-social behaviour of some misguided individuals rather than as a societal malaise that also manifests itself in groups, organizations, and state institutions (Henry and Tator 2010). As a consequence of this misconception, Canadian social attitude surveys tend to paint a picture of a racially inclusive society, a tendency, Skerrett (2008) argues, that only masks reality: "[While] [t]he existence of racial and ethnocultural discrimination in Canada is most keenly perceived and experienced by visible minority groups and immigrant visible minorities, who make up one half of Canada's total immigrant population ... census data that demonstrate inclusive social attitudes and practices in relation to diversity adds complexity to Canada's social landscape which ethnic minorities most strongly perceive as a vertical mosaic" (266).

Problematically, this illusion of inclusion may prevent transformative praxis, thereby reifying the status quo. For example, it is telling that, despite increasing diversity among student populations, the teaching force in Canada remains predominantly homogeneous – white, middle class, and monolingual. As a consequence, teachers and some of their students from diverse backgrounds, such as African Canadian children, view the world through lenses that sustain ethno-cultural schisms at all levels of the school system and, arguably, of society (Dei et al. 1997; Egbo 2001, 2009; Ghosh 2008; Ghosh and Abdi 2004; James 2010; McNeil 2011).

One question that is often asked within the Canadian context is whether or not race intersects with social positioning in any substantive way. Educational practitioners, scholars, and researchers have engaged the issue, arguing that the recognition of the salience of race is critical for improving schooling outcomes and experiences for minority students (see, for example, Dei et al. 1997; Egbo 2011; Henry and Tator 2010; James 2010; Lund 2011). For instance, Fleras and Elliott (2003) argue that, even though Canadians are ambivalent about the concept, race will remain relevant in everyday life and public policy, "not because it is real, but because people respond as if it were real.

Race matters not because people are inherently different or unequal, but because perceived differences may be manipulated as a basis for sorting out privilege and power" (52). Obviously, privilege and power are intertwined with life chances. In the final analysis, race as a social construct cannot be ignored in discourses and reform efforts that aim to improve the life chances of African Canadian children or, indeed, to engender the educational success of any racialized group's children in general. A critical starting point for this transformation is determining the requisite knowledge-base for optimizing educational outcomes.

CONTEXTUALIZING KNOWLEDGE
FOR AFRICAN CANADIAN CHILDREN

What kind of knowledge should African Canadian children (and, indeed, other minority students) acquire in schools in order to increase their life chances? Canadian writers have addressed this ostensibly simple but functionally complex question in various ways (e.g., Dei et al. 1997; Egbo 2009, 2011; James 2010; Nelson 2010). While addressing the particular case of African American children, other writers have also provided exemplars of what constitutes relevant knowledge for children of African descent (e.g., Banks 2001; Delpit 2006; Ladson-Billings 1994; Milner 2003).

To make education meaningful for African Canadian children, I distinguish between two types of knowledge that I refer to elsewhere as "non-negotiable" and "negotiable" knowledge (Egbo 2009). Non-negotiable knowledge, as the name implies, is essential knowledge that should prepare all students, regardless of background and social positioning, for living a productive life within the context of a globalized and competitive world. Negotiable knowledge, on the other hand, is knowledge that has relevance for members of particular groups (e.g., a racial, ethnocultural, or language group) and helps them to not only survive but also to thrive in society. In contrast to non-negotiable knowledge, negotiable knowledge is context-driven, based on the specific needs (epistemic, socio-linguistic, religious, etc.) of individual communities, especially in demographically heterogeneous contexts. Making education count for African Canadian children requires that both kinds of knowledge are explicitly grounded in their ways of knowing, with particular focus on the following: contextualized and critical academic knowledge, African-centred epistemologies, and community values and languages.

Critical and Contextualized Academic Knowledge

By academic knowledge, I am referring to the core curriculum that schools mandatorily teach. However, while much of this knowledge is pragmatically non-negotiable, each subject area should be culturally relevant, using content that reflects the cultural capital of all students, including that of African Canadian children. For example, while mathematics is generally a required subject for most students at the elementary and secondary school levels in Canada, the contents of the curriculum, resources, and teachers' pedagogical and instructional strategies should reflect the ways of knowing of the different groups of students in a given educational space.

African-Centred Epistemologies

In principle, Canada's official multiculturalism policy promotes identity retention. As a consequence, ethnocultural communities across the country make concerted efforts to impart their worldviews and ways of knowing to the younger generation. This is true of the wider African Canadian community as it is true of other ethnic groups. It also means that, in reality, students from diverse racial, cultural, or linguistic backgrounds (especially relatively new immigrants) typically negotiate between two sometimes incommensurate worldviews or culture bases, which I refer to as culture base1 (CB1) and culture base2 (CB2) (Egbo 2009). CB1 refers to the worldviews or cultural capital acquired through familial and home socialization, while CB2 has to do with the dominant culture that all students must acquire through schooling for full immersion and participation in society. Unfortunately, while they do not necessarily have to cause problems, the discontinuities between these two cultural frames of reference, along with the attendant *culture-switching*, create learning and culture-related challenges that sometimes lead to educational disengagement among minority students, including those from African Canadian backgrounds (Dei et al. 1997; Egbo 2009). In the case of African Canadian children, the problem is exacerbated by the fact that CB2 is either only peripherally reflected in schools' curricula or not included at all. For example, despite persistent community advocacy for the inclusion of African-centred perspectives and anti-racist education in schools' curricula, the relevant policies, with few exceptions, are annotations in policy documents and schools' curricula, as Carr (2008) observes:

When looking for tangible, comprehensive policies dealing with anti-racist education in Canada, one is struck at how little, concrete direction there actually is. There are usually preambles in policy documents inferring a commitment to equity but the actual funding, processes, staffing, content and, significantly, accountability, are not predominantly featured, nor are they transparently visible ... To underscore this point, the whole area of social justice is not generally placed on a similar plane as the multitude of areas that are formally tested, and for which generous resources are provided to develop, implement and assess curriculum, achievement and institutional standards. (11)

Not surprisingly, the absence of African-centred perspectives in official knowledge foregrounds the clarion call for the establishment of African-centred schools in black communities in Canada. Indeed, the establishment of an Africentric Alternative School (the first of its kind in Canada) within the Toronto District School Board (TDSB) in September 2009, after years of what is best described as a very contentious policy enactment process and spirited debates between supporters and critics (see for example Dei 1998; Hampton 2010; Levine-Rasky 2014; Thompson and Wallner 2011), was a recognition of the salience of African-centred epistemologies in engendering academic success and, ultimately, improving the life chances of African Canadian children.

Community Values and Languages

In addition to macro or national values, every community has its own set of values, norms, and ethos that guide members' behaviour. While schools typically teach macro or shared Canadian values that all citizens must acquire, there are values that are particular to individual communities that schools also ought to teach. Because community or micro values are integral to the identity of African Canadian children, they constitute non-negotiable knowledge in this instance, and ought to be an integral part of an empowering and inclusive curriculum.

With regards to community languages, it is important to emphasize here that, contrary to common assumptions, African Canadian communities are not homogeneous entities where everyone thinks alike or speaks the same language. Differential patterns of immigration and settlement, as well as different countries of origin, prohibit such homogeneity. For example, in addition to more recent immigrants from the Caribbean and Africa, blacks have always constituted part of the Canadian mosaic, with their presence dating back to the 1600s with the arrival of Samuel de Champlain and Mathieu de Costa, a black man from the Caribbean (see Carr 2008; Dei 2010). Subsequent to the arrival of these early African Canadian immigrants, black communities with differing cultural orientations also lived in major Canadian cities, including Toronto, Montreal, Chatham, Ontario (via the odyssey of the underground railroad), Halifax, and other major cities. As a result of these historical antecedents, a multiplicity of community or heritage languages is spoken among African Canadians. Given this linguistic diversity, it is, as a practical matter, impossible to teach all community languages in schools. This inherent difficulty notwithstanding, the overall argument here is that some languages within the African Canadian community, wherever practicable, should be integral components of the formal curriculum rather than an after-school cultural activity, as is commonly practiced. The challenge is for school systems to determine which languages have enough representation to warrant formal teaching.

A FRAMEWORK FOR CRITICAL PRACTICE

A central goal of this chapter is to provide a broad framework for critical micro-level practice. In this section, then, I turn my attention to the discussion of practical strategies and knowledge-base for making education count for African Canadian children. As I have argued elsewhere (Egbo 2009, 2011), no significant transformation can occur without co-opting teachers as critical agents of change. For example, becoming successful teachers of African Canadian children (and other minority children, for that matter) requires specific competencies such as knowledge and practice of transformative pedagogies, racial and cultural literacy, critical language literacy, and fair assessment practices.

Knowledge and Practice of Transformative Pedagogies

In so far as researchers agree that what students learn should speak to their culture bases, such knowledge and learning must also be supported with culturally responsive teaching practices (Delpit 2006; Ladson-Billings 1994; Sheets 2005; Villegas and Lucas 2002), which are inclusively described here as transformative pedagogies. Two of these pedagogies are particularly relevant to our present discussion: critical pedagogy and diversity pedagogy.

With an emphasis on how knowledge is constructed, situated, and contested within the context of power and marginality (Freire 1970; Kincheloe 2008; McLaren 2007), critical pedagogy has to do with the analysis of the relationship between knowledge and power in schools. Critical pedagogists believe that schools and their various practices are inherently politically contested spaces where oppositional discourse is silenced. As such, critical pedagogy challenges educators to become critical of orthodox understandings of what education entails, and, for the purposes of enabling critical change, to question the cannons and assumptions that underlie the curriculum. Additionally, teachers' pedagogical practices should be grounded in critical understandings of the intersections of such variables as race and gender, rather than in a view that sees both as separate entities (Henry 2009). Cumulatively, critical pedagogy challenges educational practices that privilege certain kinds of knowledge while devaluing others. Furthermore, teaching is seen as a fundamentally political and dialectical project that has the potential of either empowering or disempowering students (Egbo 2009; Kincheloe 2005).

An emergent paradigm, diversity pedagogy proposes a set of principles that emphasize the interconnectedness between culture, cognition, and schooling. According to one of its most notable proponents (Sheets 2005), teachers who teach for cultural inclusion should be able to observe and identify individual and group cultural behaviour patterns, and then apply such knowledge in identifying students' skills and competencies. These observations would, in turn, help teachers make informed instructional decisions as well as create optimal conditions for the academic success of culturally diverse students, including racial minorities. In an extensive discussion of the concept, Sheets (2005) goes on to describe how teacher competency in diversity pedagogy can positively transform the outcomes of schooling for racialized and minoritized students.

Ultimately, both critical pedagogy and diversity pedagogy help practitioners to achieve a level of awareness that can dethrone the status quo in education. Indeed, when teachers begin to ask critical questions about social structures, social spaces, structural forces, and racial injustices, they become pedagogical activists who are committed to change through their teaching practices. Most importantly, teacher agency is a prerequisite condition for making education count for African Canadian children (Egbo 2011).

Racial and Cultural Literacy

In her critically acclaimed book, in which she analyzes the interplay between race, ethnicity, and teaching and learning, Lisa Delpit (2006) argues that teachers can positively transform the lives of racial minority children if they dispense with stereotypes and cultural assumptions that are, in fact, the consequence of miscommunications and miscues when primarily white educators teach children who are racially and culturally different from themselves. While such miscues may result from a lack of understanding and exposure to other people's culture, Milner (2003) argues that they can lead teachers to "rely on stereotypical conceptions of racially diverse students – perceptions that they may have extracted from television programming, media coverage, or even family biases that still prevail in teachers' thinking about racially diverse groups ... stereotypical beliefs may force teachers to teach and to think about their racially diverse students through deficit models – whether consciously or unconsciously" (197–8).

Perhaps more problematic, colour-blindness can erroneously become an implicit antidote for racism. Even if one concedes that most people who invoke colour-blindness generally have good intentions, such claims are at best illusory, and, as Lopez (2003) argues, lead to a common perception in which

[r]acism ... [is] reduced to broad generalizations about another group based on the color of their skin. It has become an individual construction as opposed to a social and/or civilizational construct ... In this regard, racism is not necessarily connected to the larger "distribution of jobs, power, prestige, and wealth" ... but is viewed as deviant behaviors and/or attitudes in an otherwise neutral world. The belief that colorblindness will eliminate racism is not only short sighted but reinforces the notion that racism is a personal as opposed to systemic issue. (69)

Besides camouflaging racial discrimination, claims of colour-blindness are, in fact, analogous to a negation of people's identity, which can lead to what King (1991) refers to as dysconscious racism, which is "an uncritical habit of mind (including perceptions, attitudes, assumptions, and beliefs) that justifies inequity and exploitation by accepting the existing order of things as given. Dysconscious racism is a form of racism that tacitly accepts dominant white norms and privileges. It is not the *absence* [emphasis in original] of (that is, not unconsciousness) but an *impaired* [emphasis in original] or distorted way of thinking about race as compared to, for example, critical consciousness" (135). In other words, quite often, racism is normalized through a subliminal process that obscures or minimizes its inhibiting impact. Taken together, Delpit, Lopez and King's treatise above provides compelling rationale for making racial and cultural literacy required knowledge for practitioners, especially those who teach students from racially diverse backgrounds, such as African Canadian children.

Critical Language Literacy

In conceptualizing critical language literacy (CLL), I draw on Norman Fairclough's (1992) concept of critical language awareness. Consequently, critical language literacy is premised on the idea that, as a powerful technology of communication, language can be an arbiter of empowerment or oppression. But, more importantly, CLL suggests that the critical use of language is a learned or acquired practical *skill*. It follows logically that teachers, especially those who teach in contexts of diversity, should develop critical language competencies. Because language is not the benign social artifact it is often assumed to be, CLL has the potential of helping both teachers and students to understand the ways in which language, ideology, and power are connected. For example, it is through language that prejudice and negative stereotypes are conveyed. We also use language to repress, label people, or distort reality. Similarly, the language we use shapes our perceptions and our realities, as well as those of others with whom we interact (Corson 2001).

However, not all uncritical use of language is immanently obvious. Indeed, while it is easy to eliminate the more obvious biased language, sometimes the most offensive words are those that are ostensibly neutral and, therefore, latent. Take, for instance, the innocuous phrase "these people," which is commonly used in wider society. In certain contexts, it serves as the manifest evidence of binary and dichotomizing thinking that creates a culture of "us" and "them," with the implicit suggestion of the superiority of the speaker (Egbo 2009). Overall, empowering African Canadian children requires critical use of instructional and everyday classroom language (Egbo 2011; Ibrahim 2014).

Fair Assessment Practices

As a general rule, teachers are expected to use multiple assessment strategies in order to accommodate individual differences and preferred learning styles. It is simply good pedagogical practice, as we are reminded by Howard Gardner's treatise on multiple intelligences, in which he stresses the immense importance of preferred learning styles and individual differences in teaching and learning. Gardner (1999) provides a précis of his theory:

> We are not all the same; we do not all have the same kinds of minds (that is, we are not all distinct points on a single bell curve); and education works most effectively if these differences are taken into account rather than denied or ignored. Taking human differences seriously lies at the heart of the MI perspective. At the theoretical level, this means that all individuals cannot be profitably arrayed on a single intellectual dimension. At the practical level, it suggests that any uniform educational approach is likely to serve only a small percentage of children optimally. (91)

Taking individual differences into account in assessment is particularly crucial for students like African Canadian children, who, as earlier mentioned, have more than one culture base as their frames of reference. Using a variety of assessment strategies promotes learning, and, if we follow Gardner's logic, students who do not perform well on the verbal component as a result of language limitations may do well on the written or performance components, for example. Ultimately, in developing assessment strategies, educators must use approaches that are fair and bias free, particularly since assessment strategies tend to ignore cultural factors (Kelly and Brandes 2008). Exemplary assessment strategies involve paying attention to cultural difference, learning styles, and students' language competencies. Self- and peer assessment are equally important techniques for empowering learners from minority backgrounds.

CONCLUSION

The coalescing theme in this chapter is that improving the life chances of African Canadian children hinges on the nature of education they receive vis-à-vis epistemic orientation, pedagogical practices, and con-tents of the curriculum. Moreover, within their learning environments, children of African descent in Canada should see themselves as sub-jects whose history, ways of knowing, and experiences are consequen-tial. Equally important, educators who teach students from racialized backgrounds, such as African Canadian children are, should not only undertake to acquire the requisite knowledge and competencies, they should also avoid adopting an apolitical stance about issues of race and ethnicity, because such a position neutralizes teacher praxis and activism. As Pollock (2001) asserts, if educators would address the taken-for-granted assumptions about different achievement among racial groups, rather than avoiding the matter, society might be able to " better assist educators to actively refuse their programmed assump-tions that 'race group' members will achieve or fail in predetermined ways" (10).

Finally, it is worth emphasizing that, in providing African Canadi-an students more outcome-oriented education, policy-makers and ed-ucators must not fall into the trap of replacing intellectually rigorous curricula with less challenging alternatives that would only reify their disempowerment and ultimately reduce, rather than improve, their life chances.

REFERENCES

Banks, C.A.M. 2001. "Becoming a Cross-cultural Teacher." In *Multicultural Education in the 21st Century*, edited by C.F. Diaz, 171–83. New York: Addison-Wesley Educational Publishers.

Carr, P.R. 2008. "The 'Equity Waltz' in Canada: Whiteness and the Informal Realities of Racism in Education." *Journal of Contemporary Issues in Educa-tion* 3(2): 4–23.

Corson, D. 2001. *Language Diversity and Education*. Mahwah, New Jersey: Erl-baum Associates.

Dahrendorf, R. 1979. *Life Chances*. Chicago: University of Chicago Press.

Dei, G.J.S.1998. "Why Write Back? The Role of Afrocentric Discourse in So-cial Change." *Canadian Journal of Education* 23(2): 200–8.

– 2010. *Teaching Africa: Towards a Transgressive Pedagogy*. Dordrecht: Springer.

Dei, G.J.S., J. Mazzuca, E. McIsaac, and J. Zine. 1997. *Reconstructing Dropout: A Critical Ethnography of the Dynamics of Black Students' Disengagement from School.* Toronto: University of Toronto Press.

Delpit, L. 2006. *Other People's Children: Cultural Conflict in the Classroom.* New York: The New Press.

Egbo, B. 2001. "Differential Enunciation, Mainstream Language and the Education of Immigrant Minority Students: Implications for Policy and Practice." *Journal of Teaching and Learning* 1(2): 47–61.

– 2009. *Teaching for Diversity in Canadian Schools.* Toronto: Pearson Education.

– 2011. "What Should Pre-service Teachers Know about Race and Diversity? Exploring a Critical Knowledge-Base for Teaching in 21st Century Canadian Classrooms." *Journal of Contemporary Issues in Education* 6(2): 23–37.

Fairclough, N. 1992. *Critical Language Awareness.* London: Longman.

Fleras, A., and J.L. Elliot. 2003. *Unequal Relations: An Introduction to Race and Ethnic Dynamics in Canada.* 4th ed. Toronto, ON: Prentice-Hall.

Freire, P. 1970. *Pedagogy of the Oppressed.* New York: Herder & Herder.

Gardner, H. 1999. *Intelligence Reframed: Multiple Intelligences for the 21st Century.* New York: Basic Books.

Ghosh, R. 2008. "Racism: A Hidden Curriculum." *Education Canada* 48(4): 26–9.

Ghosh, R., and A. Abdi. 2004. *Education and the Politics of Difference: Canadian Perspective.* Toronto, ON: Canadian Scholars' Press.

Hampton, R. 2010. "Black Learners in Canada." *Race & Class* 52(1): 103–10.

Henry, A. 2009. "Race and Gender in Classrooms: Implications for Teachers." In *Multicultural Education: Issues and Perspectives,* edited by J. Banks and C. McGee-Banks, 183–207. Hoboken, NJ: John Wiley & Sons.

Henry, F., and C. Tator. 2010. *The Color of Democracy: Racism in Canadian Society.* 4th ed. Toronto: Nelson Education.

Ibrahim, A. 2014. *The Rhizome of Blackness: A Critical Ethnography of Hip-Hop Culture, Language, Identity, and the Politics of Becoming.* New York: Peter Lang.

James, C.E. 2010. *Seeing Ourselves: Exploring Race, Ethnicity and Culture.* 4th ed. Toronto: Thompson Educational Publishing.

Kelly, D.M., and G.M. Brandes. 2008. "Equitable Classroom Assessment: Promoting Self-Development and Self-Determination." *Interchange* 39(1): 49–76.

Kincheloe, J.L. 2005. *Critical Pedagogy Primer.* New York: Peter Lang Publishing.

King, J.E. 1991. "Dysconscious Racism: Ideology, Identity, and the Miseduca-
tion of Teachers." *The Journal of Negro Education* 60(2): 133–46.

Ladson-Billings, G. 1994. *The Dreamkeepers: Successful Teachers of African
American Children*. San Francisco: Jossey-Bass Publishers.

Ladson-Billings, G., and W. Tate. 1995. "Toward a Critical Race Theory of Education." *Teachers College Record* 97(1): 47–67.

Levine-Rasky, C. 2014. "White Fear: Analyzing Public Objection to Toronto's
Africentric School." *Race Ethnicity and Education* 17(2): 202–18.

Lund, D.E. 2011. "Examining Shades of Grey with Students: Social Justice
Education in Action." *Journal of Praxis in Multicultural Education* 6(1):
79–91.

Lopez, G.R. 2003. "The (Racially Neutral) Politics of Education: A Critical
Race Theory Perspective." *Educational Administration Quarterly* 39(1):
68–94.

McLaren, P. 2007. *Life in Schools: An Introduction to Critical Pedagogy in the
Foundations of Education*. Boston: Pearson Education.

McNeil, B. 2011. "Charting a Way Forward: Intersections of Race and Space
in Establishing Identity as an African Canadian Teacher Educator." *Studying Teacher Education* 7(2): 133–43.

Milner, H. 2003. "Reflection, Racial Competence and Critical Pedagogy:
How Do We Prepare Pre-service Teachers to Pose Tough Questions?" *Race
Ethnicity and Education* 6(2): 193–208.

Nelson, C. 2010. "Introduction." In *Ebony Roots, Northern Soil: Perspectives on
Blackness in Canada*, edited by C. Nelson, 1–13. Newcastle upon Tyne:
Cambridge Scholars.

Parker, L., and D.O. Stovall. 2004. "Actions Following Words: Critical Race
Theory Connects to Critical Pedagogy." *Educational Philosophy and Theory*
36(2): 167–82.

Pollock, M. 2001. "How the Question We Ask Most about Race in Education
Is the Very Question We Most Suppress." *Educational Researcher* 30(9):
2–12.

Sheets, R.H. 2005. *Diversity Pedagogy: Examining the Role of Culture in the
Teaching-Learning Process*. Toronto: Pearson Education.

Skerrett, A. 2008. "Racializing Educational Change: Melting Pot and
Mosaic Influences on Educational Policy." *Journal of Educational Change*
9:261–80.

Solórzano, D.G., and T. J. Yosso. 2001. "Critical Race and LatCrit Theory
and Method: Counter-storytelling." *Qualitative Studies in Education* 14(4):
471–95.

Thompson, D., and J. Wallner. 2001. "A Focusing Tragedy: Public Policy and the Establishment of Afrocentric Education in Toronto." *Canadian Journal of Political Science* 44(4): 807–28.

Villegas, A.M., and T. Lucas. 2002. *Educating Culturally Responsive Teachers: A Coherent Approach*. Albany, NY: State University of New York Press.

Zamudio, M., C. Russell, F. Rios, and J. Bridgeman. 2011. *Critical Race Theory Matters: Education and Ideology*. New York: Routledge.

8

Proposing Methodological Approaches to Elucidating African Canadian Students' Metacognition across Learning Contexts

Samson Madera Nashon

Using a microanalytic framework, this chapter proposes and discusses ways to understand the African Canadian learner (see Diallo, Ibrahim, and Thésée and Carr in this volume). More from a practical point of view (see also Egbo, this volume), the chapter attempts to offer an inclusive picture of where the education of African Canadian learners has been, where it is now, and where it is going. It is important, I am arguing, to understand how youth learn by investigating how they monitor and control their individual ways of learning. Researching this among African Canadian youth, I am also arguing, is better accomplished through employment of the dynamic and technology-enhanced methodological approaches that make it feasible to elucidate student metacognition and how it manifests across learning contexts. Research investigating African Canadian student metacognition is largely absent from the literature. Yet, understanding how metacognition manifests among this group of Canadians has the potential to inform the design of educational experiences in informal settings, given that studies focusing on classroom contexts have demonstrated the power of metacognition in promoting student independent learning, as well as deeper conceptual understanding (Anderson and Nashon 2007). Therefore, this chapter proposes and discusses the methodological approaches to understanding African Canadian student metacognition across learning contexts, firstly, by developing the meaning of metacognition and its importance to learning; secondly, by observing how it has been studied in the past, that is, by examining the strategies that have been used to elucidate its nature of manifestation during learning; and thirdly, by discussing potential strategies that can be used in studies that might seek to elucidate African Canadian students' engagement of metacognition across learning contexts (e.g., amusement parks, nature centres, museums, and aquariums). In addition, the appropriateness of the learning contexts to understanding African Canadian students and the great potential of technology to enhance metacognitive strategies will be discussed. The chapter concludes by proffering the need to employ more technology-enhanced investigations of the elusive, yet important, human construct of metacognition among African Canadian students.

THEORETICAL BACKGROUND

Metacognition is a term that has taken on various meanings, depending on a researcher's intended understanding of learners' appreciation of their own learning (Anderson, Nashon, and Thomas 2009). Consequently, there appears to be, as Larkin (2006) conveys, an inconsistent use or definition of metacognition in literature. However, Anderson and Nashon (2007) have attributed diversities in definitions to different aspects of metacognition. For this chapter, I adopt a perspective of metacognition as comprising various dimensions or aspects (Anderson and Nashon 2007; Anderson, Nashon, and Thomas 2009; Thomas, Anderson, and Nashon 2008 Nashon and Nielsen 2011). Thus, considering the differing definitions of metacognition and the underlying aspects that they subsume, this chapter proposes a methodological framework and methods consistent with this perspective, which can be useful in elucidating metacognition and similar phenomena associated with African Canadian student learning. In their review of literature, Anderson and Nashon (2007) have made a solid case for six perspectives or dimensions: *awareness* (Baird 1986; Kuhn, Amsel, and O'Loughlin 1988; Gunstone 1994), *control* (Baird 1986; Kuhn, Amsel, and O'Loughlin 1988; Gunstone 1994), *evaluation* (White 1992; Costa 1991; Bellancea and Fogarty 1993), *planning* (Bellancea and Fogarty 1993), *monitoring* (Bellancea and Fogarty 1993), and *self-efficacy* (Bandura 1998). However, recent investigation that resulted in the development and validation of an instrument, Self-Efficacy, Metacognition and Learning Inventory in Science (SEMLI-S) (Thomas et al. 2008), which can signpost students' potential to engage metacognition, has noted five dimensions/aspects as being theoretically consolidated (Aiken 1982). Three of these dimensions are described as obviously metacognitive (awareness of risks to learning, control of concentration, and monitoring-evaluation-planning), while the other two are aspects of self-regulation (self-efficacy) and learning (constructive connectivity). The SEMLI-S dimensions differ from the theoretically determined dimensions (Aiken 1982) in terms of specificity and including learning as one of the dimensions. It is argued in this chapter that this is due to the fact that metacognition, self-regulation, and meaning making (learning) might be happening simultaneously. The *knowledge connectivity* on the SEMLI-S (Thomas et al. 2008) is indicative of constructivism, which in the constructivist literature appears to be unified on the fact that learners make sense of the world or new encounters in terms of the already possessed or experienced knowledge (Kelly 1955, Driver 1983, Gunstone 1994). The SEMLI-S, which was developed based on reductionist and Rasch and factor analysis techniques, is an instrument comprising self-assessment and self-declaration of knowledge of learners' own learning process. It is intended to determine learners'/students' profiles on metacognition (awareness of risks to learning, control of concentration, and monitoring-evaluation-planning), self-regulation (self-efficacy), and learning (constructivist connectivity) profiles (Thomas et al. 2008).

It should be pointed out that the process of validating an instrument such as the SEMLI-S is also a data collection technique. The insights gained during the validation process, which in most cases are unreported, constitute a very important source of data in qualitative investigations. For example, deletion of items is often mentioned, but reasons or justifications for the action are rarely recorded. Yet, justifications for the deletion of items are important data. Through this chapter, I am contending that any action in data collection and processing does not happen without justification. These do inform the design and enactment of subsequent data collection methods, such as follow-up interviews, cognitive and affective stimulants or tasks, discussion, etc. One might wonder why data that are revealing something about an individual would be discarded just because the data are not in line with the majority of entries in the data set. For example, according to Aiken (1982), the goal of factor analysis "is to find a relatively small number of personality factors (traits) that would account for variations in scores on various inventories, and then to construct a measure of each factor" (322). But these are not the only factors that underlie the instrument. Any factor loaded with fewer than three items is typically ignored (Kim and Mueller 1978).

Although Thomas et al. (2008) extracted five factors during the analysis of data collected from 2,000 grade 8 Hong Kong students, Anderson and Nashon (2007) had discerned similar dimensions from literature: *planning, monitoring,* and *evaluation; control; awareness; knowledge connectivity;* and *self-efficacy.* In this chapter, these aspects are very important in framing any study that aims to understand African Canadian students' engagement of metacognition and what triggers such metacognitive engagement.

EPISTEMOLOGICAL POSITION ON LEARNING AND METACOGNITION: THE CONTEXT OF AFRICAN CANADIAN STUDENTS

The proposition discussed in this chapter is based on epistemological underpinnings that view learning as occurring holistically and not only in isolated contexts (Ausubel 1963; Bruner 1996), and metacognition as being dynamic and not the domain of any one single context or experience or groups of people (Flavell 1979). Consequently, learning and metacognition are viewed as processes that manifest cross-contextually, and thus can be examined across both out-of-school and in-classroom experiences. Learning is here viewed as being an idiosyncratic and a dynamic process developed through experiences that are interpreted in the light of learners' prior knowledge (Driver et al. 1997; Hodson 1986, 1998; Jenkins 1996; Kilbourn 1998; Nashon and Anderson 2004, Nashon and Adler 2012), their attitudes, and their personal background (Guerts 2002; King et al. 1994; Lave and Wenger 1991). It is also considered that learning can be interpreted as occurring at the group level, i.e., within a community of learners, and also at the individual level. Although the value of canonically correct knowledge is underscored, to understand learning and metacognition necessarily requires the examination of both canonically viable and unviable knowledge (Kuhn 1970). This is because learners' worldviews or paradigms are key influences on their perceptions or conceptions of their individual realities (Hodson 1998). Moreover, learners' personal conceptions of themselves as learners, their self-awareness, and their control of their learning processes may be both empowering and limiting factors in ways they construct knowledge. Indeed, the socio-cultural identity of the individual and the group to which the individual belongs determines, in large part, the learning tools that the individual uses to make sense of the world (Bell et al. 2000; Nashon 2003,

2004; Nashon and Anderson 2004). Additionally, this chapter considers that, to varying degrees, all learners make decisions about the strategies they employ to make meaning of the world. However, personal awareness or consciousness of the learning strategies available to them and the conditions in which they employ the strategies do vary. These considerations can further inform the design, conduct, and interpretation of any study regarding learning and metacognition among African Canadian students.

Meaningful learning (Ausubel 1963, 1968; Bodner 1986) involves, among other things, taking the responsibility for one's own learning. The process of meaningful learning, in most cases, employs the use of thinking skills or metacognition. Metacognition involves active monitoring, conscious control, and regulation of mental processes (Baird and White 1996; Baird 1986; Flavel 1987; Gunstone 1994; Mintzes and Wandersee 1998; Thomas 1999; Thomas and McRobbie 2001; Nashon and Anderson 2004; White 1993, 1998), which make it a key factor in understanding student learning processes. In this regard, Baird (1986) considers metacognition to be the awareness and control of one's own learning, and suggests that students who are metacognitive make their thoughts the object of cognition. Moreover, Kuhn, Amsel, and O'Loughlin (1988) define metacognition in terms of students' ability to not only think *with* their ideas, but *about* the ideas. On the other hand, Gunstone (1994) views metacognition as an amalgam of students' knowledge, awareness, and control that are relevant to their learning.

What seems apparent is that these authors seem to define metacognition on the basis of the mental processes that they each perceive to illuminate students' learning processes. As already stated, Gunstone (1994) says "knowledge, awareness and control are personal constructions; an appropriately metacognitive learner is one who can effectively undertake the constructive process of recognition, evaluation and where needed, reconstruction of existing ideas" (135–6). In this excerpt, Gunstone uses four constructs – *knowledge, awareness, control, recognition*, and *evaluation* – to characterize metacognition. The *evaluation* construct is described by White (1992) to be "judging whether understanding is sufficient ... [and] searching for connections and conflicts with what is already known" (157). A connection can be seen between the "searching for connections and conflicts with what is already known" (White 1992, 157) and Gunstone's construct of *knowledge*, which is described by Thomas et al. (2008) as *knowledge connectivity* to characterize aspects of metacognition. On the other hand, Thomas

(1999) eloquently observes: "[M]etacognition is ... deliberate, reflective thinking involving the individual stopping to plan, monitor and evaluate his/her cognitive processes" (46). Again, in addition to perceiving metacognition in terms of the *evaluation* construct (White 1992; Gunstone 1994), Thomas also sees metacognition as involving *planning* and *monitoring* constructs. In the same vein, Biggs (1988) simply sees metacognition as largely involving "greater self-knowledge and task knowledge" (129). For this chapter, self-efficacy (Bandura 1998) is adopted to include *self-knowledge* or *self-perception* (Anderson and Nashon 2007). Bandura defines self-efficacy simply as people's beliefs about their capabilities to produce effects.

This synthesis demonstrates the fact that metacognition is understood differently by different people, and largely seems to depend on the learning process perceived. It is possible that each of the *dimensions* is engaged differently, depending on the circumstances and the learning contexts. The dimensions allow the interpretation and development of deeper understanding of student metacognition. It is probable that the number of dimensions could be as many as there are researchers of metacognition. However, for the purpose of this chapter – which proposes an approach to studying African Canadian students' engagement of metacognition during learning across contexts such as amusement parks, museums, nature centres, and aquariums – student learning behaviour of *awareness, control, monitoring, evaluation, knowledge connectivity, planning* and *self-efficacy* are considered adequate at elucidating their metacognition across learning contexts.

In recent years, there has been a marked increase and interest in the use of out-of-school experiences in teaching and learning science. However, there have been no studies to examine African Canadian students' metacognition in relation to field trip visits to out-of-school settings, such as amusement parks. Moreover, there are very few studies that examine either how these students think about these experiences when they return to classroom environments, or how the related post-visit experiences shape their knowledge construction as well as conceptual development as a function of metacognition. Given the importance of metacognition in relation to learning, it is prudent to investigate how it influences knowledge construction and conceptual development among African Canadian students, a majority of whom are immigrants. This should not be limited only to the classroom or confines of a narrow context, but should extend in and beyond out-of-school learning contexts.

WHY INVESTIGATE METACOGNITION
AMONG AFRICAN CANADIAN STUDENTS

Understanding the characteristics of student metacognition, which in part comprises the awareness and control of the tools and strategies they use to make meaning of experiences across contexts, is important in informing the more effective design and development of learning experiences. Furthermore, it is important to study metacognition, since understanding it will illuminate the unique and idiosyncratic ways in which it manifests. Besides, metacognition has been determined to empower students to be lifelong, independent learners (Veenman et al. 2006). Also as Flavell (1979) and Nelson (1990) have intimated, metacognition has the function of monitoring and controlling of cognition, which is important in the knowledge construction process. Awareness, control, and monitoring of one's own learning process is useful in learning and for purposes of instruction and development of curriculum materials, which, in all respects, should be learner-centred. This importance should be a key consideration during the conceptualization, design, and development of any studies that might aim to frame, investigate, and illuminate African Canadian student metacognition across learning contexts.

COMMONLY USED METHODS
FOR STUDYING METACOGNITION

Various methods have been used in researching metacognition. In their review of the literature on elucidating metacognition, Veenman, van Hout-Wolters, and Afflerbach (2006) cite Pellegrino, Chudowsky, and Glaser (2001) as suggesting that metacognition can be understood by assessments that are suitable for measuring and describing metacognition. Currently, the methods being used to assess metacognition include questionnaires (Pintrich and de Groot 1990; Thomas 2003), interviews (Zimmerman and Martinez-Pons 1990), the analysis-of-thinking-aloud protocols (Afflerbach 2000; Veenman, Elshout, and Groen 1993), stimulated recall (van Hout-Wolters 2000), on-line computer-logfile registration (Veenman et al. 2003), and eye-movement registration (Kinnunen and Vauras 1995). These strategies embody Eurocentric framing. Strategies such as eye movement might be interpreted differently depending on one's sociocultural background.

It should be pointed out that these methods have pros and cons. According to Veenman et al. (2006), questionnaires, for example, can be easy to administer to large groups, whereas thinking-aloud protocols are suitable for individual assessments. Further, some of the assessment methods may be more intrusive than others. Veenman et al. (2006) further posit that it is important to determine more precisely what metacognitive knowledge or skill component can be assessed successfully by which methods. In other words, it appears that each metacognitive skill might require a different assessment method depending on the character of each. For instance, studies have shown that, though it is taken for granted that questionnaires will measure what they are intended to, such as a metacognitive activity or strategy, often the scores on these questionnaires hardly correspond to actual student behavioural measures during task performance (Veenman 2005; Veenman, Prins, and Verheij 2003). In the same vein, it can be argued that the established instruments and protocols have been framed largely with a Eurocentric focus. It is critical to develop protocols that are commensurate with the African Canadian sociocultural upbringing, which, to a large extent, influences the way in which students construct knowledge.

Van Hout-Wolters (2000) and Veenman et al. (2006) separate the assessment methods into two categories: on-line and off-line. On the one hand, off-line assessments are typically administered either before or after task performance, while on the other, on-line assessments are obtained during task performance. Therefore, according to Veenman (2005), on-line assessments are more predictive of learning performance relative to the off-line methods. This apparent discrepancy in the outcomes of the types of assessments should impress upon researchers in this field the need to consider alternative methods or designs that would provide a more accurate description of an individual student's metacognition.

This background is the motivation for proposing a plausible strategy for investigating metacognition among African Canadian students. It is important to develop a more innovative design of a study that can aim to investigate African Canadian student metacognition during learning across contexts. The design should use a multi-method approach to assess the manifestation of a student's metacognition crosscontextually. In addition, there should be inbuilt flexibilities in the study design to allow for more innovative strategies to be incorporated in the data collection procedures at various phases during the study.

In other words, experience from one phase would and should inform the design of data collection or elicitation procedures in subsequent phases, all of which should aim to improve the level of access, and capture and illuminate student metacognition.

POSSIBLE INVESTIGATION QUESTIONS

Questions aimed at investigating metacognition among the African Canadian students should be general and should seek, among other things, what learning means to them. They should inquire about the students' views of how they come to know what they know, how they understand their learning processes, and what they envision to be their main goals of going to school. In addition, questions specific to metacognition should form part of the inquiry about learning in general. Such questions might include:

1 What context-related experiences are fundamental to students' metacognition and metacognitive processes?
2 What levels of metacognition and metacognitive processes are evident among students before, during, and following experiences encountered on class field trip visits to new or unfamiliar contexts?
3 What are the attributes of the unfamiliar context experiences that result in metacognitive engagement?
4 In what ways do the metacognitive experiences in unfamiliar contexts contribute to the students' learning?
5 How do students' metacognition and metacognitive processes change as learning resulting from their unfamiliar context experiences is re-contextualized in and beyond the classroom?
6 How does metacognition vary across contexts and the learners' culture?

Investigating questions such as these could follow a diverse number of paths, provided the participants are comfortable and motivated. These could include:

1 Taking pre-measures of the students' metacognitive processing using a specially developed paper and pencil instrument;
2 Development of base-line metacognitive profiles for students;
3 Administration of interventions designed to cue students about notions of metacognition;

4 Field trip visit(s) to unfamiliar contexts (amusement parks, nature centres, aquarium, etc.);

5 Engaging the students in the in-case-context tasks that evoke or stimulate metacognitive thoughts and actions that elucidate metacognitive engagement (planning, awareness, control, monitoring, self efficacy, and constructive connectivity) (Thomas et al. 2009), which can be described and interpreted as data about metacognition;

6 Student participation in classroom-based, post-visit activities integrated with the school-based curriculum. Throughout the study, participant students should maintain reflection diaries of their experiences at the unfamiliar case-context and during and following classroom-based activities; and

7 Taking post-measures (e.g., using face-to-face interviews, group discussions or questionnaires) of student metacognition about the familiar classroom and the unfamiliar out-of-classroom context.

POSSIBLE RESEARCH JOURNEY

For rich and meaningful data, it seems reasonable to implement such a study in phases. Where a phase might involve the classroom and an unfamiliar context (typically out-of-school), for example, phase 1 might involve classroom–amusement park, phase 2 could involve classroom–science centre, and phase 3 might involve classroom–aquarium. Prior to their participating in any phase, it is prudent to determine the students' baseline conditions and behaviour so as to assess the potential of the context to stimulate their metacognitive engagements. Moreover, data collection procedures outlined above could be a valuable guide to implementing the study.

The data corpus records might include researcher field notes, video recordings of group interactions, and individual voice recordings of each of the student's conversations. These voice recordings can be captured by means of personal digital audio recorders and lapel microphones that students could wear (Anderson et al. 2009). It is helpful to have students think about their own learning by supplying them with their earlier personal conversations about the learning experience. Before the students are interviewed in small group cohorts perhaps two to three days later, these conversations can be burned onto CDs for listening, discussion, and deliberation about their metacognition and conceptual development.

DATA ANALYSIS

Data analysis should centre around (a) generating students' metacognitive scores from a specially developed paper and pencil instrument, and (b) reviewing and interpreting collectively the video and audio data of the students' interactions and conversations in each unfamiliar (out-of-school) context, post-visit interviews, in-class activities, and post-activity interviews concerning the students' knowledge construction and metacognition. These reviews could follow an iterative process of analysis, including critical reflections by those involved in the research. This process should result in rich descriptions of individuals and their respective characteristics regarding their individual learning processes and metacognition.

WHAT IS DIFFERENT IN
THIS DATA COLLECTION FORMAT?

As already discussed, various research methods or assessment tools have been used to bring about an understanding of metacognition. As Veenman et al. (2006) observed, many studies on metacognition have employed only one of the methods with mixed results. The proposed strategy allows the use of multiple methods in an attempt to capture students' metacognitive activities during learning tasks across contexts. Baseline scores are important in providing signposts to students' potential to engage the various aspects of metacognition. In other words, each participant student's level of the various aspects (dimensions) prior to participating in the remaining part of each phase of the study is a useful baseline to understand change in metacognition or learning.

IMPLICATIONS FOR RESEARCHING
METACOGNITION AND LEARNING

Researching metacognition and learning processes can be challenging for the researchers as well as for the participants. Metacognition and learning are elusive (intangible) constructs that can only be understood in terms of outcomes. The research involves an element of intrusion into the participants' personal processes of meaning making (Anderson et al. 2009). How this is understood and interpreted depends on cultural protocols of participant groups. Technology has made it possible for this to happen. For example, video- and voice-recording (using wearable technology) of the participants engaged in learning activities, and playing these recordings back to the participants for dialectic reflection, perhaps days later, offer a tremendous advantage and a leap forward in terms of data collection, analysis, and interpretation (Anderson et al. 2009).

Understanding of constructs such as metacognition and learning involves repeated review of the subjects while in the moment. Making sense of the participants' actions requires careful review of recorded incidents in a multi-perspective sense, which is made possible by technology. Furthermore, the use of technology makes it possible for the researcher to concentrate on establishing rapport with the participants and managing the research environment, as opposed to using checklists for behaviour tracking, which in itself can be very intimidating to the participants. As new technologies evolve, the quality of data collected should also evolve. Validating insights from such a study can be enhanced by involving the participants (subjects) in the interpretive process. I wish to end this chapter by describing a study on metacognition that investigated its engagement cross-contextually during science learning discourses.

METACOGNITION
AND REFLECTIVE INQUIRY STUDY

Although not specifically focusing on African Canadian populations, the studies that I have conducted on metacognition and ways of knowing have added impetus to the proposition advanced in this chapter. These studies include Metcognition and Reflective Inquiry (MRI) – Learning Across Contexts (Anderson and Nashon 2007; Anderson et al. 2009; Thomas et al. 2008; Nashon and Nielsen 2011; Nielsen et al. 2009); Canadian–East African Collaborative for the Study of East African Students' Ways of Knowing (CEACSWOK) in Science Discourses (Nashon et al. 2012; Nashon and Anderson 2013; Nashon and Madera 2013; Wright et al. 2007); and Canadian–East African Collaborative for the Study of Science Learning and Pedagogy (CEACSSLAP): The Effect of Student Learning on Science Teachers' Teaching in East Africa (Nashon and Anderson 2013a, 2013b; Nashon 2013). While the CEACSWOK and CEACSSLAP studies focus on ways of knowing and teacher change resulting from student learning respectively, they have been modelled on the MRI study. This was because one of the observations of the MRI study is about the different ways or strategies students use to understand scientific concepts/phenomena embedded in contextualized experiences. I have as such argued that understanding students' metacognition can give us insight into the ways in which they learn. Moreover, as Gunstone (1994) has intimated, one can only be metacognitive about something, such as an event, an object, a fact, or simply an encounter. The MRI study was a multinational study that investigated high school students' engagement of metacognition in Canada, Australia and China. It was evident that students' engagement of metacognitive skills was evident when the tasks required understanding of the science embedded in local contexts or use of local contexts to explain classroom science activities. In all cases, the study followed the procedures below.

Procedures

The research team, for which I was co-principal investigator, made presentations to the participating classes about our study. We shared with the class our interest, position on, and understanding of how knowledge is acquired and what metacognition is. We explained that we were interested in understanding how metacognition is deployed and what is the nature of experiences that evoke it. Further, we explained the purpose of the study and the procedures for their participation and for data collection. This presentation was always an important session, since it was when we clarified who could participate and what their role in the study would be.

The study aimed (1) to describe and explain the key field trip experiences that were key to student metacognition; (2) to determine and to describe the characteristics evident among the case study participants following a field trip experience; (3) to determine and to describe the ways in which field-trip-related metacognition contributed to the students' learning; (4) to determine, to describe and to explain how students' metacognition changed as their learning from a field trip was re-contextualized; and (5) to determine or to gain insight into how metacognition varied across learners' contexts and cultures.

We endeavoured to achieve the above aims by implementing the MRI study whereby the students completed a specially developed baseline metacognition instrument (SEMLI-S) (Thomas et al. 2009). They participated in a class field trip to Playland, Vancouver, for physics amusement experiences, and participated in group activities following the guidelines provided in the activity booklets. These students recorded their dialogues during the activity time, including reflection time (minimum of two activities, always in the same group of three). They took home recording devices and listened to their reflections and participation, and wrote their reflections, learning, and understandings in researcher-supplied notebooks, or loudly/vocally reflected and recorded on tape. Research associates followed the participants (who were wearing recording devices) everywhere during field trip activity and reflection time at the amusement park. The research associates were also filming them. The students with recording devices participated in post-visit group interviews with the researchers. Students participated in in-class, post-visit, teacher-designed activities with researcher input. (Note that those with recording devices continued to work in the groups until the end of the project.) The students participated in interviews (individually) while wearing recording devices. Six months later, the students participated in a final follow-up interview while wearing recording devices.

As participants in the study, the students went to the rides assigned by their teacher, and discussed the experiences in groups of three as directed by the activity guides and other researcher-provided items. They recorded dialogues with peers and any other loud/vocal reflections (encouraged) and informal chats with researchers and their teacher. At all times, those with recording devices always worked and reflected in their groups. They played back the recordings and reflected on the tasks and discussions of the day, reflected on recordings, and recorded or wrote in researcher-supplied notebooks. The students posed questions to their teacher, MRI team members, peers, or anyone who was connected to the learning context. All of these dialogues were recorded. Throughout the study period, the participants were required to always carry their notebooks, so that they noted down the time any thought came to their mind, the place/venue/event where this occurred, what they were doing, and what prompted the thinking. Any thought that disturbed them regarding experiences at the amusement park or any related venue, including the classroom and home, was to be similarly recorded and described.

Outcomes of the MRI Study

The MRI study generated enhanced theoretical perspectives of metacognition and conceptual learning across contexts (Anderson and Nashon 2007). Also, we are tending towards a better understanding of how students exercise and experience self-awareness and control of their own individual learning (Thomas et al. 2009; Nielsen et al. 2009). Further, I consider studies such as this as having the capacity to sensitize students about the need for and benefits of this kind of awareness and control of their own individual learning processes (Gunstone 1994). This understanding is critical to developing and offering better teacher education programs that sensitize teachers about the need for, and pedagogical benefits of, developing activities that enhance student engagement of metacognition in their learning. What the MRI, CEACSWOK, and CEACSSLAP studies have revealed is the increased level of student motivation, interest, and conceptual understanding and teacher change when student learning experiences are contextualized or grounded in students' local cultural experiences (Hull 1993; Karweit 1993; Nashon 2013; Nashon and Madera 2013; Nashon and Anderson 2013a, 2013b). These outcomes compelled the argument advanced in this chapter about studying African-Canadian students' metacognition with a view to drawing on what is around them to foster their metacognitive potential.

REFERENCES

Afflerbach, P. 2000. "Verbal Reports and Protocol Analysis." In *Handbook of Reading Research*, edited by M.L. Kamil, P.B. Mosenthal, P.D. Pearson, and R. Barr, 163–79. Mahwah, NJ: Erlbaum.

Aiken, L.R. 1982. *Psychological Testing and Assessment*. Toronto: Allyn and Bacon.

Anderson, D., K.B. Lucas, and I.S. Ginns. 2003. "Theoretical Perspectives on Learning in an Informal Setting." *Journal of Research in Science Teaching* 40(2): 177–99.

Anderson, D., and S.M. Nashon. 2007. "Predators of Knowledge Construction: Interpreting Students' Metacognition in an Amusement Park Physics Program." *Science Education* 91(2): 298–320.

Anderson, D., S.M. Nashon, and P.G. Thomas. 2009. "Evolution of Research Methods for Probing and Understanding Metacognition." *Research in Science Education* 39:181–95.

Anderson, D., G.P. Thomas, and K.M. Ellenbogen. 2003. "Learning Science from Experiences in Informal Contexts: The Next Generation of Research." *Asia-Pacific Forum on Science Learning and Teaching* 4(1): 1–5.

Ausubel, D.P. 1963. *The Psychology of Meaningful Verbal Learning*. New York: Grune & Straton.

– 1968. *Educational Psychology: A Cognitive View*. New York: Holt, Rinehart & Winston.

Baird, J.R. 1986. "Improving Learning through Enhanced Metacognition: A Classroom Study." *European Journal of Science Education* 8(3): 263–82.

Baird, J.R., and R.T. White. 1996. "Metacognitive Strategies in the Classroom." In *Improving Teaching and Learning in Science Mathematics*, edited by D.F. Treagust, R. Duit, and J. Fraser. New York: Teachers College.

Bandura, A. 1993. "Perceived Self-Efficacy in Cognitive Development and Functioning." *Educational Psychologist* 28(2): 117–48.

Bell, R.L., N.G. Lederman, and F. Abd-El-Khalick. 2000. "Developing and Acting upon One's Conception of the Nature of Science: A Follow-up Study." *Journal of Research in Science Teaching* 37(6): 563–81.

Bellancea, J., and R. Fogarty. 1993. *Catch Them Thinking: A Handbook of Classroom Strategies*. Palatine, IL: IRI/SkyLight Training and Publishing.

Biggs, J.B. 1988. "The Role of Metacognition in Enhancing Learning." *Australian Journal of Education* 32(2): 127–38.

Bodner, G.M. 1986. "Constructivism: A Theory of Knowledge." *Journal of Chemical Education* 63(10): 873–8.

Bruner, J. 1996. *The Culture of Education*. Cambridge: Harvard University Press.

Costa, A. 1991. *The School as Home for Mind*. Melbourne: Hawker Brownlow.

Driver, R. 1983. *The Pupil as Scientist?* Buckingham: Open University Press.

Driver, R., J. Leach, R. Millar, and P. Scott. 1997. *Young People's Images of Science*. Philadelphia: Open University Press.

Flavell, J.H. 1979. "Metacognition and Cognition Monitoring: A New Area of Cognitive-Developmental Inquiry." *American Psychologist* 34:906–11.

– 1987. "Speculation about the Nature and Development of Metacognition." In *Metacognition, Motivation, and Understanding*, edited by F.E. Weinert and R.H. Kluwe, 21–9. London: Lawrence Erlbaum.

Guerts, K.L. 2002. *Culture and Senses*. Berkeley: University of California Press.

Gunstone, R.F. 1994. "The Importance of Specific Science Content in the Enhancement of Metacognition." In *The Content of Science: A Constructivist Approach to Its Teaching and Learning*, edited by P. Fensham, R.F. Gunstone, and R.T. White, 131–46. Washington, DC: Falmer Press.

Hodson, D. 1986. "The Nature of Scientific Observation." *School Science Review* 68(242): 17–29.

Hodson, D. 1998. *Teaching and Learning Science: Towards a Personalized Approach*. Buckingham: Open University Press.

Hull, G. 1993. "Hearing Other Voices: A Critical Assessment of Popular Views on Literacies and Work." *Harvard Education Review* 63(1): 20–49.

Jenkins, E. 1996. "The Nature of Science as a Curriculum Component." *Journal of Curriculum Studies* 28(2): 137–50.

Karweit, D. 1993. *Contextual Learning: A Review and Synthesis*. Baltimore, MD:

Center for the Social Organization of Schools, Johns Hopkins University Press.

Kelly, G.A. 1955. *The Psychology of Personal Constructs: A Theory of Personality.* New York: Norton.

Kilbourn, B. 1998. *For the Love of Teaching.* Toronto: The Althouse Press.

Kim, J.-O., and C.W. Mueller. 1978. *Introduction to Factor Analysis. What It Is and How to Do It.* Beverly Hills, CA: Sage.

King, E.W., M. Chipman, and M. Cruz-Janzen. 1994. *Educating Young Children in a Diverse Society.* Boston: Allyn and Bacon.

Kinnunen, R., and M. Vauras. 1995. "Comprehension Monitoring and the Level of Comprehension in High- and Low-Achieving Primary School Children's Reading." *Learning & Instruction* 5:143–65.

Kuhn, T.S. 1970. *The Structure of Scientific Revolutions.* 2nd ed. Chicago: University of Chicago Press.

Kuhn, D., E. Amsel, and M. O'Loughlin. 1988. *The Development of Scientific Thinking Skills.* San Diego, CA: Academic Press.

Larkin, S. 2006. "Collaborative Group Work and Individual Development of Metacognition in the Early Years." *Research in Science Education* 44(2): 1–6.

Lave, J., and E. Wenger. 1991. *Situated Learning: Legitimate Peripheral Participation.* Cambridge: Cambridge University Press.

McManus, P.M. 1993. "Thinking about the Visitor's Thinking." In *Museum Visitor Studies in the 90s,* edited by S. Bicknell and G. Farmelo, 108–13. London: Science Museum.

Mintzes, J.J., and J.H. Wandersee. 1998. "Reform and Innovation in Science Teaching: A Human Constructivist View." In *Teaching Science for Understanding: A Human Constructivist View,* edited by J.J. Mintzes, J.H. Wandersee, and J.D. Novak, 30–58. San Diego, CA: Academic Press.

Nashon, S.M. 2003. "Teaching and Learning High School Physics through Analogies in Kenyan Classrooms." *Canadian Journal of Science, Mathematics, and Technology Education* (CJSMTE) 3(3): 333–45.

– 2004. "The Nature of Analogical Explanations High School Physics Teachers Use in Kenya." *Research in Science Education* 34:475–502.

– 2013. "Interpreting Kenyan Science Teachers' Views about Effect of Student Learning Experiences on Their Teaching." *Canadian Journal of Science, Mathematics and Technology Education* 13(3): 213–31.

Nashon, S.M., and J.D. Adler. 2012. "Constructivist, Analogical and Metacognitive Approaches to Science Teaching and Learning." In *Contemporary Science Teaching Approaches: Promoting Conceptual Understanding in Science,* edited by F. Rnek and I.M. Saleh, 15–26. Charlotte, NC: Information Age Publishing.

Nashon, S.M., and D. Anderson. 2004. "Obsession with 'G': A Metacognitive Reflection of a Laboratory Episode." *Alberta Journal of Science Education* 36(2): 39–44.

– 2013a. "Interpreting Student Views of Learning Experiences in a Contextualized Science Discourse in Kenya." *Journal of Research in Science Teaching* 50(4): 381–407.

– 2013b. "Teacher Change: The Effect of Student Learning on Science Teachers' Teaching in Kenya." *International Journal of Engineering Education* 29(4): 839–45.

Nashon, S.M., and E.K. Madera. 2013. "Instrument for Assessing Disposition for Contextual Learning of Science of Students in East Africa." *Sage Open* (2013): 1–23. doi:10.1177/215824401394862.

Nashon, S.M., and S.W. Nielsen. 2011. "Connecting Student Self-Regulation, Metacognition and Learning to Analogical Thinking in a Physics Problem-Solving Discourse." *Education Research Journal* 1(5): 68–83.

Nashon, S.M., S. Ooko, and F.B. Kelonye. 2012. "Understanding, Interpreting and Profiling Kenyan Students' Worldviews of Science Learning." *Journal of Technology and Socio-Economic Development* 1(1): 346–52.

Nelson, T.O., and L. Narens. 1990. "Metamemory: A Theoretical Framework and New Findings." *The Psychology of Learning and Motivation* 26:125–41.

Nielsen, W.S., S.M. Nashon, and D. Anderson. 2009. "Metacognitive Engagement during Field-Trip Experiences: A Case Study of Students in an Amusement Park Physics Program." *Journal of Research in Science Teaching* 46(3): 265–88.

Pellegrino, J.W., N. Chodowsky, and R. Glaser, eds. 2001. *Knowing What Students Know: The Science and Design of Educational Assessment*. Washington, DC: National Academy Press.

Pintrich, P., and E.D. de Groot. 1990. "Motivational and Self-Regulated Learning Components of Classroom Academics Performance." *Journal of Educational Psychology* 82:33–40.

Thomas, G.P. 1999. "Developing Metacognition and Cognitive Strategies through the Use of Metaphor in a Year 11 Chemistry Classroom." PhD diss., University of Technology.

– 2003. "Conceptualisation, Development and Validation of an Instrument for Investigating the Metacognitive Orientation of Science Classroom Learning Environments: The Metacognitive Orientation Learning Environment Scale—Science (MOLES-S)." *Learning Environments Research* 6:175–97.

Thomas, G.P., D. Anderson, and S.M. Nashon. 2008. "Development and Validity of an Instrument Designed to Investigate Elements of Science Stu-

dents' Metacognition, Self-Efficacy and Learning Processes: The SEMLI-S."
International Journal of Science Education 30(13): 1701–24.

Thomas, G.P., and C.J. McRobbie. 2001. "Using a Metaphor for Learning to
Improve Students' Metacognition in the Chemistry Classroom." *Journal of
Research in Science Teaching* 38(2): 222–59.

Van Hout-Wolters, B. 2000. "Assessing Active Self-Directed Learning." In *New
Learning*, edited by R. Simons, J. van der Linden, and T. Duffy, 83–101.
Dordrecht: Kluwer.

Veenman, M.V.J. 2005. "The Assessment of Metacognitive Skills: What Can
be Learned from Multi Method Designs?" In *Lernstrategien und Metakogni-
tion: Implikationen für Forschung und Praxis*, edited by C. Artelt and B.
Moschner, 75–97. Berlin: Waxmann.

Veenman, M.V.J., J.J. Elshout, and M.G.M. Groen. 1993. "Thinking Aloud:
Does It Affect Regulatory Processes in Learning." *Tijdschrift voor Onderwijs-
research* 18:322–30.

Veenman, M.V.J., F.J. Prins, and J. Verheij. 2003. "Learning Styles: Self-Reports
versus Thinking Aloud Measures." *British Journal of Educational Psychology*
73:357–72.

Veenman, M.V.J., B. Van Hout-Wolters, and P. Afflerbach. 2006. "Metacognition and Learning: Conceptual and Methodological Considerations."
Metacognition and Learning 1:3–14.

White, R.T. 1992. "Implications of Recent Research on Learning for Curriculum and Assessment." *Journal of Curriculum Studies* 24(2): 153–64.

– 1993. "Insights on Conceptual Change Derived from Extensive Attempts
to Promote Metacognition." Paper presented at the annual meeting of the
Educational Research Association (AERA), Atlanta.

– 1998a. "Decisions and Problems in Research on Metacognition." In *International Handbook of Science Education*, edited by B.J. Fraser and K.G.
Tobin, 1207–12. London: Kluwer Academic Publishers.

– 1998b. "Research, Theories of Learning, Principles of Teaching and Classroom Practice: Examples and Issues." *Studies in Science Education* 31:
55–70.

Wright, H.K., S.M. Nashon, and D. Anderson. 2007. "Re-thinking the Place of
African Worldviews and Ways of Knowing in Education." *Diaspora, Indigenous and Minority Education* 1(4): 239–46.

Zimmerman, B.J., and M. Martinez-Pons. 1990. "Student Differences in Self-
Regulated Learning: Relating Grade, Sex, and Giftedness to Self-Efficacy
and Strategy Use." *Journal of Educational Psychology* 82:51–9.

9

Triple Whammy and a Fragile Minority within a Fragile Majority: School, Family and Society, and the Education of Black, Francophone Youth in Montreal

Gina Thésée and Paul R. Carr

INTRODUCTION:
TO BE YOUNG AND BLACK IN MONTREAL

In Quebec, young black francophones are principally from the Caribbean. Of this group, approximately 90 per cent are of Haitian origin, either first-, second- or third-generation. From the initial waves of Haitian immigration to Quebec in the early 1960s, and, especially, since the massive levels attained in the mid-1970s, the Haitian experience in education has been the subject of a number of debates and studies that have underscored numerous and recurring problems. These studies present an unhealthy and disconcerting educational portrait: low academic achievement, the need for French-language support programs, over-representation in special needs classes, under-representation in the academic streams leading to higher learning, drop-outs and school failure for many, and lower levels of graduation, etc., especially in comparison with those of Quebecois heritage (known in French as *de souche*) or other immigrant groups (McAndrew and Ledent 2009). Similarly, the mainstream media has been effective, willingly or unwillingly, in propagating myths, stereotypes, and misrepresentations of young Haitians as gang members, delinquents, and undesirables.

With regard to health issues, these youth also are at greater risk than many other groups of young people for contracting sexually transmitted diseases and experiencing teen pregnancy (Adrien 2011). According to Adrien (2011), this is due in large part to the combined effects of risky behaviour related to gender roles and sociocultural norms of the communities in which these youth live; they often have negative role models and multiple sexual partners, and they reject birth control and usage of condoms, among other things. Despite the existence of sex education courses at school, the knowledge of, and discourse about, potential issues and problems is not matched by behaviours.

Along with the education and health problematics, there is the equally disconcerting issue of the family and social context, which, in some cases, leads to children being placed in, or condemned to, youth centres, unemployment, and over-representation in prison. For example, one study in 1997 noted that, of the 993 young immigrants placed within protective settings, some 426 were of Haitian origin (Tillus 1999). Several sociocultural and family factors have been identified to help explain this situation: culture shock (resistance vis-à-vis authoritarian parents), disadvantageous soci-economic conditions (poverty and enhanced family responsibilities), precarious family dynamics (disproportionate single-mother households), non-integration and weak recognition of socially diverse situations (including within the family, at school, and within society), and the general negative public image of the Haitian community within the Quebecoise society (leading to stigmatization and devalorization) (Tillus 1999). The combined schooling, educational, professional, social, and economic experiences of Haitian youth in Quebec reveal and underscore a situation of permanent crisis.

Undoubtedly, Quebec is not the only place where such a situation exists, and the proximity to the United States makes Quebec and Canada geographic centres in which constant comparisons are made, usually with excessively critical assessments being made about the neighbour to the south. Elsewhere, Carr and Lund (2007) have documented how whiteness and white power and privilege play out within the Canadian context, underscoring the prevalence within the Canadian socio-political context of visceral racism south of the border, combined with a supposed kinder, more decent multicultural society that is more tolerant, progressive, and welcoming within the northern part of the continent. Interestingly, in their work throughout their whiteness project, which involved presentations, papers, interviews, an award-winning book, and other community linkages, Carr and Lund found that the topic, concept, and vocabulary did not translate easily, or at all, into French. In fact, although their book contained a broad range of chapters from leading and emerging scholars across Canada, including male and female, white and diverse racial minorities, Aboriginals and others, it was not possible to include a French-language, francophone vantage-point. In Europe and elsewhere through the French-language Association for Intercultural Research, this chapter's authors have made presentations on the subject of intercultural relations and whiteness, and have encountered resistance and even sometimes hostility, which relates to the ways the language, culture, geography, ideology, and politics have difficulty in crossing borders. This contextualization is significant here, because the Quebec polity and social context is often at odds with, and in opposition to, the English-language Canadian world, which has been highly influenced by the US in myriad ways.

Within this context, where there is a clear problem and malaise, one needs to ask how many studies – qualitative, quantitative, and otherwise – we need to fully document and elucidate the problematic. What level of "statistical significance" is required to understand the issue? Moreover, what is required to take meaningful action? The goal here is not to answer these questions but, rather, to frame them differently. For example, is it possible, or was it possible, to conceive the problematic differently? Given the multiple particularities concerning the context for African Canadian youth within the French-language context, should we be astonished that there are recurrent socio-educational deficits and worrisome outcomes from many within the community?

In light of the sensitive nature of this problematic – in conjunction with the serious individual and collective short- and long-term implications for the ensemble of Haitian communities in Quebec, as well as within the broader Diaspora, not to mention in Haiti as the country of origin – we believe that it is fully appropriate and essential to ask why this problem needs to exist, as well as to explore the socio-educational dynamics underpinning it. It is equally important to interrogate the informal and formal educational experiences of these young, African Canadian francophone youth, especially in relation to the contribution made by schools and other formal institutions, the diverse black communities themselves, professional associations, and, significantly, the families raising these young people.

To pursue our analysis, we have developed a theoretical and conceptual framework inspired by the tenets of critical pedagogy and postcolonial theories to elucidate the diverse socio-educational perspectives, dynamics, and concerns that African Canadian youth of Haitian origin in Quebec face. We focus on three significant dimensions (race, social class, and gender), and three other connected variables (migration history; academic and professional experience; and cultural and community experience [religion, links to Haiti, etc.]). We are motivated to not only understand better the underlying conditions and realities of this problem but also to be able to advocate for greater levels of sensitization, participation, engagement, and concern for young Haitian youth.

THE BLACK COMMUNITIES
IN AND FROM MONTREAL

Mathieu da Costa is recognized as the first black to be on Canadian soil alongside the renowned French explorer Samuel de Champlain in 1604. This fact is at odds with the generally accepted contention that Canada, and, indeed, Quebec, are white spaces, colonized, cultivated and populated only by whites. Of course, the thousands of years of life on this geographic space of Aboriginal peoples, the First Nations, needs to be evacuated from the hegemonic mainstream perspective in order to accept the white premise, but, once having done so, the racialized diversity in Canada is then formally, officially, and vociferously suppressed. Da Costa was a Métis of African origin, a navigator, linguist, and participant in numerous voyages between Europe, Africa, and the New World. His talents as an interpreter and translator with the Mi'kmaq people were greatly appreciated by the Dutch, the Portuguese, and the French. Champlain is said to have been accompanied by da Costa as he founded the city of Quebec in 1804, but it is difficult to validate this affirmation, given the ways that history has been written. Four hundred years after its foundation, under the gaze of black militants, Quebec City named a street in honour of Mathieu da Costa. It could be considered that da Costa is the founding father of Canadian multiculturalism, and, in addition, has inspired, to some degree, interculturalism within the Canadian context (Fehmiu-Brown 2011; Historica Canada n.d.).

Without question, the most legendary and historic figure of the black community in Montreal is Marie-Josèphe Angélique, a black slave who was accused of having purposely burned down a hospital and forty-five homes in the city on 11 April 1734. A litany of prejudice gathered steam to provide credence to a rumour that Angélique had set the fires in retaliation against her female owner, and also to cover the traces of her escape with her lover. The criminal trial is perhaps the most spectacular known under the French regime, and despite the contradictory testimony and the absence of eye-witnesses, the young slave was tortured into confessing the crime, ultimately condemned by the testimony of a child, and publicly executed on 21 June of the same year (Fehmiu-Brown 2011). In February 2012, a small park in Montreal, close to the Champ-de-Mars subway near Old Montreal where she lived, was inaugurated in Angélique's honour. This young black woman from Montreal, unjustly condemned, can be seen as an emblem of black history by the black community.

Today, in Metropolitan Montreal, the majority of blacks (85 per cent), anglophone and francophone, reside primarily in a number of areas in the eastern and western parts of the city. In the predominantly francophone areas, the eastern quarters such as Montréal-Nord, Rivière-des-Prairies, Saint-Michel, and Saint-Léonard are generally known to be largely populated by the Haitian community, where there are many commercial interests (grocery stores, hair salons, music stores, markets, caterers, etc.). Other areas in the metropolitan space, such as Côte-des-Neiges and Parc-Extension, as well as the suburbs of Laval in the north and Longueuil in the south, also have Haitian populations with a corresponding commercial presence. African immigration, the majority of which is francophone and started to intensify in the 1990s, is primarily situated in the west of the city in places like Côte-des-Neiges and Notre-Dame-de-Grâce. Black anglophone communities are primarily congregated in the western part of the city in Côte-des-Neiges, Petite-Bourgogne, Pointe-Saint-Charles, Saint-Henri, and Verdun. It is important to highlight that, in these areas, one black person out of every two lives under the poverty line (Torczyner et al. 2010). With the exception of Laval, property ownership is lower for blacks than for other groups in the population, determined to be a meagre 38 per cent versus 63 per cent in the rest of the population (Torczyner et al. 2010). Property ownership is considered to be an important factor in the creation of wealth, economic security, and generation heritage. It is also important to highlight here that residential (racial) segregation is much less pronounced in Canadian cities than in American ones (Labelle et al. 2001).

According to the 2006 Canadian census, from 1996 to 2006, the size of the Montreal black community increased by 38 per cent to 170,000 people, with four out of ten born in Canada, one out of six being of African origin, and four out of ten being born in the Caribbean, of which 75 per cent were born in Haiti. In Montreal, the black community is the largest contingent of what is considered the "visible minority" community. The average age in these black communities is much lower than the population at large, the birth rate is higher, and, proportionately speaking, the rate of black families having three or more children is three times higher than that of the broader population (27 per cent versus 9 per cent) (Torczyner et al. 2001).

The family context for the black community of Montreal is also marked by financial vulnerability and affective stability, sometimes directly connected to the fragile linkages with the extended family and single-parent female households, teenage parenting relationships, and other situations that can lead to hardship. Single-parent households within black families in Montreal are two times greater than that of the population at large: in 2006, 42 per cent of children under fourteen years of age lived in such a family, as opposed to 18 per cent for the broader population; 47 per cent of children under fifteen years of age lived below the poverty line as compared to 21 per cent for the broader population (Torczyner et al. 2010). There is also a linkage between single-parenting and area of residence: a large percentage of these single-parent black families in poverty live in areas where housing, property values, and options are less favourable than elsewhere in the city, areas such as Montréal-Nord et Saint-Michel. What might explain this situation, in part, is the recent immigration that advantages black women over black men (54 per cent versus 46 per cent). In addition, in relation to interracial couples, 62 per cent involve black men as opposed to 38 per cent for black women (Torczyner et al. 2001). The effect of immigration policies promoting the arrival of women before or without their spouses is to separate families and to deprive them of natural social and family networks. In sum, in general, black women are poorer than the general population, in spite of their age, level of education and training, and language. They are often found in employment that is less desirable, more poorly remunerated and frequently in the service sector, and they have additional responsibilities within the home and related to the extended family. In 1996, as an example, 30 per cent of the revenue received by black females in Montreal came through government transfers (Torczyner et al. 2001). The over-representation of black women seeking protection from conjugal violence is another factor in trying to disentangle the lived realities of individuals within the black francophone community, as well as a factor in attempting to draw a composite, a profile of the collective experience for black youth as a group.

THE POLITICAL-LINGUISTIC CONTEXT IN QUEBEC

Quebec is a French-speaking province in Canada, with roughly seven million francophones, making it the French centre for cultural life in the country, and also constituting a fragile linguistic minority within the rest of largely English-speaking Canada, and even more so when the US is factored into the equation. Cultural and linguistic assimilation, combined with formal laws, cultural and systemic discrimination, educational challenges, and the seduction of hegemonic English-speaking (especially American) culture, frame the Quebec context in a multitude of ways. Who is Quebecois? Who can become Quebecois? How long does it take to become a Quebecois? Must one be a francophone to be considered Quebecois? Must one also be white, Christian, and of French-language stock extending back to the origins of the founding of Quebec? The complexity of identity and identity formation is fundamental to this discussion. On the one hand, Quebec could be considered a minority context in relation to its quest to preserve its culture, however that is defined, and in relation to its language, which at the same time could be directly connected and also disconnected. But Quebec could also be considered a majority culture that has a certain control and authority over its own laws, culture, and language. Within Quebec, then, what is the relationship between the majority white population and the minority black population? For the purposes of this chapter, we ask what this relationship is, particularly with the Haitian population, which is largely French-speaking and does not align itself with the English-speaking community. Are Haitians in Quebec African Canadians, African Quebecois, blacks, Haitians, or simply Quebecois, or some other formulation? Does it matter if they are first-, second-, third- or fourth-generation, as is now the case for many families of Haitian origin in Montreal? Some of the second-, third- and fourth-generation youth and others of Haitian origin in Montreal do not speak Creole (the de facto language of Haiti that is, in large part, connected to French), have never visited Haiti, and may or may not have direct linkages, relations, and interests in and with Haiti.

This discussion is intended to help us construct a linguistic as well as a racialized and gendered identity for those of Haitian origin in Quebec, one that is nuanced, complexified, and integral to the debate around interculturalism, multiculturalism, and democracy (Thésée et al. 2011). While many trends, data-sets, and collective realities provide insight into Haitian youth identity, we are also cautious to not essentialize the diverse Haitian realities that pervade the Haitian and Quebec cultural spaces. To complete any portrait of this community, as alluded to earlier, social class is useful as a fundamental marker of life experience, opportunity, and perspective, not to close off potential developments, changes, and border-crossing but to simply accentuate that it plays a critical role in determining lived realities. Thus, education becomes pivotal to facilitating change and transformation for the individual, for the community, and for the society.

THE SOCIO-EDUCATIONAL AND SOCIO-PROFESSIONAL CONTEXT

Even as educational achievement levels have improved for black communities in recent years, including graduation rates, they still lag behind the success rates experienced by other communities. Formal education being the key to professional success, black youth need to be assured of the same opportunities, support, and experience as others.

Young Blacks

Black youth twenty-five years of age and younger represent 43 per cent of the black communities in Montreal compared to 29 per cent of the population. From those who arrived in the early 1960s to fourth-generation people of Haitian origin, the youth represent a diverse population, generally bilingual or trilingual, dynamic and growing; yet they face ongoing and significant socio-educational challenges. For example, in 2006, 38 per cent of this fifteen- to twenty-year-old group did not complete high school studies; 19 per cent of those in the labour market were unemployed; and the vast majority (96 per cent) earned less than $25,000. The higher level of poverty forces youth to leave formal education earlier, to suspend their studies, or to work while they are studying, all of which exposes them to further socio-economic vulnerability (Torczyner et al. 2010).

The newly arrived Haitian immigrants may be immediately locked into special education or second-language classes. The connection between their parents and the school may be limited or difficult. Decisions made in the early days will have a resultant effect for years to come. Dropping out could then become a logical and acceptable option. Despite visible signs, indicators, and demands from the community, the "at-risk" designation is often not enough to lead to concrete, far-reaching, and systemic reforms (Torczyner et al. 2010). The integration of blacks within the interculturalism model is not directly addressed with regard to anti-racism, and many important variables and concerns are not addressed.

Quebec language policies focus on formal education, notably, the obligation to attend French-language elementary and secondary schools in order to make Quebec more resolutely and majoritarily francophone. Bill 101, adopted in 1977 by the separatist Parti Quebecois government, sought to force immigrants to be educated in French as an attempt to break the traditional tendency for immigrants to integrate within the English-language education system, and, subsequently, the broader English-language community and cultural life. The English-language black community, among whom many were unilingual anglophones, were extremely marginalized and disadvantaged as a result of this legislation. The English-language black community interpreted Bill 101 as a sign of ethnocentrism on the part of the Parti Quebecois (Labelle n.d.).

Community Structures and Associations for Blacks in Montreal

The linguistic barrier along with the geographic dislocation became factors underscoring the lack of broader black community development between anglophones and francophones. Sustainable partnerships were not developed, and language became a fundamental component in dividing peoples who have many common experiences.

Black Youth in the Socio-educational Context in Montreal

Several studies (McAndrew and Ledent 2009; Torczyner et al. 2001, 2010) present an alarming educational portrait for black youth in Montreal. However, comparative studies, including McAndrew and Ledent (2009), present a vastly different educational situation for English- and French-speaking black youth with regard to demographic, socio-educational, and socio-economic characteristics. Within the French-language sector, students from black communities are considered to be the most "at-risk" and vulnerable, and within that group, creolophone and anglophone students from the Caribbean appear to be the most disadvantaged. Francophone students from Africa and the Caribbean exhibited better results than the "at-risk" students above, but still under-performed other immigrant groups. Within the anglophone sector, students appear to have performed better, but still face barriers and challenges. The two linguistic sectors have differences, but equally engage with similar results based on racial lines (McAndrew and Ledent 2009). The major findings from this research are the following: close to one-quarter of students from black communities at the secondary school level have a gap of two or more years in learning for their age level; they are much more frequently labelled with a learning disability; they have a lower level of graduation after five, six, and seven years; they have great linguistic support needs; they have lower levels of continuation on to studies after secondary school, and they experience less advanced achievement at higher levels than the broader population.

At the secondary level, black anglophones from Africa, as well as francophones from other regions outside of Haiti, experience more success within the formal education system. However, when juxtaposed with the broader population, the situation in general for black youth in Montreal is disconcerting, and there is a need for a range of measures from a range of sectors (McAndrew and Ledent 2009). Two types of recommendations flow from the research. The first set relates to general measures that affect all students, including the need to fight the trend leading to dropping out, to provide homework and linguistic support, and to address other indicators that characterize disadvantaged social conditions. The second concerns problems associated specifically with black communities, which should be complementary to the variable noted in the first set of recommendations (McAndrew and Ledent 2009).

The authors of that study made several recommendations, many of which were adopted by the Ministère de l'Éducation du Loisir et du Sport du Québec (MÉLS), school boards, and other governmental agencies, black community associations, and other cultural and professional associations. Some of the initiatives identified by the black Community Demographic Study Group include: the development of programs to assist with homework; the development of learning materials on black history for teachers; the implementation of specially designed summer schools by the Haitian community; diverse learning, after-school, and pedagogical programs created by community organisms; the establishment of a Haitian teacher consultative group to respond to concerns generated by schools; and the consolidation of black community interests as a means of providing recommendations to the government in relation to students of African origin (Torczyner et al. 2010).

Although many initiatives were taken by a range of actors, these socio-educational measures were implemented largely at the immediate local level, and thus did not affect the overall system or the vast number of students in need (Torczyner et al. 2010). In addition, where the support was most required, within families and communities and with the students themselves, researchers were critical of the lack of tangible, meaningful, and critical investments at those levels (Torczyner et al. 2010). Based on their analysis, some researchers concluded that 1) an overarching policy framework is too limited and needs to be more expansive and comprehensive; 2) a veritable inter-/multicultural pedagogy needs to be developed; 3) greater partnerships between schools and community groups is required; 4) improved relations are required between schools and black youth and their parents; 5) greater training and professional development for school personnel is required in relation to black youth; 6) an enhanced school culture that cultivates cultural diversity, equity, and antiracism is necessary; 7) enhanced school leadership that responds to the preceding points is required; and 8) a range of systemic, holistic and multidimensional strategies on the part of government, school systems, community groups, and families should be put in place (Torczyner et al. 2010).

DISCUSSION

This chapter has sought to provide a portrait of what we have characterized in the title as a "triple whammy and a fragile minority within a fragile majority." The black community in Montreal, like elsewhere, whether it be in Toronto, New York, London, Paris, Rio de Janeiro or elsewhere, is complex, multi-layered and complicated. Many factors help us determine the shape and contours of the problematic. We have privileged three central factors – race, class, and gender – and further added the fundamental variable of migratory-path/migratory-history (when they emigrated to Canada as well as the conditions enveloping that journey), academic and professional experience, and cultural and community experience (religion, links to Haiti, etc.). We can see a clear connection to other groups in the black Diaspora internationally, and the problems we have highlighted are not entirely unique. There are shortcomings, problems, and issues that have been highlighted more readily in other jurisdictions, and this may be explained in part by the socio-political context in Quebec, and, more broadly, within the French-speaking world. It may be easier to raise such issues within the English-speaking and/or anglophone world, and academic literature in those contexts may be more critical and open. However, this is not to say that the problem of black youth's education experiences should not be explored or critiqued in Quebec. Rather, we believe that more studies of a comparative nature involving black diasporic and other groups would be extremely helpful in developing policy and other strategies.

The Canadian reflex to boast that the situation south of the border is much worse discounts how racism is systemically embedded within the Canadian psyche, albeit differently than in the US (Carr and Lund 2007). Understanding the positionality of language and the Quebec polity is an important piece of this equation. When language is not considered the problem – for instance, for those who speak French fluently, as is the case for the vast majority of Haitians in Quebec – we need to interrogate what other factors lead to differentiated educational experiences and outcomes. The variables we have privileged should provide ample reflection for policy makers, community leaders, educational officials, administrators and teachers, and others in five significant areas that we believe will lead to great democracy in education: pedagogy, curriculum, educational policy, institutional culture, and epistemology.

The problems facing black youth in Montreal require critical and innovative solutions that challenge hegemony, whiteness, and mainstream educational thinking. The French-language context involves some concerns that are different than those in other parts of Canada and the US or elsewhere in the world, but the fundamental issues are the same. Broad-based reforms, research, practices, and engagement are required in Montreal in order to overturn an unacceptable and deleterious situation for many students and their families in the black community.

REFERENCES

Adrien, A. 2011. *Facteurs de Risque aux Infections Transmissibles Sexuellement et par le Sang chez les jeunes Québécois d'origine haïtienne: Étude Exploratoire.* Québec: Direction de santé publique.

Carr, P.R., and D.E. Lund. 2007. *The Great White North? Exploring Whiteness, Privilege and Identity in Education.* Rotterdam: Sense Publishers.

Centre justice et foi. 2009. "En Vue de L'action: Portrait de la Communauté Haïtienne au Québec." Accessed 16 January 2015, http://cjf.qc.ca/userfiles /file/Haiti_Portrait-pour-action.pdf.

Fehmiu-Brown, P. 2011. *Ces Canadiens Oubliés.* 3rd ed. Montreal: Éditions Aquarius.

Historica Canada. n.d. Accessed 3 February 2015, https://www.historica canada.ca/fr.

Icart, J.-C. 2006. "Pour Une Pleine Participation des Communautés Noires à la Société Québécoise." *Vivre ensemble* 13(46). Accessed 3 February 2015, http://www.cjf.qc.ca/upload/ve_bulletins/942_a_Icart_No46.pdf.

Labelle, M., D. Salée, and Y. Frenette. 2001. "Incorporation Citoyenne et/ ou exclusion? La Deuxième Génération Issue de L'immigration Haïtienne et Jamaïcaine." *Rapport de recherche*. Montréal: Fondation Canadienne des relations raciales et Université du Québec à Montréal. Accessed 5 February 2015, http://www.criec.uqam.ca/Page/Document/textes_en_lignes /Rapport_Labelle_Salee_Frenette_01_Jeune.pdf.

Lafortune, G. 2012. "Rapport à l'école et aux savoirs scolaires de jeunes d'origine haïtienne en contexte scolaire défavorisé à Montréal." PhD diss., Université de Montréal. Accessed 3 February 2015, https://papyrus.bib .umontreal.ca/jspui/bitstream/1866/8479/2/Lafortune_Gina_2012_these .pdf.

McAndrew, M., and J. Ledent. 2009. *La Réussite Scolaire des Jeunes des Communautés Noires au Secondaire*. Montréal: Université de Montréal (CEETUM).

Potvin, M. 2008. "L'expérience de la deuxième génération d'origine haïtienne au Québec." Accessed 3 February 2015, http://canada.metropolis.net/pdfs /Pgs_can_diversity_spring08_f.pdf.

– 2012. "Trajectoires Scolaires des Jeunes D'origine Haïtienne au Québec." *Revue d'éducation de l'Université d'Ottawa* 1:8–9. http://education.uottawa .ca/assets/publications/Revue_Edu_2012_Fr_F/files/assets/seo/page8.html.

Thésée, G. 2003. "Le Rapport au Savoir Scientifique en Contexte D'acculturation: Application à L'étude de L'expérience Scolaire en Sciences D'élèves du Secondaire D'origine Haïtienne." PhD diss., Université du Québec à Montréal.

Thésée, G., N. Carignan, and P.R. Carr, eds. 2010. *Les Faces Cachées de la Recherche Interculturelle*. Paris: L'Harmattan.

Thésée, G., and P.R. Carr. 2012. "The 2011 International Year for People of African Descent (IYPAD): The Paradox of Colonized Invisibility within the Promise of Mainstream Visibility." *Journal of De-colonization, Indigeneity, Education and Society* 1(1): 158–80.

Tillus, M. 1999. "Le Placement des Jeunes D'origine Haïtienne et L'approche Milieu." *Revue professionnelle Défi jeunesse*. Accessed 24 February 2015, http://www.centrejeunessedemontreal.qc.ca/pdf/cmulti/defi/defi_jeunesse _9906/placement.htm9.

Torczyner, J. 1997. *Diversity, Mobility and Change: The Dynamics of Black Communities in Canada*. Montreal: McGill.

Torczyner, J.L., and collaborators. 2001. *L'évolution de la Communauté Noire Montréalaise: Mutations et Défis. Rapport de recherche.* Accessed 13 January 2015, https://www.mcgill.ca/mchrat/fr/demographics.

Torczyner, J.L., and collaborators. 2010. *Caractéristiques Démographiques de la Communauté Noire Montréalaise: Les Enjeux du Troisième Millénaire, 2010.* Accessed 13 January 2015, http://www.mhaiti.org/sites/default/files /documents/Créer%20'Document'/etudedemognoire2010.pdf.

10

"Who Owns My Language?"
African Canadian Youth, Postcoloniality, and the Symbolic Violence of Language in a French-Language High School in Ontario[1]

Awad Ibrahim

So, I always wonder, you know, when do we own the language we speak? I know I speak Wolof, but is French not my language or what? Who owns my language?

> A grade 9 male student, originally from Senegal

[O]ne can testify only to the unbelievable. To what can, at any rate, only be believed; to what appeals only to belief and hence to the given word ... [here] when we ask others to take our word for it, we are already in the order of what is merely believable.

> Derrida 1996, 20

To testify to the unbelievable – that which is symbolic in nature and which is felt but hard to talk about – is indeed tremendously difficult, especially in postcoloniality. We are always almost there, but "the unbelievable" eludes language. As soon as we speak it, we are dealing with emotionality; it slips away. But we must speak it. When we do, however, we are constantly told, "That's just unbelievable!" Then we are left wondering if this response is an exclamation, a questioning, or a reminder. Yet, this chapter dares to ask if, having fully mastered the colonial language (French in this case), postcolonial subjects can ever speak with authority. In other words, at what point do we own the language we speak?

By way of an answer, similar to Nashon's (Chapter 8 in this volume), this chapter tells the story of a group of French-speaking refugee and immigrant continental African youth who attend an urban, Franco-Ontarian high school in southwest Ontario, Canada. They arrive at French-language schools with a highly valued variety of French, *le français parisien* or Parisian French. As Monica Heller (2006) showed, the linguistic variety of French spoken in Ontario is both devalued and unauthorized in schools. However, Heller explains, most teachers in Franco-Ontarian schools speak this "devalued" variety of French. Hence, I am arguing, society enters a "linguistic war," in which the struggle is no longer about language per se, but about power.[2] And in the context of this chapter, it is about race and language ownership. I will show that, because of race and legal status, this highly symbolic capital that African youth bring with them to Franco-Ontarian schools seems to become an unauthorized norm, a liability, and a burden rather than an event to celebrate. Continental African students are denigrated, classified, and streamed in either lower grades or in general levels, where their chances for advanced or university studies are limited. "It was unbelievable how they spoke," one teacher exclaimed, expressing what Ben Rampton (1995), within the British context, calls *deceptive fluency*. According to this notion of deceptive fluency, Rampton explains, even though they may sound British and are born in Britain, South Asians cannot be native speakers of English. Therefore, as this view would have it, their fluency or British accent is deceptive. For Jacques Derrida (1996), this is an exemplary moment of "performative contradiction," an antinomy, if you like, one about which he would have declared, "Yes, I only have one language, yet it is not mine" (2).

THEN, WHO OWNS LANGUAGE?

Though strongly worded, Derrida (1996) is worth quoting at length here; after all, he is our referent in intersecting authority-language-symbolic power. For Derrida, language is, and has always been, in the plural, and any claim especially by "the master" to its possession can only be that: a claim.[3] In fact, Derrida (1996) declares, "the master himself" [*sic*] is no longer:

> [C]ontrary to what one is often most tempted to believe, the master is nothing. Because the master does not possess exclusively, and naturally, what he calls his language, because, whatever he wants or does, he cannot maintain any relations of property or identity that

are natural, national, congenital, or ontological, with it ... [And] because language is not his natural possession, he can, thanks to that
very fact, pretend historically, through the rape of a cultural
usurpation, which means always essentially colonial, to appropriate
it in order to impose it as "his own." (13)

As we shall see, one has to be very careful in using the language of coloniality within the Franco-Ontarian context where I conducted the current research. The discourse of coloniality, especially when understood
subalternly, does not lend itself easily here, and the situation is tenu-
ous, if not confusing, at best. When subalterns speak, said Spivak (1999),
they are not heard. They are subaltern not because of total social im-
mobility or for inherent reasons; they are subaltern because they are
spoken for; they are authored and already talked about. Hence their silence is made possible if not expected: "Here is a woman who tried to
be decisive in extremis. She 'spoke,' but women did not, do not, 'hear'
her. Thus she can be defined as a 'subaltern' – a person without lines of
social mobility" (28).

So picture this: It is Canada, an officially French-English bilingual
country, and one of the most prominent countries worldwide in implementing bilingualism and multiculturalism. The study's population
is French-language speakers in Ontario, an English-language speaking
province that is situated next to Québec, the only French-language
speaking province besides New Brunswick, which is the only bilingual
province in Canada. As we know, the so-called *français canadien*, or
Canadian French, is older even than Canada as a nation. It goes back to
fifteenth-century France, and has unique lexical, morphological, syn-
tactic, and phonetic characteristics (Heller 2006; Mougeon and Beniak
1991). Ontario has the highest French-language-speaking population
outside Québec (Statistics Canada 2013). It is known as *Franco-Ontarien*
or Franco-Ontarian, comprising anywhere between 4.3 to 5 per cent of
Ontario's population, and it is concentrated primarily in Eastern Ontario, especially Ottawa. Franco-Ontarians are exceptionally savvy in
using the apparatus of the state and in social and political mobilization. They pride themselves on this mobilization ability, and refer to
themselves as *francophones de souche* (old or "original" French) to distinguish themselves from other francophones (e.g. Arabic speakers,
Haitians, or West Africans). Thanks to activism and the Canadian Charter of Rights and Freedom, which guarantees as prominent a place in
Canada for the French language as it does for English, Ontario has
twelve French-language school boards (both public and Catholic), a

number of community colleges, and four universities that offer programs in French. The University of Ottawa is fully bilingual, attracting a sizeable number of Ontario's francophone population.

Francophone de souche is as much a linguistic, historical, and cultural reference as it is a racial one. It is a term commonly used for white Europeans who speak French and are part of the earlier settlers in Canada. They speak varieties of French that are similar to Québec French, but are still quite distinct. Some of the distinct linguistic features of Franco-Ontarian French (FOF) include, among many others, 1) simplification (e.g., third-person plural that is cited as first-person singular: *ils veulent* [they want] turned into *ils veut* [they wants]); 2) the use of *sontaient*, a non-standard variant of *étaient* [were], the standard third-person plural imperfect form of the verb *être* [to be]; and 3) the common use of the possessive *à* in lieu of *de* (e.g., *la voiture à mon père* [my father's car], whereas the "standard" use is *la voiture de mon père*) (Mougeon and Beniak 1991). It is significantly important to note that these are mostly non-standard features which, as we shall see, create a very peculiar situation. On the one hand, internally, it creates a Franco-Ontarian linguistic community, with its social bond and intra-community recognition, but, on the other, it becomes a simultaneous mechanism and a technology for exclusion.

For instance, oddly enough, those who speak standard French may feel either excluded or highly valued. The "lack," as Édouard Glissant (1981) might put it, is a better description for those who feel excluded. Postcolonial subjects, Glissant (1981) explains, are constantly identified by and reminded of their lack of language possession. Language is locked in as a possession of a nation, a culture, and a group of people. It belongs to "them," and identity (Franco-Ontarianness in this context) is no longer regarded as a being-of-the-entity [*l'être de l'étant*], a being-that-is-always-to-become (Derrida 1996; Ibrahim 2008), but, as a fait accompli, is an ontology whose essence and features are already known and non-changing. It may be a hyphen-identity in this context – Franco *and* Ontarian – but it is still purely "French."

This is precisely why the real or imagined Frenchness is highly valued symbolic capital (Bourdieu 1991). But for it to function as such, Frenchness has to have the "right ingredients" in linguistic, cultural, and racial terms. French, it seems, is a convoluted term, referring mostly to white Europeans *belonging* to or *citizens* of France. The rest, as Derrida (1996) put it, are the "Francophones *belonging*, as we strangely say, to several nations, cultures, and states" (10; original emphasis). They are hyphenated: Franco-Maghrebian, Franco-Antillais,

Franco-Senegalese, etc.[4] Because of this hyphen, or maybe thanks to it, they go through moments of mourning, when they speak a language – masterfully indeed – that they are told is not theirs. The source of this work of mourning (Todd 2003) is in the psychic tension, in which, in many postcolonial moments, French is the only language francophones speak, or they master French better than their mother tongues. "I only have one language," Derrida (1996, 1) declares, and "it is not mine."

Such "exclusions," Derrida continues, come to leave their marks on colonial as well on postcolonial subjects and their identity formation. They create a "disorder of identity" that is best captured in Paulo Freire's *Pedagogy of the Oppressed* (2000). In this disorder, despite her/his presumed superiority, the so-called possessor of language enters the work of mourning as much as the oppressed. Oppression and exclusion, Freire contends, indeed affect the oppressed as they do the oppressor, and raise the following Derridean (1996) questions on language possession, which I will address subsequently: "But who exactly possesses it [language]? And whom does it possess? Is language in possession, ever a possessing or possessed possession? Possessed or possessing in exclusive possession, like a piece of personal property? What of this being-at-home [*être-chez-soi*] in language toward which we never cease returning?" (17).

SEASON OF MIGRATION TO CANADA

In *Season of Migration to the North*, Tayyib Salih (1991) tells the story of Mustafa Sa'eed. Originally from the Sudan, Sa'eed is a postcolonial subject who finds himself in Britain. He goes through identity translation and re-configuration, whereby he ends up in a Third-Space, a split-subject between two cultures, languages, and ways of being (Ibrahim 2008). This is also the case with my research subjects. In 2007, I conducted a small-scale research study in an urban Franco-Ontarian high school in southwest Ontario, Canada. This research was a follow-up to an earlier study conducted between January and June 1996 (Ibrahim 2014).

Both in 1996 and 2007, the research was a critical ethnography that looked at the lives of a group of continental Francophone African youth and the formation of their social identity. Besides their gendered and racialized experience, their youth and refugee status was vital in their *moments of identification* (Ibrahim 2008): where and how they were interpellated in the mirror of their society (cf. Althusser 1971; Bhabha 1994). In other words, I demonstrated that, once in North America, these youths were faced with a social imaginary in which they were already blacks. This social imaginary was directly implicated in how and with whom they identified, which in turn influenced what they linguistically and culturally learned and how they learned it. What they learned, as I have showed elsewhere (Ibrahim 1999), was black English as a Second Language (BESL), which they accessed in and through black popular culture. They learned by taking up and repositing the Rap linguistic and musical genre, and, in different ways, by acquiring and rearticulating the Hip-Hop cultural identity (Ibrahim 1999, 2014).

In the present study, the research participants were a group of continental Francophone African youth in a small, French-language high school, which I will refer to as Marie-Victorin or MV, in southwest Ontario, with a school population of approximately 400 students from various ethnic, racial, cultural, religious, and linguistic backgrounds. (All names in this chapter are pseudonyms.) In addition, French, English, Arabic, Somali, and Farsi were also spoken at the school. This group of continental Francophone African youth varied, first, in their length of stay in Canada (from one to two years to five to six years); second, in their legal status (some were immigrants, but the majority were refugees); and, third, in their gender, class, age, linguistic, and national background. They came from places as diverse as Democratic Republic of Congo (formerly Zaïre), Djibouti, Gabon, Senegal, Somalia, South Africa, and Togo. With no exception, all of the African students in MV were at least trilingual, speaking French, English, and an African language as a mother tongue. Given their postcolonial educational history, significantly, most African youths in fact came to Franco-Ontarian schools already possessing the highly valued symbolic capital: *le français parisien* (Parisian French, also known as *français standard* or *français international*).

ETHNOGRAPHY AND HOSPITALITY

[I]s there anything worse, said Nietzsche, than to find oneself facing a German when one was expecting a Greek?

                                        Deleuze and Guattari 1994, 109

As a critical ethnographic research project, I spent over six months in 1996 and three months in 2007 engaged in the research: I attended classes, talked to students in my research, and observed curricular and extracurricular activities two or three times per week. I audio- and video-taped classes and natural conversations, visited their houses, played basketball (a game dominated by African students) and became the basketball team coach, and was invited for picnics. In short, I literally lived with the students. What is more, my own background as a continental African also helped me to decipher their narratives and experiences. Clearly, we shared a safe space of comfort that allowed us to open up, speak, and engage freely.

Of this growing continental francophone African population in Franco-Ontarian schools (Ibrahim 2014), I ended up choosing ten boys and six girls for extensive ethnographic observation inside and outside the classroom and inside and outside the school, and I interviewed all sixteen. Of the ten boys, six were Somali speakers (from Somalia and Djibouti), one was Ethiopian, two were Senegalese, and one was from Togo. Their ages ranged from sixteen to twenty years. The six girls were all Somali speakers (also from Somalia and Djibouti), aged from fourteen to eighteen years. Interviews were conducted either in French or English, and French interviews were translated into English. Here, language was a crucial part of this comfort zone, this safe space.

This space was built against the backdrop, first, of a total absence of diversity in the teaching, personnel or administration staff (with the exception of one teacher of Haitian descent), and, second, the traumatic psychic experience of exclusion, discrimination, and symbolic violence that students had experienced (see Ibrahim 2008). Before the 1990s, MV had not experienced such a mass of diversity, especially the continental African presence. Thus, teachers had no experiential knowledge about how to interact with African youth in either comfortable or informed ways. Intentionally or not, students made it clear that there was a serious race-relation problem in the school. This problem manifested in three different ways:

1 *The host as hostage*: Here, one is hosted, but only conditionally. In Jacques Derrida's (2000) language, there are two forms of hospitality: conditional and unconditional. In the former, one is hosted, but with certain conditions, restrictions, choices, and possibilities. Omer (M, 19, Ethiopia),[5] who came to Canada by himself when he was fifteen years old, exemplifies this situation. Omer was living in a shelter at the time of the interview; yet he enthusiastically was longing and planning to go to Laurentian University. Following an Althusserian (1971) language, Omer conceives this conditional hospitality as interpellation: "Hello there! You are Black; you can't do anything. Muslims, you can do nothing. This is what [is] astonishing to me. It is already seen [what Blacks and Muslims can or can-

not do]" (Omer, French-language interview). As Gayatri Spivak explained above, here the subalterns are already "talked" about and authored, and hence their silence is either made or expected.

2 *Undemocratic decisions*: This happens when students *feel* they are not consulted on matters related to their lives. These decisions, then, are perceived as discriminatory and insensitive, if not plain racist. For instance, because all school teachers and personnel are white and Christian (except for one Jewish teacher), when the school decided that it was no longer permissible to do mid-day Muslim prayer, the decision was read in multiple ways, including as being racist. Aziza (F, 18, Somalia) described it thus: "So ... they met ..., they agreed, like we were nothing at all. They said, 'Oh, who cares!' you see. 'We have to just tell them not leave the class, because our class is more important than their pray ... '" (Aziza, French-language group interview).

3 *The minute and the trivial*: This is the third and final way of racialization wherein *non-appartenance*, non-belonging or rejection, is seen as an accumulative memory of small details that, when put together, tend to leave students with a clear message that they are not trusted or wanted, or that they are deviant. Listen to Aziza again when she explains that even their names become a burden. The teacher's repetition of how African students' names should be pronounced becomes a marker that sets them apart:

> I am going to give you an example. A female teacher always gives the absent sheet [*la feuille d'absence*], always to white students. Moreover, teachers are going to know the names when they know the, for a teacher always knows the names of all the students in class. He is going to know more the names of the white students than the names of African students. "What's your name again? Bûralé? How do you want to me to pronounce that, Bûr-ralé, Boralé?" You see things like that. It's a bit, it gives it gives you pain here [pointing to her chest]. This is like, these things are small small, but they can be big, which can also be something catastrophic you see. And you, you have to live with this everyday you see. (Aziza, French-language group interview)

All three examples above are illustrative of what Howard Winant (2004) calls racialization or racialized experiences. They are insidious, convoluted, hard to pin down, but psychically and painfully felt. As well, they are best captured as symbolic violence (Bourdieu 1991).[6]

The beauty (and, I recognize, the irony of the term) of symbolic violence in this case is that it works through slippage; that is, when the perpetrators are confronted or called up to answer to their deeds, they can escape by saying: "We didn't know; indeed we had the best intentions; we wanted to treat African students like any other students" (see also Graham and Slee 2008 and their notion of "benevolent humanitarianism"). *Intentions matter only in their final effect*, as we know. That is, in socio-psychic terms, how one makes people feel matters as much, if not more, than one's intentions. Whether this symbolic violence is intentional or not, African students in MV have built an experiential memory that is not so pleasant to remember, and is strongly expressed in language.

RACE-IN(G)-LANGUAGE:
LE FRANÇAIS PARISIEN ILLEGITIMATELY SPOKEN

In MV, it is clear that race (read: blackness, in this case) is experienced in at least three different ways, as we saw above, and with variable degrees of emotional intensity. My contention in this section is that language is central to this experience. Given their postcolonial education, African students, by and large, arrive at school fluent in, and armed with, the highly valuable symbolic capital: *le français parisien*. Interestingly enough, as is noted many times by Heller (2006), the role and the mandate of the French-language schools in Ontario is to introduce students to this variety of French as well as to the variety spoken by middle-class Franco-Ontarians. However, when African students come to school with this capital, there is astonishment and disbelief on the part of teachers and school counsellors. Their language, it seems, is *deceptively fluent*: they cannot be so fluent and speak the language with such mastery! This skepticism stems from the fact that, as Bourdieu (1991) would have said, the "legitimate" language is spoken by an "illegitimate" speaker: a refugee who is imagined to be, at least in the dominant media representations, pitiable rather than astonishing and enviable. This mistrust of the linguistic capital possessed by African students has led to a patronizing attitude that is easily open to a racialized, if not bluntly racist reading. Without naming it as such, students were aware of both the process of racialization and how it illegitimizes their speech. In my group interview with them, female students reflected on this situation thus:

AMANI: The teacher could not stop thanking me every time I speak and tells me "Here, your French, you can, it is different than

the others. How that happens, where did you learn that? Are you
sure that you are not in the wrong stream?" [This was a general
level course.][7] You know, things like that. And then, she was really
surprised you know. I told her "No, I know what I have to know
for my level, my my ... " [interrupted]

AZIZA: And then she was very impressed when we said that we
learn our French in our country. And then things like that, and
then she said, "Really, in your country, there is really this system?"

SAMIRA: "Are there professors who speak French like that? But
my God you have *l'accent français!*" But of course we have *l'accent
français*; there were teachers that taught us, no? And then this: "You
are coming from Somalia oh, we never heard that in Somalia people speak French with ... " [interrupted]

AZIZA: "Really in Somalia you have this system?" You know, *they
don't accept that.* (Aziza and Samira, French-language group interview, italics added)

In my individual interview with Aziza, she expands on how teachers'
disbelief is patronizing and grossly disturbing, especially given its racial
connotation:

The first day when I wrote my [evaluation] test, of my French level,
he [the counselor] was really surprised because I spoke an excellent
French. The good and rich French; you know when you live in
Africa? He was really surprised, you see. "You have an excellent
French," you see! Because that is new you see, *an African who speaks
a good French, much better than they do.* It is a bit [too much? unbelievable?] you see. (Aziza, individual French-language interview,
italics added)

In spite of their "good," "rich," and "excellent" French, continental
African students are disproportionately streamed in the general,
non-college-bound level. This disproportionate number is noted by
the students themselves. Using his ethnographic gaze, Musa (male, 19,
Djibouti) observed that "the majority of African students who are in
Marie-Victorin take general level courses." Although not all African
students are in the general level, it is noteworthy that, without a question from me to this effect, Musa introduced this observation to the
discussion during my focus group interview with the boys. Building
on their memory of how schools functioned in Africa, African students were not fully aware of the difference between fundamental, gen-

eral, and advanced level courses. In Africa, according to the boys in my group interview, all students go to the same class to perform the same academic task.

The girls, on the other hand, seemed to believe that it is the boys who are streamed more in the lower levels; because of lack of statistical information, I can neither confirm nor overrule this observation. Nonetheless, I made the same ethnographic observation. Boys' presence in general level was substantially higher than the girls': close to 90 per cent of students in that level were boys while fewer than 10 per cent were girls. When asked why this was so, the girls hypothesized that it has to do with the exclusivity the boys make between sports and academic performance. According to the girls, the boys always view becoming successful as an athlete as being opposed to doing well academically. When one is doing one's homework successfully, one is seen as a "nerd," a term connected to what Ogbu and Fordham (1986) call "acting White." The girls had seen these boys "back home," where they were "first class" students. Something had happened that caused them to see academics in opposition to athleticism.

AWAD: I have noticed that at the school, especially there is a very very strong majority [of the African students] who are present in the general level.

ASMA: That I know why. You know why?

AWAD: Why?

ASMA: The majority are the boys. The majority are the boys, they want *basketball*. *Dream Team*, I love the basketball [a girl talking]. Yes, wait.

OSSI: Yah, what does that mean?

AWAD: Yes, yes, what does that mean?

ASMA: They really want, they really could, I know these boys. They are really good. I remember in my country, they were really intelligent students.

AZIZA: First class.

ASMA: Yes, they know, they know. They know their academics; they know how to do this, how to do that. The problem is that if I start doing my homework, and I am a boy, this means I am a nerd. (Asma, Awad, Aziza, and Ossi, French-language group interview)

The gendered answer was exceptionally interesting here. When I asked the boys the same questions about why they dichotomize academics and athleticism, on the one hand, and why they are disproportionately represented in general level, non-university-bound courses, there was an unanimous response that indicated that 1) their racialized experience, 2) school counselling, 3) being refugees and 4) living on their own were reasons for their streaming and sense of alienation. Mukhi (male, 18, Djibouti) summed it up thus: "Si tu allais faire un sondage, ça vient souvent de l'orientation ou des personnels" ["If you conduct a survey, the reason stems either from counselling or school personnel"]. Taking the role of the African elder, Musa (male, 19, Djibouti) expressed the African students' agony concerning living on their own, working through the immigration papers, and dealing with their social workers:

> The African students, they have a lot of problems. Here, the Canadians don't have problems, they have their parents, there is that. We, we have problems. You, you are late, she [the principal] sends you home. You go home for three or four days. We, we can't afford that because there is the immigration that calls us: "You have to come to see me today." You have to sign your cheque, things like that. There is back and forth. So, you have to go to the immigration, you have to go to, your, how do you call it, social worker? (Musa, French-language group interview)

Expanding on Mukhi's notion of school personnel and their role in student streaming in the general level, Musa continued his contention and elder role:

> But the majority of the African students who are at Marie-Victorin, every time I see them, they take general level courses. I don't know why.
> "Why are you taking a general level course?" [explaining how he talks to other younger students]
> "It's Madame Robert [the principal] who gave it to me."
> "But, gee Madame Robert, [let her] go to hell, and take an advanced level course," I said. (Musa, French-language group interview)

In my field notes dated 5 February 1996, I wrote, "Musa came up to me requesting if I can offer an English-language tutoring course because he thinks that African students have problems with English." What is significant in all of this is the fact that, first, Musa unselfishly is looking after other younger African students, and, second, Musa's hopes are high that students can do much better. He knows they can do much better.

CONSEQUENTLY:
MAKING LINKAGES AND CONCLUSIONS

Consequently, anyone should be able to declare under oath: I have only one language and it is not mine; my "own" language is, for me, a language that cannot be assimilated. My language, the only one I hear myself speak and agree to speak, is the language of the other.

Derrida 1996, 25

At this point, I am sure my "gentle reader" (as W.E.B. Du Bois would have called you) may be wondering if the connection was made between race, language, postcoloniality, and authority of speaking. I certainly hope so. I have to admit though, tersely and speculatively, the chapter is meant to be food for thought, which sometimes is more provocative than a French three-course meal. In the context of the education of African Canadian children, my intent was to show how, given students' racialized bodily experience, students' speech is illegitimized, despite its highly symbolic value. This is what I am referring to as "symbolic violence." This is closer to Foucault's (1979) notion of punishment, whereby the bodily experience is replaced with the psychic experience. That is to say, one is left questioning not only one's speech and language but even one's subjectivity (not to say humanity). Derrida (1996) talks about himself as an Algerian-Jew who has nothing else but French to "speak": "In what language does one write memoirs when there has been no authorized [language]? How does one utter a worthwhile 'I recall' when it is necessary to invent both one's language and one's 'I'?" (31).

African students, it seems, are left with the same question: Can we ever speak with authority? They are to invent both their language and their subjectivity. Here students were conscious of what is involved in this (re)invention, this linguistic return, in which one spells one's own name and names oneself. This process involves the following.

1 A full mastery of the rules of the game, what Bourdieu (1991) would call the "market of exchange." In any market, Bourdieu explains, there are currencies or capitals that are needed; there are

rules about how to exchange these capitals, and, he emphasizes, the players along with the rules determine the value of capital. Hassan (male, 17, Djibouti) was fully aware of his role in the school as a "market of exchange" and of the capitals he possesses: "So, there are all these structures and differences that you have to play with [*jouer avec*]. Such include the fact that you have to have the competency of playing with others, you have to know how to play with others" (Hassan, French-language individual interview). Clearly, we do not all enter the game the same way, nor with the same capital. Nonetheless, "gaming the system" or knowing how to play the game (i.e., system) is essential for Hassan.

2 Once aware of exclusion and discrimination, or knowing how the system works and how it excludes people, one is under the ethical responsibility to "out" it, to talk about, and to turn it around to one's own benefit. To do so, however, one can work within the "system," from the inside. Hassan articulates it thus: "To begin with, there are all these stereotypes about black people. There is discrimination and all that, OK! The only way to combat discrimination is outing [or publicizing] discrimination. Why do we have all this [discrimination]? We have to play their games to our own benefit. We don't have to do the impossible you know" (Hassan, individual French-language interview).

Since one is working with(in) the system, the "game" if you like, one does not look for alternative markets and identities – as did the boys when they chose basketball as opposed to volleyball, and Hip-Hop as opposed to dominant identities. Instead, one chooses to affirm one's identity from within the particular *authorized, legitimized*, and *dominant* market and identity. Yet, Hassan is mindful of the fact that, in the case of blackness, there are no guarantees, even when one possesses the market's required credentials and capitals. That is why, he adds in the same interview, "if you come in [for an interview] with a tie, or with a suit, with your PhD, they are probably going to accept you more than before." By "they," one may argue, Hassan is referring to the power bloc: those who have a larger control of the market, and who set themselves as the norm, the yardstick against which all is measured. Given their benefit from the dominant structure, "they" have little incentive and lucrative investment in imagining others differently, especially black people, and in decentring themselves. For to do so is to question one's own power, and in some cases, to give all or some of it up.

3 As educators, finally, and especially as anti-racism workers, we need
   to deconstruct the social structure of domination, discrimination,
   and negation. Otherwise, some are damned to struggle all their
   lives and to find themselves in the periphery of power, with little
   or no resources and capitals. Thanks to these hegemonic structures,
   black/African youth, by and large, find themselves putting in twice
   the effort to reach an average position (at least as defined by rules
   of the market). They carry the burden of "proving" themselves,
   which means, in some cases, they have to dichotomize the school
   and the schooling process on the one hand, and, on the other, their
   personal desires, history, language, and culture. One way out of this
   dichotomy, Hassan argues, is to "flip the script." That is, in place of
   failure, one emphasizes pedagogies of hope, possibility, and success; one talks about the unsaid, the absent, and the silenced:

> And the only way to do it [prove ourselves to others?] is not to
> conform or buy into stereotypical data like: "Oh 50 per cent of
> African youth had failed, they can't do it." What has to happen
> is to show them that 50 per cent had passed, not only to show
> them the 50 per cent that failed. But they only see the part that
> failed; they don't look for the part that passed. We have to show
> them the part that passed; that's what we have to do; and this is
> one of my objectives: to do more in this regard, to leave a dream
> ... (Hassan, individual French-language interview)

To materialize this dream, Hassan is placing the onus squarely on
himself. He is willing to "sacrifice" and take up that burden, and
he knows the price he has to pay. As the old African saying goes, If
the spirit is high, the body can only feel its height/weight. That is
to say, the body does not have too many choices when there is a
will, since we are guided by our will, not our bodies. In Hassan's
words, "I am sacrificing enormous amount of time. I have been in
a chain of committees for example, so there are always prices to pay
... Personally, I know I sacrificed: I missed evenings and there is my
mother, anxious [debordée]. 'You come really late at night. Why do
you stay after school, occupied with so much work?' she says, you
see!" (Hassan, individual French-language interview).

Hassan's spirit of sacrifice, personal responsibility, and vision are
vital in the struggle against exclusion and discrimination. However,

the institutional and systematic nature of racialization, discrimination, and exclusion motivates us to think not only how discrimination takes place but also, significantly, how it tends to reproduce privilege, especially white privilege (Graham and Slee 2008). As Peggy McIntosh (1998) argues, for the longest time we have tended to think about discrimination and racism and their effects on the victim. She contends that we need to think about discrimination and racism as technologies of power that end up reproducing privileges, ways of thinking, being, and speaking. To conclude, Hassan's mother is absolutely right in asking, "Why do you personally, my son, sacrifice so much?" Both Hassan and his mother need also to ask, "Why do we as African and black people have to prove who we are and what we have to anyone?" In an Obama era, this latter question seems more than ever urgent, since the silenced are yet to speak, and to speak with authority. They love, but their love is yet to be heard as a creative margin for a radical pedagogy of hope, love, and desire.

NOTES

1 A slightly modified version of this chapter appeared as Awad Ibrahim, "Will They Ever Speak with Authority? Race, Post-coloniality and the Symbolic Violence of Language," in *The Power in/of Language*, ed. David Cole and Linda Graham (Chichester, UK: Wiley-Blackwell, 2012), 68–84.

2 To clarify, there are two varieties of French that are talked about here: *français de France* and *français canadien*. I refer to the former as *"français parisien"* (Parisian French) and the latter as *"français de souche"* (original or old French, a term used both in Quebec and Ontario to refer to "original" French settlers and their language). In the Franco-Ontarian context, the Parisian French is highly valued, whereas *français de souche*, the variety spoken by most Franco-Ontarian schoolteachers, is both marginalized and discouraged. For further discussion, see the section in this chapter titled "Then, Who Owns Language?" For now, however, one may argue that we are dealing with "racialized class conflict," where classism and racism are expressed through linguicism, that is, in the variety spoken and valued. Interestingly enough, Franco-Ontarian teachers speak *français de souche*, which they in turn devalued. This is a phenomenon of cognitive dissidence, if not a schizophrenic moment, one in which one devalues what one speaks. However, when continental African youth arrived at the school with their *français international* (which I am provocatively calling *français parisien*), as we shall see, they were told, "That's just unbelievable!"

3 In reality, "language" is and has always been plural. For Derrida (1996), the French language, for example, always had (and still has) multiple speakers, accents, and daily expressions. However, it was standardized as it was written, thus attempting to eliminate its multiplicity. This standardization, Derrida argues, is part of a colonial project, where even people within France who spoke a variety of French were brought into the project of the Republic, which is assumed to have one language, one accent, and one voice.

4 When it comes to Franco-Ontarians, notions of coloniality, postcoloniality and oppression are exceptionally complicated. Franco-Ontarians are a French-speaking minority in Ontario. They struggle as much as any minority does, and historically have been prevented from teaching their language or opening French-language schools (Heller 2006). Yet, presently they have unearned privileges that others must struggle either for or against: whiteness, language, (institutionalized) power, school and social institutions, and, above all, the protection of the state. Because of these privileges, the population of my research (continental francophone Africans) finds itself a minority within a minority. Put simply, Franco-Ontarians do feel that their language variety is not as valued as *le français parisien* or *français de France*, but they ally themselves with this privileged symbolic capital by naming themselves *Français de souche* [original or old French], hence creating a complex situation where the oppressed or dispossessed can be an oppressor or a possessor, and where the very notion of oppression and exclusion is no longer a unidimensional idea.

5 Each student pseudonym is followed by their gender, age, and country of origin. I will also indicate whether the interview is individual or group, or in French or English.

6 Violence is, by definition, violent, no matter the shape or form. In Bourdieu's (1991) language, however, "symbolic violence" is no less violence or violent. It is "symbolic" only in that it works at the psychic and intangible level. It is conceived in relation (not in opposition) to material and bodily violence. The two forms of violence, for Bourdieu, are complementary, go hand-in-hand, and can/do converge one into the other. (See also his notion of "symbolic" and "material" capital.)

7 In Ontario, there are two streams: general and academic. The former leads students either to vocational schools or community colleges, whereas the latter leads to university studies. Despite their language mastery, most African students find themselves in general level, as we shall see, which itself becomes part of their experience with the process of racialization.

REFERENCES

Althusser, L. 1971. *Lenin and Philosophy*. London: New Left Books.

Bhabha, H. 1994. *The Location of Culture*. London and New York: Routledge.

Bourdieu, P. 1991. *Language and Symbolic Power*. Cambridge: Harvard University Press.

Dei, G., I. James, L. Karumanchery, S. James-Wilson, and J. Zine. 2000. *Removing the Margins: The Challenges and Possibilities of Inclusive Schooling*. Toronto: Canadian Scholars' Press.

Deleuze, G., and F. Guttari. 1994. *Thousand Plateaus: Capitalism and Schizophrenia*. London and New York: Continuum.

Derrida, J. 1996. *Monolingualism of the Other, or, the Prosthesis of Origin*. Stanford: Stanford University Press.

– 2000. *Of Hospitality*. Stanford: Stanford University Press.

Foucault, M. 1979. *Discipline and Punish: The Birth of the Prison*. New York: Vintage Books.

Freire, P. 2000. *Pedagogy of the Oppressed*. New York: Continuum.

Glissant, E. 1981. *Le Discours Antillais*. Paris: Seuil.

Graham, L., and R. Slee. 2008. "An Illusory Interiority: Interrogating the Discourse/s of Inclusion." *Educational Philosophy and Theory* 40(2): 277–94.

Haney-Lopez, I. 2006. *White by Law: The Legal Construction of Race*. New York: New York University Press.

Heller, M. 2006. *Linguistic Minorities and Modernity: A Sociolinguistic Ethnography*. London: Continuum.

Ibrahim, A. 1999. "Becoming Black: Rap and Hip Hop, Race, Gender, Identity, and the Politics of ESL Learning." *TESOL Quarterly* 33(3): 349–69.

– 2008. "The New *Flâneur*: Subaltern Cultural Studies, African Youth in Canada, and the Semiology of In-Betweenness." *Cultural Studies* 22(2): 234–53.

– 2014. *The Rhizome of Blackness: A Critical Ethnography of Hip-Hop Culture, Language, Identity and the Politics of Becoming*. New York: Peter Lang.

McIntosh, P. 1998. "White Privilege: Unpacking the Invisible Knapsack." In *Race, Class, and Gender in the United States*, edited by P. Rothenberg, 165–9. New York: St Martin's Press.

Mensah, J. 2002. *Black Canadians: History, Experiences, Social Conditions*. Halifax: Fernwood.

Mougeon, R., and E. Beniak. 1991. *Linguistic Consequences of Language Contact and Restriction: The Case of French in Ontario, Canada*. Oxford: Oxford University Press.

Ogbu, J., and S. Fordham. 1986. "Black Students' School Success: Coping with the 'Burden of Acting White.'" *The Urban Review* 18(3): 98–116.

Rampton, B. 1995. *Crossing: Language and Ethnicity among Adolescents.* London and New York: Longman.

Salih, T. 1991. *Season of Migration to the North.* Nairobi: Heinemann.

Spivak, G. 1999. *A Critique of Postcolonial Reason: Toward a History of the Vanishing Present.* Cambridge: Harvard University Press.

Statistics Canada. 2013. Transcript of the Chat Session on Education and Labour Data, 2011 National Household Survey, http://www.statcan.gc.ca /sc-rb/chat-clavarder/2013-06-28-eng.htm. Accessed 4 October 2013.

Todd, S. 2003. *Learning from the Other: Levinas, Psychoanalysis, and Ethical Possibilities in Education.* Albany: State University of New York Press.

Winant, H. 2004. *The New Politics of Race: Globalism, Difference, Justice.* Minneapolis: University of Minnesota Press.

Yon, D. 2000. *Elusive Culture: Schooling, Race, and Identity in Global Times.* New York: State University of New York Press.

11

The Alchemy of Sport and the Role of Media in the Education of Black Youth

Carl E. James

During the opening weeks of 2013, Torontonians were provided with news reports of gun violence that took the lives of young people, many of them not yet twenty years old. Perhaps to boost attention to the kinds of people involved in the violence, Marcus Gee's (2013) *Globe and Mail* article, "We Can't Keep Tiptoeing around Black-on-Black Violence," opined:

> Much has been said about the fact that three youths shot to death in Toronto in the past few weeks were all a mere 15 years old. Quite a bit has been said about the fact that they all died in public housing. Very little has been said about another fact – all three were black. Street violence is taking a tragic toll on black men and boys in this city. Both as victims and as perpetuators, they are caught up all too often. If you pick up the paper or turn on the computer after reports of a shooting, stabbing or violent robbery, chances are the face staring out at you will be black.

Among the platitudes that reporters seem obliged to reveal about young black victims are those related to their athletic aptitude. For instance, in the case of one youth, *The Toronto Star* reported, "He was known as a star athlete – No. 7 – with a promising future in football, studious with a wide, toothy smile always plastered on his face" (Pagliaro 2013). This promise of a future in sport is a pervasive and long-standing prize that is usually held out for black youth, especially for those living in marginalized communities, as were these fifteen-year-olds (see James 2012a; Bimper and Harrison 2012). This is why athletic activities are usually provided for young people, especially boys, living in economically disadvantaged, marginalized, and racialized communities.

THE PROMISE OF SPORT
AND THE MIS-EDUCATION OF BLACK YOUTH

Putting aside the fact that a young black student athlete has a better chance of becoming a professor than a "star athlete" in the NBA, for instance (see Price 2010),[1] the evidence also indicates that, even though a student athlete completes high school and university, perhaps even with graduate degrees, questions about his academic abilities and competence remain. Such questions tend to be informed by constructs of athletes, and black athletes in particular, as jocks who are more athletically rather than academically able, and hence are less motivated by, or invested in, intellectual activities; consequently, it is assumed that they are less likely to excel scholastically. Important here is the role of the media, and, more generally, the society, in their construction of black youth as athletes (see James 2012b) and in awarding kudos to young people for their athletic prowess and achievements. Indeed, it should not be surprising that, confronted with media reports of black students winning athletic scholarships to US colleges and universities, and/or making it to such organizations as the NBA, young black student athletes would aspire to these post-high-school opportunities.

Furthermore, apart from an achievement in sport, how else would a black youth come to the attention of Canadians and of Canada's Prime Minister? And how else would a black youth make the front page of the national newspaper or the line-up in the evening's national television news? Clearly, medical student Ayodele Odutayo, one of three University of Toronto students (or one of eleven Canadian students) to win a 2013 Rhodes Scholarship to study at Oxford University,[2] did not receive publicity or front-page recognition similar to that of basketball star Andrew Wiggins, whom the media headlined for weeks as "the country's top basketball prospect" (Parker 2012), "a name to remember ... the best high school player in the continent" (Malchelosse 2012), "a Canadian basketball phenom" (Brady 2013), and the "Canadian ... named top high school basketball player in US" (CTV News 2013).[3] *Sportsnet* trumpeted, "The rise of Andrew Wiggins: The best high school baller on earth" (Zurum 2012). Additionally, the *Canadian Press* (2013) reported,

Highly-touted Canadian basketball prospect Andrew Wiggins has won the Naismith Trophy as the top high school player in the United States.[4] Wiggins, who plays for Huntington Prep in Huntington, W. Va., was named this year's winner on Monday. The 18-year-old from Vaughn, Ont. ... has yet to decide where he'll attend college next fall.

The award caught the attention of the Prime Minister Stephen Harper, who sent out a congratulatory message to Wiggins on his Twitter account. "Just heard the news that the best High School basketball player in the United States is Canadian Andrew Wiggins. Congratulations @22wiggins!" tweeted Harper. Wiggins responded: "@pmharper Thank you sir, I appreciate your support."

Interestingly, as reported, Wiggins had been attending high school in the United States when he received the top basketball honour. (He had moved there a year earlier.) Nevertheless, as the headlines above indicate, Canadian media had been covering his progress for weeks. For instance, reporting on Wiggins's recent appearance at a high school basketball game at McMaster University in Hamilton, Ontario, *The Globe and Mail* reporter Rachel Brady (2013) wrote: "Spectators packed the gym so tight, they overflowed into the aisles, peeked through the windows above to see him, and lined up afterward to get his autograph. A media mob befitting a major game piled into a conference room to interview him. Everyone was there to see the next great thing" (Brady 2013). And as a retort to Huntington Prep School head coach's affirmation of Wiggins's "genetic gift" and "how good he actually is right now," CBC reporter, Marie Malchelosse (2014) rejoined, "And, he's a Canadian," seemingly to ensure that her television viewers did not forget that this "top" basketball player was one of "us."

This is the societal context in which, according to Marcus Gee (2013), "Black-on-black violence is a disfiguring stain on the face of the city's multicultural success," but we are also invited to celebrate "a Canadian" becoming the best basketball player in the United States. How might we understand the adulation that black male bodies receive for their athleticism and the simultaneous ridicule, fear, and resentment that the same bodies seem to spawn in a place that Gee describes as "a welcoming and liberal city"? The use of the term "welcoming" is significant, in that it signals the status and relationship of the speaker to those spoken about. So, how can black bodies be identified as Canadians at some times, while at other times, they are foreigners to be welcomed? Our main concern here is to understand how a society that sees young black men as "perpetuators" of violence can, at the same time, to borrow Ferber's (2007) observation, admire and worship them as athletes (12).

In this chapter, using media representations, I explore the role of media in helping to shape the athletic life interest and educational trajectory of young black male students. I concur that sports offer students the opportunity to develop many skills, such as discipline, hard work, determination, independence, self-confidence, self-esteem, working collegially and collaboratively, the ability to deal with losing, and knowing how to live up to expectations. But in a society where race operates to mediate the educational, career, social, employment, and economic outcomes of individuals, these acknowledged and well-posited benefits are not likely to operate in the same way for black young men as they do for white young men. Accordingly, the potential and possibilities that sports offer black youth must be read in the context of the persistent inequities that exist in society and that are sustained through racialization, racism, and discrimination.

Theories of colour-blindness, social reproduction, and social and cultural capital – all key components of neoliberalism – inform our analysis of the role of sport in the education and schooling outcomes of black male students. Writing about how elements of "White supremacy and new racism reinforce popular representations of black male athletes," Ferber (2007) asserts that "[b]lack male bodies are increasingly admired and commodified in rap, hip hop, and certain sports, but, at the same time, they continue to be used to invoke fear" (12). Therefore, conceptualized within the contours of colour-blindness, the athletic interests, academic performance, and aspirational outcome of black students are invariably mediated by the racialization, racism, and discrimination that they experience through the practices of teachers, coaches, and individuals with whom they interact. The fact is that the seemingly enthusiastic support of the athletic interests and capabilities of black youth operate within the societal and institutional "White supremacist constructions of Black masculinity," leaving intact the mainstream or dominant racist constructs and discourse of black males, including athletes (Ferber 2007, 12; see also Bimper and Harrison 2012).

Therefore, we need to be concerned about the ways in which the schooling and educational process perpetuate and/or reproduce values, norms, and beliefs that sustain social and economic hierarchical

systems, class relations, aspirational patterns, and educational outcomes. Additionally, notwithstanding the interconnection of institutional structures (e.g., schools) and an individual's exercise of agency,
reproduction theorists draw attention to how the social and cultural
capital of individuals, educated in a schooling context that privileges
"academic credentials and experiences" of middle and elite members
of society who are mostly white, help to determine mobility opportunities and individual outcomes (Singer and May 2010). For instance, in
their study of how an African American, male high school basketball
player "from a low SES background [was] complicit in the reproduction of his social position in society by aspiring to a career as a professional basketball player," Singer and May write that, among many of
their male participants, the "lack of cultural capital" and "their myopic
focus on sport participation" are particularly disadvantageous, since
the interlocking effects of race and class often compound the obstacles
that black student athletes face (310; see also Harper, Williams, and
Blackman 2013). Furthermore, the "double bind of marginality," as
Singer and May contend, operates against black youth attaining the
mobility they seek, especially when they lack "the necessary athletic
skills, appropriate knowledge, and social networks for attaining [their]
athletic goals," particularly in an education system from which they
have been excluded and from which they might never obtain the "resources that helps [sic] one to develop the skills necessary for achieving
social mobility" (311).

But it is not only to the schooling and education systems that we
must affix our critical gaze with regard to how black boys and young
men are sold the idea that it is through sport that will they be able to
obtain the education, career, financial stability, and social mobility to
which they aspire. In fact, media play a significant role in manufacturing, selling, and (in)forming the aspirations of young Canadian black
male athletes. For instance, the allure of "going south" on athletic scholarship is something that media and coaches tend to promote in ways
that so entice black Canadian students especially, they make significant
efforts towards this end; they commit large amounts of time to sports
over their academic work, going from school to school, completing
high school in the US, and overlooking the possibility of attending university in Canada (James 2005; Miller 2012). Evidently, these black male
athletes are not alone in their choice of this narrow pathway toward
achieving their educational aspirations and ultimate upward social mobility, for teachers, coaches, parents, and others, also "buy into" this

(among others) media-manufactured athletic dream and its inherently limited possibilities for some youth.

Scholars have long scrutinized the persistent role of the media in routinely manufacturing, recycling, and reinforcing what is perceived as "evidence" – or as common-sense ideas – that eventually becomes part of the dominant discourse or is embedded in the popular imagination of society members (Ferber 2007; Henry and Tator 2006; Welsh 2009). In their "agenda setting" role, as Henry and Bjornson (1999) put it, the media focus on particular topics while ignoring others. Furthermore, as van Dijk (2000) contends, in modern information societies, "media discourse is the main source of people's knowledge, attitudes and ideologies," and as such, with other institutions (and elite group members) in society, plays a "discursive and symbolic" role that has powerful influences on the lives of most people (36). Gorham (1999) also proffers that "the repeated presentation of social groups in particular ways in the media are partly responsible for the effects of how audience members think about people in those groups" (230). He concludes that, by "repeatedly and consistently" presenting racial stereotypes, the media "influence our interpretations of media content in a way that supports dominant racial myths" (Gorham 1999, 244). In the case of black youth, the everyday presentation of images that represent them as highly accomplished athletes serves as a "truth" that common sense would dictate their observance of or faithfulness to athletics as a route to educational and social success.

In what follows, I reflect on how athletics, as a social and educational tool and as a seemingly favourable and assuring "aspirational capital," is encumbered by a set of racialization factors that structure the potential, opportunities, and possibilities of black young athletes. "Aspirational capital" refers to capital that provides "hope in the face of structured inequality" to young people who often do not have alternative "means to make [their] dreams a reality" (Yosso 2005, 77). Therefore, multiculturalism policies and practices notwithstanding, athletes are not immune from the hegemonic ways in which race, class, and gender intersect to mediate their educational, career, and social trajectory and outcomes. Consequently, despite the adulation, media-hype, role-models, and media and coaches' insistence on scholarship opportunities, in a society where race matters, athletes and former athletes, like their non-athletic peers, are left to navigate and negotiate the same inequitable and discriminatory structures that often limit their opportunities and outcomes. The reality is that, informed by the neoliberal ideology of individualism, choice, competition, and entrepreneurship (Connel 2010), student athletes and their parents, bolstered by teachers, coaches, and media reporters, come to live with the idea that race (or skin colour) has nothing to do with the athletic participation and performance of student athletes, since it is their choice to play sports. Working with this notion in the remainder of this chapter, I discuss how the illusion of choice, incongruity of individualism, and paradox of competition in a stratified educational context with limited resources and inequitable opportunities account for black student involvement in sports – sometimes to the detriment of their academic potential.

THE NEOLIBERAL SCHOOLING CONTEXT

In a contribution to the *Handbook of Research in Social Foundations of Education*, I engaged the questions: "Why is the school basketball team predominantly Black? And what does that say about educators' role in 'leveling the playing field'?" (James 2011). Understandably, the question comes from my observations of the over-representation of black students on their high schools' basketball teams – even in cases where they represent a very small proportion of the school population. I suggested that, while, on the one hand, black students' participation in sports might be seen as "encouraging," in that it indicates that they are actively engaged in their school and its activities, on the other hand, it should be a concern, since in many ways, their participation in sports conceals the tendency of sports to be used as "a divergence from, rather than an enhancement of, their academic performance" (James 2011, 450).

Furthermore, if black students tend to find school alienating, marginalizing, unresponsive and/or irrelevant to their needs and interests (Smith 2010), then "choosing" to play sports is often more a product of the schooling conditions and opportunities than a representation of their interests, talent, and/or skills. And insofar as sports provide a means by which student athletes "gain recognition, build self-confidence, derive benefit from idolization, and qualify for postsecondary education scholarships" (James 2011, 456), it is understandable that sports would be seen as a viable alternative to engage school and to attain the necessary education and occupation for social mobility. In this regard, the overrepresentation of black students on their schools' basketball teams (and, indeed, on other teams such as track-and-field and

football) is not merely a result of their interests or skills but of their neoliberal schooling that emphasizes individual responsibility, equality
of opportunity, freedom to pursue whatever one wishes, competition as
a "naturally occurring social good," and the achievement of wealth
through hard work and self-discipline (Braedley and Luxton 2010). This
educational ethic is encouraged and sustained through the many media
accounts that present sports as a mechanism that can instil discipline,
enhance academic performance, inspire high educational aspirations –
particularly to attain athletic scholarships to US colleges and universities – and that can be used as a pre-emptive strategy to address anti-
social, oppositional, troublesome, and/or "bad boy" behaviours among
black youth. In the remainder of the chapter, I make reference to print
media sources in my examination of how sports is proffered as a means
of *escaping* a "tough" neighbourhood life, as having a relationship to
genetics, and as a "road" to upward social mobility with the help of
US scholarships.

The Way out of Canada's "Tough" Neighbourhoods

In showing the power and capacity of athletics, the *Globe and Mail*
basketball reporter, Michael Grange (2007), under the headline "From
Jane and Finch to Ivy League; After Living in a Tough Toronto Neighbourhood, Andre Wilkins Is Well Prepared for Any Challenge at
Cornell," writes:

> Andre Wilkins knows life at the intersection of Jane and Finch in
> northwest Toronto. He's heard the gunfire. He knows what it
> means to live in a place divided, where venturing to the "wrong"
> housing complex or crossing the street can earn you a beat down
> or worse. He's even been caught up in the ripple effect of crime
> and suspicion and been questioned by police for nothing more
> than being young, male and black ... The road from Jane and Finch
> to the Ivy League is at the very least the road less travelled. For a
> basketball player, it might be the road never travelled, at least that
> anyone can remember.

Grange continues to tell of the attraction that sports had for Wilkins,
who, according to his "single" mother,[5] "stood on his own since kindergarten." And reflecting on his journey to the point of winning the scholarship at twenty years old, Wilkins commented that at the age of "16 or

17 years," he looked for a job – "I applied for everything" – but was unable to get one even at McDonald's. And while "for a day" he thought about "street life" with "the money, the clothes, the cars," he did not acquiesce to that temptation, because the consequences of "jail or worse" meant that "[i]t's not worth it." In addition to his high school coach, who suggested that "neighbourhood" is no barrier to success, the coach at Cornell University saw Grange as an example, a role model. As the coach said, "We don't have a lot of what I call three-car garage guys. But Grange's a little different because he comes from an extremely rough background and has made it on his own. I want him at this university because he deserves it, but I want him here because the university needs guys like him here, too."

A means to a "good" education and to getting out of the "tough" neighbourhoods also involves attending the "right" high school and taking the advice of the coach, as Keaton Cole did. Now in Toronto, having completed a four-year degree in sociology at Western Carolina University, Cole attended a high school that was about twenty miles from his Jane and Finch neighbourhood, because, as he told *Toronto Star* reporter David Grossman, "As an undersized player, I wanted to overcome obstacles, play on a school team known across the country, get a U.S. scholarship, be around the best players and, if I was fortunate, become one of them one day." At 5-foot-8, and "frustrated with his small size in a big man's game," Cole is said to have "thought about quitting high school basketball," but, accepting the advice of his coach, did not. Cole went on to become "one of the top teenage point guards in the country," besides being "unanimously chosen by game officials, fans as well as high school and university coaches" – consulted by the newspaper – in the "top five senior players from more than 200 high schools hoops teams in the Greater Toronto Area." The message being communicated about Cole's educational and career journey seems to be captured in the words of the new coach of his former high school: "He [Cole] proved what a great deal of commitment and hard work can do" (Grossman 2008).

The sense of what can be achieved through the discipline that sports provides was also central to the hockey program introduced by the principal of the same neighbourhood middle school. Writing about the hockey program at the middle school, the *Toronto Star* reporter Debra Black (2009) headlines that the program was "designed to keep children skating in the right direction, away from trouble." The educators believed that if they do not get to their "at-risk" students, especially black males, early, "they may be lost to gangs, crime and drugs."[6] So, even though basketball would have been the sport of choice for these students,[7] hockey – the principal's "passion" – was used to teach them, in the words of the principal, that "anything is possible." This message was reinforced by *role models* like former NHL player Tony McKegney,[8] who, in his speech to a school assembly, recounted his years as a successful professional hockey player, becoming "the first black player in the NHL history to score 40 goals in a season." McKegney told his young listeners of his "struggles" with racism in his elementary and high schools – "as the only black person" – and on the ice. He indicated that he dealt with racism by ignoring it, and used "athletics as a way to get accepted." For the school principal and teachers, then, McKegney, among others, was evidence of the possibilities that hockey affords. Indeed, the principal pointed out that hockey was a way to teach students "life skills," such as how "to work as a team," and how to deal with struggles and not "give up." He admitted that the students will be "faced with hardship and obstacles," but he expects that they will learn to "persevere," working with values such as "respect, discipline, listening and fun." And according to one teacher, "Hockey gave them something to do, something to learn, something to accomplish, something to strive for."[9]

It's All in the "Genes"

The evidence that media, educators, "role models" and others bring forward about young people who live in disadvantaged, difficult or "at-risk" communities is that, through the discipline and ethics of sports, these young people are able to achieve social mobility as long as they are prepared to work hard, persevere, take advice, be responsible, and have hope. Closely aligned with this individualism ethos is the biological construct of athleticism (see Ferber 2007; James 2005). In fact, in many of the broadcast and newspaper accounts of the accomplishments of student athletes, references are made by reporters, coaches, parents and athletes alike – either in jest or certainty – to the role that genes or physiology plays in their lives and trajectories. For instance, Rachel Brady of the *Globe and Mail* observes, "After all, Wiggins is the beneficiary of exceptional athletic genes" (2013). Similarly, picking up on Huntington Prep School head coach assertion that Wiggins "is very instinctual on the court ... he's been given a little bit more genetics because his IQ for the game is very very good,"

CBC reporter Marie Malchelosse, after proclaiming, "And he is Canadian," goes on to say, "Basketball is in his blood. His dad Mitchell played six years in the NBA for the Houston Rockets. His mother Marita Payne won two silver medals for Canada in the Los Angeles Olympic Games. Wiggins grew up in the Toronto area. He was basically born with a ball in his hands. A basketball star? For sure" (Malchelosse 2012).

And very early in his article on Andrew Wiggins – described as "The Canadian Jordan," "the great hope north of the border" and "the Canadian basketball phenom considered the best high school-aged player in the world" – Pete Thamel (2013) goes on to reference the athletic background of Wiggins's parents, suggesting he would have inherited his skills and abilities from them.

His [Wiggins] genetic credentials are impeccable. Mitchell Wiggins played in the NBA for six seasons and played professionally for nearly 15. Marita Payne-Wiggins won two silver medals for Canada in the 1984 Olympics.[10] Andrew Wiggins flashes sprinter speed in the open floor, boasts a 44-inch vertical and his dunking ability has made him a YouTube sensation. His Go-Go gadget arms and quick feet give him the tools to become an elite-level NBA defender.

Thamel also adds that "Andrew Wiggins's work ethic and motor have yet to catch up to his athleticism and raw ability (Thamel 2013). And to this profile, Mike George, the co-founder of the CIA Bounce (a Toronto-based youth basketball organization) that competes in the AAU (Amateur Athletic Union) program, adds, "If you're doing a test tube baby and putting together a genetically made boy, he'd be the perfect genetically made baby" (Thamel 2013). Thamel also writes of Wiggins: "While it's hard when he's already being anointed a future NBA All-Star, there's debate as to whether he possesses the killer instinct and love of the game to become an elite NBA player" (Thamel 2013).

Just as Andrew Wiggins's athletic prowess was genetically linked to that of his father and mother, so, too, was Julian Clarke's. This is represented in the *Toronto Sun* headline "The Clarkes Reach for the Top: Dad Norman and Son Julian Were Both Blessed with Basketball Smarts and a Genius of Knowing What Is Important" (Lankhof 2010). Columnist Bill Lankhof begins,

A generation ago, Norm Clarke, the Canadian-born son of immigrant parents from Jamaica became one of Toronto's most celebrated high school athletes. It started him on his journey from modest playgrounds of York, to the national team and a U.S. basketball scholarship at St. Bonaventure University – a most rare and treasured thing for any Canadian in the 1970s but especially for someone who otherwise might not have afforded such a grand education.

And Clarke Sr, now a high school teacher and coach, is quoted as saying, "My parents were blue-collar workers. Long hours. Shift work. Lots of times I went home and they weren't there and we had to learn to fend for ourselves. They gave us the best they could based on their experiences and their limitations of education and not being able to get a better job. They didn't have much. But they worked hard to give us what they could." Buried in this narrative of the immigrant family making good in Canada with the help of sport is the role of genetics. In fact, Lankhof writes that "Julian's mother still holds high school track records in Sault St. Marie where she grew up"; and Clarke Sr is quoted as suggesting that competition is "in both our genes pools that we don't want to lose."

Further, in the same month, and two years before Wiggins came into the spotlight, news reports were chronicling the successes of Cory Joseph and Tristan Thompson, describing them as "among the brightest high school basketball stars in North America, soon to be playing prime-time minutes for two of the top Division 1 schools in the NCAA" (Wolstat 2012). Journalist Ryan Wolstat referred to Joseph and Thompson as having "natural athletic gifts." But while these two players were not reported to have parents with similar accomplishments, as is often the case, there were signals in the athletes' stories that athleticism runs in the family. For instance, Joseph is reported to have an older brother with whom he played and "won back-to-back provincial championships" (Wolstat 2012). Besides, it is not uncommon to hear of coaches and scouts recruiting siblings on the basis of one sibling's athletic interest and skills (James 2005).

The Ultimate Reward Is Scholarships to a US School,
Especially an "Ivy League" University

It's estimated that as many as 100 Canadian teenagers – primarily boys from the Toronto area, though there are girls and boys from every region of the country – are chasing their hoop dreams in the United States, often as early as the ninth grade.

Michael Grange, *Globe and Mail*, 7 March 2010

In the stories of almost all the student athletes featured in news reports is their attainment of athletic scholarship to US colleges and universities (before going on to the NBA). Such an award has been described as, in the case of Wilkins with his Cornell University scholarship, "the road less travelled" (Grange 2007), or for Norman Clarke, "a most rare and treasured thing for any Canadian" (Lankhof 2010). All of the basketball players mentioned in this chapter had received or were expected to receive athletic scholarships to US postsecondary institutions. Indeed, this is the dream or prize that all "serious" student athletes pursue, singularly and uncompromisingly, with the encouragement and support of coaches, educators, and parents (see James 2005; Miller 2012).[11] Because of this goal, student athletes like Cole, as mentioned earlier, travelled significant distances across the city to a high school that they believed would provide them the training, support, and exposure necessary to win the all-important athletic scholarship. Many others, like Joseph, Thompson, and Wiggins, elected to attend high school in the US (see above quote, Grange). Recall that Wiggins was, for two years, a student at Huntington Prep School in the US when he was named top high-school basketball player in the US.

This flight to the US of many – if not most – "star" Canadian high school athletes, especially basketball players, was the subject of two *Globe and Mail* articles by reporter Michael Grange. The articles are titled "Bound for Glory; Hype and Big Dreams Are Seducing More and More Canadian Teenagers to Leave Home for Mega-Money High-School Basketball Programs in the U.S." (2010a) and "Making Run for the Border; Part 11: Canada Basketball Faces Tall Order in Keeping the Best High School Roundball Talent from Heading South" (2010b). In the 5 March article, Grange (2010a) examines the situation and comments of Cory Joseph and Tristan Thompson, writing,

> [they] could be any other Canadian high school kids with big dreams, making their way through Shakespeare, but imagining a

brighter stage. The difference? The pair of 18-years-olds are already on that stage, starring for one of the best high school basketball teams in the United States, their stories splashed all over the internet, the hype spilling over. At the end of this month they will become the first Canadians in more than 20 years to play in the McDonald's High School All-American game, an honour they'll share with everyone from LeBron James to Michael Jordan. Next month they'll lead No. 3-ranked Findley Prep in the ESPN RISE National High School Invitational – the unofficial high school championship of the United States – to defend the title they won last year.

For their part, attending high school in the US with an athletic program was seen as providing them, as Joseph puts it, "more exposure." Likewise, Thompson explains that he left home at sixteen years old because of his desire "to play North Carolina or Kentucky or Texas." This desire, he admits, dates back to "the first time" he saw these teams on television. "I want to play for those programs," he said. "It's not like there aren't good programs in Canada. I just wanted more. I wanted the highest competition out there and that's Division 1, so I made that my goal" (Grange 2010a).

According to reporter Grange, the attraction of migrating to the US also has to do with inadequate resources, insufficient understanding of requirements, and lack of opportunities in Canada that would enable student athletes to qualify for scholarships, "and a desire on the part of some players to find safer and more stable places to play and study than they have at home." For, as Grange adds, "Many of the kids ... are from immigrant minorities, from tough neighbourhoods and less-than-ideal home situations." On this point, the founder of the Toronto-area organization CIA Bounce notes, "There has been a lot of crime in some of those neighbourhoods, no doubt about it ... For some parents, they see it like sending their kids to boarding school, it gives them a sense of security" (Grange 2010a). But in many cases, the exposure, full scholarships, and satisfactory living conditions do not materialize. In fact, as Grange also writes, some of these youth experience situations in which they are "essentially fending for themselves at schools with dubious academic standing and scant record of developing elite basketball players" (Grange 2010a; see also CBC 2012). Nevertheless, student athletes and their parents do feel that the "sacrifice" is necessary if they are to realize their mobility dreams. Take for instance, what Joseph and his mother had to say: "It's really tough mentally to come down here ... You go through a lot of ups and downs, and the downs are hard because you're alone. [But] my mom told me ... in order to get to your highest level, you have to make sacrifices." Joseph's mother admits to having "doubts about having her youngest son leave Canada in Grade 11 to play basketball in the United States." But for Thompson's parents, "it wasn't a hard decision," because they felt that their son was "mature" for his age and "needed a challenge" playing with the "tough ones" (Grange 2010a).

Interestingly, there is a paradox to going south seeking to win "what is widely considered to be a golden ticket for elite Canadian athletes," to quote *Toronto Star* reporter, Rachel Mendleson (2012). For as Grange indicates, this well-accepted aspiration is premised on the logic that "[i]f playing basketball in the United States is good, then staying at home is bad" (Grange 2010b).[12] What, then, is at stake if Canada loses its best athletes to the United States? Coaches will not able to organize competitions with strong competitive teams that effectively capitalize on the abilities and skills of players, thereby supporting their success. After all, in order to qualify for prep school in the US or win scholarships to US universities, athletes must experience strong competitive players at home. There are significant implications here for black student athletes and their parents, many of whom live in the communities that are featured so prominently in the discourses of coaches, educators, and recruiters. Indeed, what many of these black youth do not hear about are the experiences of the many youth for whom the athletic and educational systems have failed to provide the promised opportunities. This information is needed if student athletes are to come to the realization that athletic scholarships to a US school should not or cannot be considered the ultimate reward or essential route to upward social mobility.

CONCLUSION – WHAT IS AT STAKE?

I started this chapter by referencing reports of gun violence that is affecting the lives of a number of young black men, and by pointing out the proclivity of the media and members of society generally – particularly educators, service providers, youth leaders, parents, and even the youth themselves – to present sports as a means by which we might be able to address "the ills" that plague young black men. It is held that sports can instil in young black men discipline, responsi-

bility, self-control, and hope, leading to enhanced educational performance, high aspirations, and social mobility, regardless of their
schooling, family, and neighbourhood. Genetics aside, there is no
denying that sports is important for physical health, and as discussed,
it also teaches hard work, determination, dedication, communication, teamwork, leadership – skills needed to adapt to challenging
situations and to deal with stress and deadlines. And there are qual-
ities such as confidence, perseverance, and self-pride that are gained
in concert with a level of arrogance and entitlement, the latter of
which, in the case of black youth living in a racist society, when dis-
played with related attitudes and behaviour, could prove disadvantageous for them.

I argue that the values, expectations, and behaviours learned through
sports are rooted in the neoliberal assertions of individualism: individual choice, personal responsibility, hard work, self-discipline, colour-
blindness, and free enterprise (Braedley and Luxton 2010). These values
are embedded in the culture of societal institutions (educational, athletic, and others), and, by extension, resonate with and are implemented by individuals (especially "role models") who work with the
youth. As such, the situation of black youth is considered to be more a
product of individual choices and the "black community" than a result
of the economic, political, cultural, and social structures that created
and sustain the situation. Sports serve as a useful tool to deflect or mask
the duplicity of institutions and the hegemonic structures of inequity,
alienation, marginalization, and racialization. In reality, sports do little
to "level the playing field," but do more to keep alive the "common-
sense hegemonic ideology" (Luxton 2010, 210) that success is possible
in its competitive arena where the false message of genetic, aptitude,
athletic skills, and the "rational choices" keep student athletes (and their
parents) believing in the dream.

Sufficiently socialized through the messages from their coaches,
teachers, parents, role models, and media about the possibilities sports
offer them, many black student athletes in Toronto go from one high
school to another; some migrate to the US, "sacrificing" the comforts
of home and family to attend prep school with the hope of eventually
winning an athletic scholarship. Parents similarly sacrifice through financial commitments and by sending their teenage sons to be raised by
unknown coaches, dormitory monitors, and role models; in the process,
they unwittingly become part of the capitalist venture of certain prep
schools, colleges, universities, and wealthy business people. This "per-

verse individualism," as Luxton (2010) says of another situation, works
to keep active the promise of an athletic career, and as a consequence,
immobilizes student athletes, thereby making it difficult for them to envision alternative routes to their educational and career goals. "Their
sense of individual agency," says Luxton, "is reduced to a notion of
choice," leading to the assumption "that their circumstances are a result
of poor choices they have made, rather than that the choices available
were problematic or wrong" in the first place (180). In fact, in today's
schooling, educational, and athletic context, black students are subjected to what Sukarieh and Tannock (2008) might say is "a culture of
responsibilisation and entrepreneurship ... [with] a politically neutered
and context-free set of 'skills': tolerance, accepting the other, teamwork,
respect of work for its own sake, work ethic, stability, dependability, motivation, persistence, self-discipline and self-confidence" (309). It is also
a context in which, if the youth fail to succeed in sports through their
own efforts, skills, and physiological makeup, they are expected then
to accept their deficiencies – that they lack the necessary athletic skills
(and genes) and commitment – and therefore should work on themselves (see Sukarieh and Tannock 2008). Essentially, with young people
and their parents intensely focusing on individual efforts, skills, genetics, interests, and aspirations, they leave unacknowledged the accountability, role, and responsibility of educational institutions, social
agencies, athletic bodies, and governments to equitably and justly respond to the needs, interests and aspirations of black youth.

NOTES

1 According to William Price (2010), in the US, young men have "only a .03%
    chance" of a pro-career in basketball. This means that, of the almost 156,000
    male, high school senior basketball players, only 44 will be drafted to play in
    the NBA after college, and only 32 women (.02%) out of just over 127,000 fe-
    male, high school senior players will eventually be drafted. And referencing
    Price, Becky Bratu (2012), a staff writer with NBC News, states: "The odds of a
    high school senior basketball player being drafted to play in the NBA after
    college are a slim 1 in 6,864,000."

2 *The Toronto Star* reporters Noor Javed and Kamila Hinkson (7 January 2013)
    start their article by saying that the three winners "will join the likes of the
    world's most influential intellects, writers and policy makers like Bill Clin-
    ton, Naomi Wolf and Bob Rae." And they go on to point out, "The Rhodes
    scholarship is considered one of the world's most prestigious and competi-
    tive academic awards and is given to 11 Canadians each year."

3 Other news reports that put out the same refrain include *Yahoo Sports*, whose article about Wiggins came under the headline "Canada's Andrew Wiggins, U.S. High School Basketball Player of the Year, Now Mulling His College Choice" (Neate Sager, 26 February 2013). And Pete Thamel, in *Sports Illustrated*, raised the question, "Andrew Wiggins has elite talent, but there are questions about whether he has the drive and desire to become a star player at the next level" (7 February 2013).

4 *Canadian Press* indicated that the "Naismith Award winner is selected by basketball journalists from around the United States and is based on the 2013 high school season. Past winners include LeBron James (2003), Kobe Bryant (1996) and Jason Kidd (1992)."

5 It was also reported that Andre has a younger brother.

6 As if to give readers a full sense of what the educators are up against, Black (2009) also writes that the school is mere blocks from the high school where Manners had been shot in 2007. "Many of the students," she continues, "come from troubled homes, without adequate supervision and financial resources. Some have no place to go after school ... It is a high-risk community, but also one of great potential."

7 According to Black, for many black youth, hockey was "a 'white man's sport.' Basketball was their passion. It mirrored what they saw around them. Black men on television played basketball; in their neighbourhood they played b-ball or maybe soccer. These kids knew nothing about hockey. And most of their parents couldn't afford the steep fees and hefty equipment costs of the game" (*Toronto Star*, 21 March 2009).

8 McKegney played with the Buffalo Sabres, the Quebec Nordiques, and the St Louis Blues.

9 The notion of sports *rescuing* "at-risk" young black males living in "at-risk" neighbourhoods is a recurring theme in the assertions of youth workers and service providers – some of whom fancy themselves as "role models." These assertions are reported in a number of newspaper articles, often with images of black males with sport equipment (e.g., a basketball or football) in a related space. For instance, Toronto mayor Rob Ford is quoted as saying to the *National Post* in 2008 that he was "absolutely sure" that playing on the high school football team he coached saved a player in question from "death or jail" (Daniel Dale, *Toronto Star*, 8 March 2013). And in an article titled "Going through Hoops to Reach At-Risk Youth," reporter Betsy Powell tells of a "surrogate father/counselor/coach/ and co-founder of the Neighbourhood Basketball Association," a charitable agency that caters to "black at-risk youth, aged 13 to 18, who live in priority neighbourhoods." The agency focuses on youth who are "high school dropouts or youth in and out of trouble with the law" (*Toronto Star*, 5 August 2011).

10 Lori Ewing (*The Globe and Mail*, 31 March 2013) expressed a similar idea saying: "Wiggins, the fourth of six children, also boasts impeccable genetic credentials. His dad Mitchell played in the NBA. His mom Marita
Payne-Wiggins was a sprinter, helping Canada to a pair of relay silver medals
at the 1984 Olympics. She still holds the Canadian record in the 200 metres
and shares the 400 record with Jillian Richardson."

11 The recent (2012/13) Ontario teachers' job action created a crisis for some student athletes who were on the path to winning an athletic scholarship. For example, the *Toronto Star* reported that the teachers' "work-to-rule could hurt
students' chances of landing a coveted U.S. sports scholarship" (Rachel
Mendleson, 20 December 2013). Mendleson tells of Luke Barrett, a grade 12
student, whose pursuit of a US basketball scholarship "has been all-consum-
ing for the Toronto student and his single mom, who has stretched her fi-
nances to improve his odds of landing the what is widely considered to be a
golden ticket for elite Canadian athletes."

12 Grange (7 March 2010b) reports that Canadian coaches see this as a false logic.

REFERENCES

Bimper, A.Y., and L. Harrison. 2012. "Meet Me at the Crossroads: African
American Athletic and Racial Identity." *Quest* 63(3): 275–88.

Black, D. 2009. "Scoring Hockey Pride at Jane-Finch." *The Toronto Star*, 21
March. http://www.thestar.com/life/parent/2009/03/21/scoring_hockey
_pride_at_janefinch.html.

Brady, R. 2013. "Andrew Wiggins: A Canadian Basketball Phenom." *The Globe
and Mail*, 18 February.

Braedley, S., and M. Luxton. 2010. "Competing Philosophies: Neoliberalism
and the Challenges of Everyday Life." In *Neoliberalism and Everyday Life*,
edited by S. Baedley and M. Luxton, 3–21. Montreal & Kingston: McGill-
Queen's University Press.

Bratu, B. "11 Things More Likely to Happen Than Winning the Powerball
Jackpot." *NBC News*. Accessed 28 November 2012. http://usnews.nbcnews
.com/_news/2012/11/28/15510840-11-things-more-likely-to-happen-than-
winning-the-powerball-jackpot?lite.

Canadian Broadcasting Corporation (CBC). 2012. "The Fifth Estate: Fast
Break." Accessed March 2016. http://www.cbc.ca/fifth/episodes/2011-
2012/fast-break.

Canadian Press (CP). 2013. "Highly-Touted Basketball Prospect Andrew Wiggins Has Won the Naismith Trophy as Top High School Player in the United States." Accessed 26 February 2013, http://www.cbc.ca/sports/basketball
/nba/canadian-basketball-prospect-wiggins-wins-naismith-award-1.1370357.

Connel, R. 2010. "Understanding Neoliberalism." In *Neoliberalism and Everyday Life*, edited by S. Braedley and M. Luxton, 22–36. Montreal & Kingston: McGill-Queen's University Press.

CTV News. "Canadian Andrew Wiggins Named Top High School Basketball Player in the U.S." Accessed March 2016. http://www.ctvnews.ca/sports /canadian-andrew-wiggins-named-top-high-school-basketball-player-in-u-s-1.1172170.

Dale, D. 2013. "Don Bosco Alum Says Rob Ford Was Wrong to Say He'd Be 'Dead or in Jail' without Football." *The Toronto Star*, 8 March. http://www.thestar.com/news/city_hall/2013/03/08/don_bosco_alum_says_ rob_ford_was_wrong_to_say_hed_be_dead_or_in_jail_without_football .html.

Ewing, L. 2013. "Canadian Phenom Andrew Wiggins Faces Pressure as High School Showcase Looms." *The Globe and Mail*, 31 March. Accessed April 2016. http://www.theglobeandmail.com/sports/basketball/canadian-phenom-andrew-wiggins-faces-pressure-as-high-school-showcase-looms /article10588290/.

Ferber, A. 2007. "The Construction of Black Masculinity: White Supremacy Now and Then." *Journal of Sport and Social Issues* 31(1): 11–24.

Gee, M. 2013. "We Can't Keep Tiptoeing around Black on Black Violence." *The Globe and Mail*. Accessed 22 February. http://www.theglobeandmail .com/news/toronto/we-cant-keeptiptoeing-around-black-on-black-violence /article8907404/.

Gorham, B.W. 1999. "Stereotypes in the Media: So What?" *The Howard Journal of Communications* 10:229–47.

Grange, M. 2010a. "Bound for Glory." *The Globe and Mail*, 5 March. http://m.theglobeandmail.com/sports/basketball/bound-for-glory/article 1209439/?service=mobile.

– 2010b. "Making a Run for the Border." *The Globe and Mail*, 7 March. http://m.theglobeandmail.com/sports/basketball/making-a-run-for-the-border/article1493032/?service=mobile.

– 2007. "From Jane and Finch to Ivy League." *The Globe and Mail*, 23 June. http://www.theglobeandmail.com/sports/from-jane-and-finch-to-ivy-league/article1087913/.

Grossman, D. 2008. "Little Guy Cole Has Big Talent." *The Toronto Star*, 9 March. http://www.thestar.com/sports/amateur/2008/03/09/little_guy_cole_has _big_talent.html.

Harper, S.R., C.D. Williams, and H.W. Blackman. 2013. *Black Male Student Athletes and Racial Inequities in NCAA Division 1 College Sports*. Philadelphia: University of Pennsylvania, Centre for the Study of Race and Equity in Education.

Henry, F., and M. Bjornson. 1999. *The Racialization of Crime in Toronto's Print Media: A Research Project*. Toronto: Ryerson Polytechnic University.

Henry, F., and C. Tator. 2006. *The Colour of Democracy: Racism in Canadian Society*. Toronto: Harcourt Brace.

James, C.E. 2005. *Race in Play: Understanding the Socio-cultural Worlds of Student Athletes*. Toronto: Canadian Scholars' Press.

– 2011. "Why Is the School Basketball Team Predominantly Black?" In *Handbook of Research in the Social Foundations of Education*, edited by S. Tozer, B.P. Gallegos, A.M. Henry, M.B. Greiner, and P.G. Price, 450–9. New York: Routledge.

– 2012a. *Life at the Intersection: Community, Class and Schooling*. Halifax: Fernwood Educational Publishing.

– 2012b. "Students 'At Risk': Stereotyping and the Schooling of Black Boys." *Urban Education* 47(2): 464–94.

Javed, N., and K. Hinkson. 2013. *University of Toronto Students Snag Three Rhodes Scholars Spots*. 7 January. http://www.thestar.com/yourtoronto /education/2013/01/07/university_of_toronto_students_snag_three_rhodes _scholars_spots.html.

Lankhof, B. 2010. "The Clarkes Reach for the Top: Dad Norman and Son Julian Were Both Blessed with Basketball Smarts and a Genius of Knowing What Is Important." *The Toronto Sun*, 30 March. http://www.torontosun .com/sports/columnists/bill_lankhof/2010/03/30/13416941.html.

Luxton, M. 2010. "Doing Neoliberalism: Perverse Individualism in Personal Life." In *Neoliberalism and Everyday Life*, edited by S. Braedley and M. Luxton, 163–83. Montreal & Kingston: McGill-Queen's University Press.

Malchelosse, M. 2014. "Canada's Andrew Wiggins Tops 2014 NBA Draft Prospects." CBC Sports. Accessed 20 June 2015. http://www.cbc.ca/player /Sports/Top+Stories/ID/2322181885/.

– 2012. "Andrew Wiggins, a Name to Remember." CBC Radio-Canada. Accessed March 2016. http://ici.radio-canada.ca/sports/plussports/2012/12/04 /004-basket-wiggins-malchelosse.shtml.

Mendleson, R. 2012. "Work-to-Rule Could Hurt Students' Chances of Landing Coveted U.S. Sports Scholarships." *The Toronto Star*, 20 December. http://www.thestar.com/news/gta/2012/12/20/worktorule_could_hurt _students_chances_of_landing_coveted_us_sports_scholarships.html.

Miller, D. 2012. "Placing Canadian Black Student Athletes in the Race for US Athletic Scholarships." Paper presented at North American Society for the Sociology of Sport (NASSS). Annual Conference, New Orleans.

Pagliaro, J. 2013. "Family Mourns 15-Year-Old Teen Tyson Bailey Fatally Shot in Regent Park as Police Detail New Evidence." *The Toronto Star*, 2 March.

http://www.thestar.com/news/crime/2013/01/28/family_mourns_15yearold
_teen_tyson_bailey_fatally_shot_in_regent_park_as_police_detail_new
_evidence.html.

Parker, B. 2012. "Andrew Wiggins Coolly Handles the Pressure of Being the
Country's Top Basketball Prospect." *The Washington Post*, 10 December.
Accessed March 2016. https://www.washingtonpost.com/sports/high-
schools/andrew-wiggins-coolly-handles-the-pressure-of-being-the-countrys-
top-basketball-prospect/2012/12/10/b3ab5198-4303-11e2-9648-a2c323a991
d6_story.html

Powell, B. 2011. "Going through Hoops to Reach At-Risk Youth." *The Toronto
Star*, 5 August. http://www.thestar.com/news/crime/2011/08/05/going
_through_hoops_to_reach_atrisk_youth.html.

Price, W.J. 2010. "What Are the Odds of Becoming a Professional Athlete?
United States Sports Academy." *The Sport Digest*, 23 January. http://www.the
sportdigest.com/archive/article/what-are-oddsbecoming-professional-athlete.

Sager, N. 2013. "Canada's Andrew Wiggins, U.S. High School Basketball Player of the Year, Now Mulling His College Choice." *Yahoo*, 26 February.
Accessed March 2016. https://ca.sports.yahoo.com/blogs/eh-game/canada-
andrew-wiggins-u-high-school-basketball-player-163434497.html.

Singer, J.N., and R.B. Buford May. 2010. "The Career Trajectory of a Black
Male High School Basketball Player: A Social Reproduction Perspective."
International Review for the Sociology of Sport 46(3): 299–314.

Smith, C.C., ed. 2010. "Anti-racism in Education: Missing in Action." *Our
Schools/Our Selves* 19 (3).

Sukarieh, M., and S. Tannock. 2008. "In the Best Interests of Youth or Neoliberalism? The World Bank and the New Global Youth Empowerment Project." *Journal of Youth Studies* 11(3): 301–12.

Thamel, P. 2013. "The Canadian Jordan, Andrew Wiggins the Great Hope
North of Border." *Sports Illustrated*, 7 February. Accessed March 2016.
http://www.si.com/college-basketball/2013/02/07/andrew-wiggins.

Van Dijk, T.A. 2000. "New(s) Racism: A Discourse Analytical Approach." In
Ethnic Minorities and the Media, edited by S. Cottle, 33–49. Milton Keynes,
UK: Open University Press.

Welsh, E.T. 2009. "Representations of Race and Gender in Mainstream Media
Coverage of the 2008 Democratic Primary." *Journal of African American
Studies* 13(2): 121–30.

Wolstat, R. 2012. "GTA Teens Are Lighting Up the U.S. The Mild One Cory
Joseph Arrived First and Then Came the Wild One Tristan Thompson."
The Toronto Sun, 2 April. http://www.torontosun.com/sports/basketball
/2010/03/09/13174601.html.

Yosso, T.J. 2005. "Whose Culture Has Capital? A Critical Race Theory Discussion of Community Wealth." *Race, Ethnicity and Education* 8(1): 69–91.

Zurum, D. 2012. "The Rise of Andrew Wiggins: The Best High School Baller on Earth." *Sportsnet*, 13 December. Accessed March 2016. http://www.sportsnet.ca/magazine/the-rise-of-andrew-wiggins-the-best-high-school-baller-on-earth/.

12

Marginalization of African Canadian Students in Mainstream Schools: Are Afrocentric Schools the Answer?

Edward Shizha

INTRODUCTION

The foundations of education and schooling in Canada are based on Eurocentric worldviews, ways of knowing, cultural capital, and pedagogical practices. Canada is regarded as an open and tolerant multicultural society that is receptive to cultural differences. However, when it comes to education and schooling, multiculturalism becomes contentious and questionable. The school curriculum in mainstream or Canadian public schools favours the ideology of the dominant Anglo-Canadian culture while marginalizing minority cultures. Among the marginalized cultures are the African Canadian worldviews and their fundamental cognitive orientations. Decades of research have documented African Canadian students' struggles in public schools, and scholars have examined reasons for African Canadian youth disengagement from the school system. While many factors contribute to this academic disengagement, one must be careful to generalize one reason over another (Dei et al. 1997). However, this chapter conceptualizes African Canadian youth's academic disengagement to be a result of cultural dissonance, racism, and discrimination perpetuated by the Canadian education system. One solution to overcome the marginalization of African Canadian students and their cultures in the mainstream schools has been the opening of publicly funded Afrocentric schools, with the first of such schools having been opened in January 2009 by the Toronto District School Board (TDSB).

There are arguments for and against Afrocentric schools. While some people argue that the schools are a progressive strategy to address and promote the academic achievement of the "failing" African Canadian youth, others see them as regressive and promoting self-segregation, stigmatization, and educational apartheid. This chapter argues that, while Afrocentric schools, theoretically, might promote African Canadian students' self and cultural identity and improve their academic performance, the schools have unintended consequences, and may be accused of being dysfunctional to social integration and national unity. The chapter provides a theoretical discourse for and against Afrocentric schools, and concludes that transformational changes should be made to the Canadian mainstream school curriculum to promote cultural and knowledge inclusivity. An inclusive curriculum, which is culturally and pedagogically responsive to the needs of diverse students, challenges the conservative and conformist educational environment by organizing itself around a holistic model of common principles, while making the curriculum inclusive of the totality of students' lived experiences.

THE RACE ISSUE

It is worth noting from the onset that, in this chapter, I do not intend to use the racialized categories "black" and "white" in terms of people's biological, anthropological, or genetic attributions. I deliberately avoid using these racial categories, because I do not believe that there are people whose pigmentation reflects those colours. Racial categorization of people is a legacy of colonial and historical "slave–master" relationships. Race is primarily socio-political, and racial categories are perpetuated and reinforced by racist attitudes and prejudices. It is my argument, however, that race is not mainly a biological matter but primarily a socio-political construct that emerged from colonialism and slavery.

The sorting and classification of people into races in contemporary society has generally been done by powerful groups for purposes of maintaining and extending their own power. From the dominant groups' views (Eurocentric in Canada), racial distinctions are a necessary tool of dominance. They serve to separate the subordinate people as the "Other" (those who have experienced subjugation, slavery, exploitation, and miscegenation). Because of biological or cultural characteristics, which are labelled as inferior by powerful groups in society, minorities are often singled out for differential and unfair treatment. Biological characteristics do not define racial groups; rather, these groups are defined by how they have been treated historically, politically, economically, and socially. Society assigns people to racial categories, not because of science or fact, but because of opinion and social experience. The construction of race is a synthesis of contradictions born from social relations and contradictory forces (Du Bois 1986). It is the differential and unfair treatment of "Otherized" racial categories that gave rise to Afrocentrism and Afrocentric schools. Unfortunately, even people of African origin have consciously or unconsciously accepted these otherized racial labels, which need deconstruction. Consequently, the terms "Africans" or "people of African origin" and "Europeans" or "people of European origin" (the geographical origins of one's ancestors) will be used throughout this chapter.

AFROCENTRISM: THE CONCEPT

The contributions of African scholars have been remarkable, but often overshadowed by politics of invisibility resulting from a lack of information and intentional distribution of misinformation (Rivera 1995) about the achievements of minority groups in society. Because of political invisibility, minority groups sometimes feel a sense of powerlessness and neglect. Invisibility is a trap that leads to resignation and retreatism from the mainstream society. Even in the field of education, the discourse on educational theory and practice on the school achievements (success or failure) of African Canadians have not been a priority in the mainstream Canadian education system. Subsequently, Afrocentrism arose out of this concern.

Afrocentrism is a controversial but popular movement in schools and universities across North America, as well as in African American and Canadian communities. It is a theoretical, ideological, and nationalist perspective that arose from the oppression of people of African origin, particularly in the United States of America (USA). The origins of Afrocentrism lay in the African American nationalistic fight for recognition, acknowledgement, and emancipation. The ideology is grounded in historical thought and the continued marginalization of African history, culture, and symbolisms in the mainstream North American society, particularly in the education system. Advocates of Afrocentrism argue that the contributions of various African people are largely ignored, downplayed, or discredited due to the legacy of colonialism and slavery's pathology of "writing Africans out of history" (Andrade 1990, 91). Andrade cites Hegel's racist (mis)representation of Africa as outside history as an indication and reflection of the archival gaps that imperialism produces. She argues, "Although Africa's silence in hegemonic European historical discourse should be acknowledged, its absence from the world history must of course be rejected" (1990, 91).

Afrocentric ideology, as a cultural and political thought, seeks to deconstruct, transform and reconfigure the misconstrued and misconceptualization of Africans and people of African origin in the Diaspora. At its most fundamental level, Afrocentrism argues that "[m]any African-Americans, particularly children and youth, suffer from an ethnic identity crisis and that rediscovering West African and Egyptian philosophies holds the promise of cultural transformation for *people of African origin* [*original term substituted*]. Building ethnic pride, strengthening knowledge about African history, and fostering a worldview that values community, balance, and harmony is one promising strategy to improve the quality of life for *people of African origin*" [*original term substituted*] (Ginwright 2004, 17). The Afrocentric idea as a cultural configuration, Dragnea and Erling (2008) contend, stems from an intense interest in psychological location as determined by symbols, motifs, rituals, and signs; a commitment to finding the subject-place of Africans in any social, political, economic, architectural, literary, or religious phenomenon; a defense of African cultural elements as historically valid; a celebration of centredness and agency that eliminates pejoratives about Africans or other people; and a powerful imperative from historical sources to revise the collective text of African people.

Molefi Kete Asante (2003, 2008), who is regarded as the "father" of the Afrocentric ideology, argues that Afrocentrism encourages African Americans to discard their recent history, with its inescapable Eurocentric domination and so-called "European supremacy," and instead to embrace an empowering vision of their Africanness and the history of their ancestors (specifically and controversially, Egyptians) as the source of western civilization. Asante (2008) uses Afrocentrism as a cultural perspective that examines and explores the existential reality of African people in order to present an innovative interpretation on the modern issues confronting people of African origin in contemporary society. Asante (2003) defends the necessity for African people to view themselves as agents and subjects instead of objects on the fringes of Europe, and proposes a more democratic framework for human relationships. Charles Mills (1997) argues that Eurocentrism and Afrocentrism are both the outcome of a history of racist practices and assumptions that serve to actively exclude or denigrate the perspectives and ideas of those whom the dominant culture labels "sub-persons."

While some Africanists support Afrocentrism as an ideological discourse that helps Africans in the Diaspora understand their history, origins, and ethnic identities (Dei 2006), others reject the idea that it explains African American history. Walker (2001) labels it "therapeutic mythology" for healing the "psychological wounds" of African Americans to promote their self-esteem by creating a past that never was. Controversially, Walker insinuates that Afrocentrism is not historical but a form of nationalism. In fact, he argues that the origins of Afrocentrism lay in African American nationalism of the Romantic era, but he rejects it as history. For Walker, Afrocentrism is simply bad history which promotes a feel-good myth of the past in tackling problems that still confront people of African origin in a racist society. Walker claims that historians should help African American students to appreciate their "own real history" that offers them an identity worthy of enormous pride and to avoid pursuing "distortions of the past" in the name of identity. Walker's argument and prescription rob African Americans and/or African Canadians of their full history. He seems to allude that their history is limited to the contemporary experiences in North America, and that what happened before their ancestors came to North America is not history but mythology!

Another criticism of Afrocentrism is that it reverses racism as it distances people of African origin from the mainstream society. Because it re-invents hierarchies of knowledge and promotes unequally the belief that ancient Africa was the source of cultural and intellectual achievements that have been systematically denied or suppressed by Europeans, Afrocentrism is questioned on its neutrality. It is, in this respect, alleged to be an inversion of the perceived racial hierarchies of Eurocentric history. Perhaps, it could be described as "Eurocentrism in an African face." Furr (1996) criticizes Afrocentrism for being racist and highly conservative and divisive. According to Furr, it victimizes students of African origin who are almost exclusively exposed to the ideology (assuming that non-Africans are excluded from the Afrocentric discourse). In addition, Afrocentrism is perceived by critics as based on a misrepresentation of history that lacks historical truth. Its foundation is based on early Egyptian civilization, without taking into consideration the inventions and early civilizations of Africans in sub-Saharan Africa. The omission of sub-Saharan African historical inventions, civilization, and intellectual achievements is in itself viewed as racism. However, given the popularity of Afrocentrism and its spread through the academic community and popular culture, anyone teaching in multicultural schools or interested in multiperspective methodologies should educate themselves about Afrocentrism.

RATIONALIZING AFROCENTRIC SCHOOLS

Many African Canadian parents and communities are highly dissatisfied by the treatment their children receive in mainstream schools. They are not happy with pedagogical practices in schools, the curriculum content and its portrayal of minority groups, and the interaction between their children and mainstream teachers who are mainly of European origin. There is a cultural mismatch and dissonance between school knowledge and the culture of minority students that result in African Canadian students failing. As a result, minority students continue to remain behind students of European backgrounds. In addition, there is a high dropout rate among African Canadian students. One argument for setting up an Afrocentric school in Toronto was to curb the excessive 40 per cent dropout rates among Toronto District School Board's 30,000 African Canadian students (Hopper 2011).

Promoting Academic Achievement

It is an acknowledged fact that mainstream schools fail students of minority backgrounds. Dei (2006) argues that, despite its notable successes, the public education system fails many students, as evidenced by the disengagement, failure, and high dropout rates for African Canadians, Aboriginal, and other minority youths. He suggests a "re-visioned schooling" model in the form of African-centred schools that, according to supporters, affirm identities and myriad experiences of learners by providing a holistic education. The general belief among parents of African Canadian students is that mainstream teachers are insensitive to the history and culture of minority groups, and that this accounts for the high failure and dropout rates among African Canadian students. African voices have been speaking in Canada for a very long time; yet, their discourses are pushed back to the margins. Many students and parents are challenging mainstream schools to be more inclusive in their academic practices. Dissatisfied with mainstream practices, African Canadian educators and community groups are increasingly mobilizing to define their own educational agenda, and to seek alternative models and approaches for educating their children.

According to the British educational theorists Frank Reeves and Mel Chevannes (1983), mainstream psychological and sociological frameworks have participated in the ideological construction of underachievement among students of African origin (as cited in Henry, 1993). The internalization of an "inferior status" plays an undeniable role in the academic achievement (Fordham and Ogbu 1986; Shannon and Bylsma 2002) of students of African backgrounds who often come from lower-income families, and some of those students may be learning English as a second language. These factors militate against school achievement. Some researchers have found that, when students of African origin exhibit their potentialities, abilities, and competencies, they are accused by their colleagues of "acting European" (Fordham and Ogbu 1986).

Schools and teachers should address the specific learning needs of diverse students in their care. Durden (2007) supports an African-centred education for its specific instructional practices that address the unique learning styles of African Canadian students, and advocates for a curriculum that is rooted in the reality and history of African people. Studies have found that minority students encounter less opportunity to learn, inadequate instruction and support, and lower expectations from their schools and teachers (Haycock 2002; Mubenga 2006). Accordingly, offering students of African backgrounds an African-centred education is a means of providing adequate education to students who may be at risk (Marks and Tonso 2006). The solution to "their" underachievement is having schools that cater for "their" specific cultural needs. Supporting Afrocentric schools, Dragnea and Erling (2008, 3) argue that "African-centered education is committed to cultural as well as academic and social goals." Teachers teach students about their culture, about life, and about their role in society and the world, while maintaining high expectations.

Institutional Racism

One justification for establishing Afrocentric schools is that institutional racism is a trademark of mainstream schools in North America. According to Macpherson (1999), "Institutional racism is the collective failure of an organization to provide an appropriate and professional service to people because of their colour, culture, or ethnic origin. This can be seen or detected in processes, attitudes, and

194   *Edward Shizha*

behaviour that amount to discrimination through unwitting prejudice, ignorance, thoughtlessness, and racist stereotyping which dis-
advantages people in ethnic minority groups" (cited in McKenzie
and Bhui 2007, 649). Institutional racism also refers to "ways in
which racist beliefs or values have been built into the operations of
social institutions in such a way as to discriminate against, control
and oppress various minority groups" (McConnachie, Hollingsworth,
and Pettman 1988, 24). Often, institutional racism is covert or even
unrecognized by the agents involved in it. Race and racism inform
our subjective realities and structure unequal material relations in
contemporary Canadian society. Arguably, racism systemically per-
vades institutions within Canadian society and permeates our being
and consciousness. Unfortunately, mainstream teachers of European
origin employ individualization, blame the victim, and situate racism
as a student's problem to avoid implicating themselves or their
school within racism. The majority of schools in Canada are controlled, managed, and administered by those who are in power because of their racial and economic backgrounds. The dominant and
powerful socio-racial groups live and experience life from a privileged position and it is, indisputably, difficult for them to understand
others' experiences of prejudice, discrimination, marginalization, mis-
judgement, misinterpretation, and mistreatment.

By virtue of their skin pigmentation, mainstream teachers and school
administrators label students from minority backgrounds as inherently inferior to mainstream students despite the success of minority
students under difficult and unfriendly school socio-cultural environments. The skin pigmentation of people of European backgrounds
is erroneously associated with power and intellectual capabilities.
According to Delpit (1995), power relations are enacted in the classroom, and there are codes or rules for participating in power; that is,
there is a "culture of power" whose rules reflect the rules of the culture
of those who have power. These aspects of power indicate that power
is experienced differently with minorities not participating in the "culture of power." The founding of Afrocentric schools came out of the
realization that those with power were failing African Canadian students by foisting their cultural codes and cultural power on minority
students. Clearly, African students and parents felt that the students
were being treated unfairly, making the students feel intellectually and
socially incompetent.

Those who support Afrocentric schools emphasize the need for the
schools to embrace anti-discrimination and anti-racist initiatives. These

initiatives are regarded as efforts that will address race-based, national origin, and ethnic discriminatory actions (Rivera 1995). With these initiatives, schools will be able to expand critical awareness and thinking and to enable both teachers and students to challenge stereotypes, misconceptions, and ignorance. In Canada, the Afrocentric School in Toronto is perhaps an empirical example of an anti-racist initiative. Its purpose is to fight against racism and marginalization in an attempt to secure a positive, future space for African Canadian children (Allahar 2010). Some Canadians argue that the multicultural discourse within multiculturalism as a Canadian policy allows racial and ethnic groups to practise their culture; therefore, the policy takes care of anti-racism and anti-discrimination. According to Leman (1999),

"Multiculturalism" in Canada refers to the presence and persistence of diverse racial and ethnic minorities who define themselves as different and who wish to remain so. Ideologically, multiculturalism consists of a relatively coherent set of ideas and ideals pertaining to the celebration of Canada's cultural mosaic. Multiculturalism at the policy level is structured around the management of diversity through formal initiatives in the federal, provincial and municipal domains. Finally, multiculturalism is the process by which racial and ethnic minorities compete with central authorities for achievement of certain goals and aspirations. (n.p.)

Multiculturalism, as a policy and in practice, tends to reinforce structural differences and ethnic inequalities. As Allahar observes, "As a capitalist society where social inequality is a structural feature of the wider economy and polity, and also as a society in which systemic racism is an acknowledged reality, the ideology of multiculturalism clashes with the lived racism experienced by working-class immigrants of color, and it is in this context that leaders of the Caribbean diaspora in Canada have based calls for the creation of a [African]-Focused School" (Allahar 2010, 57).

Schools that emphasize both a cross-cultural curriculum and multiple pedagogies nurture valuable experiences in students and acknowledge the contributions of every social group in a multicultural Canada. Students are culturally heterogeneous, and there is no place for racism, discrimination, prejudice, and racist attitudes. These schools are seen as models of anti-racist education. Further, Dei (2006) contends that success for African Canadian students and the ability to root out symbolic violence will flow from this vision of education. The Afrocentric ideology transforms schools from an "ordinary" learning setting to learning narratives that are based on multi-stories of teachers, students, and members of the community who envision the school as a socially just place.

Cultural Recovery

African people living both on the mainland and in the Diaspora have a strong attachment to their continent, their culture, and their spirituality. Their beliefs, ideological worldviews, ways of knowing, epistemologies, ontologies, preferences, and practices are shaped and guided by their culture. What identifies Africans from others is their rootedness in African spirituality, cultural belongingness, and indigeneity. The term "Afrocentric" refers to a framework or ideological perspective that places Africa at the centre of "political, economic, cultural, and spiritual life" (Ginwright 2004, 17). African-centred thought among Africans in the Diaspora is a response to what Clovis Semmes defines as "European cultural hegemony" (1995, 12). Afrocentrism is viewed as a form of cultural nationalism (Moses 1996) through which Africans in the Diaspora could redress the effects of cultural hegemony. It is a political project that deconstructs the universality of Eurocentric cultural knowledge. As cultural nationalism and a political project, Afrocentrism rejects the dominant framework that edifies Europe as the origin and centre of all modern knowledge. Afrocentric schools came into existence as a response to Moses's cultural nationalism.

African-centred schools, just like Islamic schools or German schools, are considered as schools that provide an alternative education to the mainstream public schools. Dei (1994) argues that the basic principles of African-centred schools are the social, political, cultural, and spiritual affirmation of Africa and its historical ties. These principles among the African Diaspora communities are crucial to the educational objectives of their schools. Kofi Lomotey adds to this argument by stating, "African-centered education enables African American students to look at the world with Africa as the center. It encompasses not only those instructional and curricular approaches that result in a shift in a student's worldview, but engenders a reorientation of their values and actions as well" (1992, 456).

The rationale behind establishing these schools is that they allow African students to identify with their culture and history and to learn more effectively, because the schools are culturally grounded and will be able to link issues of individual or group identities with what goes on at school. Afrocentric educators believe that centring students within their own cultural frames of reference helps them to connect emotionally, politically, socially, ideologically, and spiritually to the learning process (Agyepong 2010). According to Dei (2005), an Afrocentric school is an alternative system of education whose objective is to promote student engagement by providing an atmosphere that is culturally compatible and free from negative racial and cultural biases.

African-centred pedagogy focuses on generating self-knowledge, critical thinking and consciousness in the midst of a European supremacist reality (Murrell 2002). Resting on the importance of education as a means of liberation and social action for people of African descent, those within African-centred education posit that education provided to students of African descent becomes a primary means of transforming the current realities of African people (Maat and Carroll 2012). It is an educational setting that deconstructs Eurocentric hegemony in the administrative structures, school curriculum, teaching staff, and the epistemological foundation. Altogether, an African-centred curriculum challenges the universality of Eurocentric philosophies, worldviews, and ways of knowing and experiencing the world. The school emphasizes Afrocentric ontologies and epistemologies in curriculum development and pedagogies. Afrocentric education "is understood as the critical analysis of African[a] life, history and culture from the perspective of African[a] people, with the ultimate goal of changing the life chances of African[a] people" (Maat and Carroll 2012, 1). In all probability, Afrocentric education and schooling provide some kind of holism which is useful when attempting to clearly discuss the overall interpretation of knowledge orientations in the classroom. They replace or counter-act the cultural misorientation (Kambon 2005), psychological misorientation (ya Azibo 1989), and materialist depression (ya Azibo and Dixon 1998) that attempt to describe specifically the psychology of African people (Maat and Carroll 2012). As many African-centred scholars have maintained, the spirituality of African people is a defining characteristic that uniquely reflects their lived reality.

Identity Politics

African Canadian youths struggle with their identity; therefore, membership with Afrocentric ideology and institutions is their gateway to socio-cultural belongingness and identity politics (James 2010). Africans in the Diaspora are conspicuous because of their racial identities, and, as such, a diasporic identity is easily related to the notion of "soft primordialism" (Allahar 1994), where a socially constructed, imagined cultural sense of belonging can assume the strength of blood ties and can come to inform political action (Allahar 2010). "Soft" primordialism views primordial attachments (blood or culture ties as bonds of identity) as evolving from history and a myth of a common homeland rather than from blood ties or cultural heritage (Joireman 2003). Essentially, this means that the defining elements of ethnic/cultural identification are psychological and emotional rather than biological.

African students in mainstream schools struggle with their identity, and both students and mainstream teachers react to this identity-perception gap (the "gap" between the desired identity and the perceived identity). Mainstream teachers are likely to misinterpret the identity and self-perceptions of African Canadian students. According to Toshalis (2010, 15), "urban teaching is identity work. In classroom situations, teachers (and students too) confront social, psychological, and political challenges as they try to promote the achievement of hundreds of students who emerge from a multiplicity of backgrounds." These misperceptions lead to mislabelling of African students as incapable, dull, passive, rude, and unteachable. The cultural differences and different ideological worldviews shared by teachers and students appear to create a gap between what teachers teach and how African students learn. The function of ideological worldviews is "not to offer us a point of escape from our reality but to offer us the social reality itself as an escape" (Žižek 1999, 45). Teachers struggle to understand that they, like African students, are also "cultural beings and that their conceptions, decisions, and actions are culturally shaped and mediated. They sometimes do not recognize the salience and centrality of their own culture, and how it is woven through their work as teachers" (Milner 2010, 1). As teachers negotiate classroom relationships with their students across cultural, racial, linguistic, and socio-economic differences, they expose constructed identities and perceptions, which, if negatively reinforced in everyday encounters and interactions, might become a hindrance to academic performance and achievement, particularly among minority students.

Interactions between teachers and African Canadian students in public schools generate anxieties, especially when students face questions about who they are, who they should be, how they want others to see them and how others want them to be. In one of his seminal works, *The Souls of Black Folks* (1903), Du Bois (as cited in Wiggan 2010) elegantly discusses the veil that separates African Americans and people of European origin, and the "two-ness" or double consciousness that most African Americans face in the US as they are constantly forced to see themselves through the eyes of the "Other" (Euro-Americans) and are compelled to measure themselves against that "Other." Du Bois argued that this "two-ness" creates a great level of stress and discomfort in the lives of African Americans, because the racialized perceptions of the other remain a permanent feature in their psychology. The struggle with their identity conjures immense identity crises among students. Explaining the challenges of identity crises, Toshalis (2010) argues,

> The modern, Western constructions of identity as a singular, cohesive, durable "me" across multiple domains sometimes loses its explanatory power when teachers confront the ways their students interpret, label, and evaluate them differently than they do themselves. This may be why teachers so often express the need for what is suggested in the epigram – secure and stable identities that can withstand myriad interpersonal interactions that occur in classrooms on a daily basis, some of which may be prejudicial. (17)

African Canadian students and other minority students experience prejudicial interactions and interpretations of their behaviour because of the Western constructions of identity, which tend to be biased and politicized. Minority students are vulnerable to misrepresentations and to the insensitivity of teachers. They experience a form of insecurity that produces a sort of paralysis in their interactions with the teacher and other mainstream students, which disrupts their participation in classroom activities such that they are not free to express their opinions and ideas. Canadian schools create, recreate, and reinforce curricular and school environments that are inundated with European (Anglo-Saxon) cultural biases. Hence, Afrocentric schools provide African Canadian students with a sense of identity and common experience.

CRITICISM OF AFROCENTRIC SCHOOLS

While Afrocentric theorists see the positive outcomes from Afrocentric schools, there are criticisms that are levelled against the system.

Segregation or Separatist System

One major criticism of Afrocentric schools is that they introduce segregation and a separatist schooling system within the Canadian multicultural society. According to Winks (1997), the schools may represent a regression to the historical, race-based educational segregation. Given the mere fact that Afrocentric schools are likely to exclude other racial groups, they may act as gated communities. The community gates act to protect those inside from unwanted encounters with the otherness of others (Flusty 2004). Those who argue against Afrocentric schools insist that the isolation caused by this "educational apartheid" will harm and isolate African Canadian students in the long-run (Thompson and Thompson 2008), when the students fail to integrate into the mainstream society. Mainstream schools that are multiracial and multicultural are perceived to play the role of preparing young ones for Canadian society. On the other hand, segregated schools enclose the daily lives of students from the broader society, replacing wider interaction with limited subcultural interactions. Fredericks (2010) claims that belongingness is experienced in everyday relations as constructed within the exclusionist schools. While the importance of the everydayness of belonging and attachment cannot be ignored, the schools create barriers to rich experiences found in multicultural schools or mainstream schools.

Stigmatization or Stigmatism

Isolating students within their own ethno-racial schools opens them to possible stigmatization. According to Allman (2013), stigma and the act of stigmatizing are common and recognizable forms of social exclusion resulting from prejudices. Students from Afrocentric schools are likely to face and experience prejudice and stereotypes. They may be labelled as "those students" (the "us" and "them" phenomenon) and experience other negative inferences about their abilities and scholarly aptitudes. Stigma lead certain individuals to be "systematically excluded from particular sorts of social interactions because they possess a particular characteristic or are a member of a particular group" (Kurzban and Leary 2001, 187). The latent effect of Afrocentric schools is promoting the functionality of "outsiderness." Either those participating in the schooling system will view those in the mainstream schools as outsiders, or those students in Afrocentric schools will be perceived by the mainstream society as outsiders.

Stigmatization occurs when the evaluation of the students' school performance and outcomes gets discredited. The fact that Afrocentric schools have not been well received by some members of Canadian society, and even by some among African-Canadian communities, is a matter of concern and will result in the stigmatization of the schools and students.

Diversity among African Canadians

African Canadians are not homogeneous. There is no universal acceptance and agreed definition of an African Canadian. For example, there is reluctance and disdain among some Jamaican Canadians to be classified as African Canadians. African culture or Caribbean culture is not universal among people of African origin. Among the African Canadians, there are those who are from the African continent and the Caribbean and those who are born in Canada. Even among those from the continent, their ethnic cultures are diverse. Therefore, those opposed to Afrocentric schools question how these schools cater for this diversity. As Thompson and Thompson (2008, 47) report, "While advocates of the plan have failed to address the many diversities encapsulated within the umbrella of 'African-Canadian,' critics are quick to point out that a hegemonic [European] power structure cannot be resolved by [African-Canadian] retreat." Even within the Afrocentric school system, the proliferation of cultural differences may lead to cultural conflict and a collision of ethnic cultures. What mechanisms are in place to avoid cultural conflict in order to promote co-existence and tolerance? In his prescient article "Identity and Culture," Deloria (1981) argues that inter-ethnic relations are premised on power relationships. Weaker ethnic communities are likely to be marginalized or to get assimilated by the stronger ethnic groups, and the once-vital subcultures might lose their vigour and distinctiveness. Measures have to be taken to make sure that the schools are truly multiethnic and that there is "equal" representation of ethno-cultural knowledge within the curriculum.

CONCLUSION

While having a separate schooling system, such as Afrocentric schools, could alleviate the learning difficulties of African Canadian students, there is a need to rethink and revision the education system, curriculum, teaching personnel, and pedagogical practices. Afrocentric schools are a short-term solution to the academic needs of minority students. They do not provide a permanent solution that benefits all students regardless of their racial affiliation. Afrocentrism should be applied across the official curriculum in all schools. An inclusive curriculum that provides and promotes a transformative approach to education is desirable. A transformative approach "actually changes the core and the nature of the curriculum by infusing (not just by addition) multiple views and perspectives into the curriculum – so that the curriculum is not representative of only one dominant view or way of experiencing the world" (Milner 2010, 44). Afrocentric schools tend to lose the focus on deconstructing the mainstream curriculum. When it is applied selectively and/or exclusively to particular schools, it defeats the purpose for which it has been designed. We live in an inclusive society where African Canadian students interact with students of other racial and ethnic identities. Mainstream schools that teach and present curriculum material to their students from multiple perspectives enrich their students and prepare them for the contemporary Canadian multicultural society. The curriculum should strive to create new forms of discourse about African Canadian worldviews, intellectual achievements, and historical contributions.

Educational transformation should have an impact on education by implementing an inclusive curriculum, changing the biased language used in schools to reflect a holistic universe that incorporates conversations originating from Africa, Asia, Europe, the Caribbean, and the Americas. Schools should found a renaissance based on commitment to fundamental ideas of diversity, agency, centredness, and cultural location. A transformative curriculum gives all students (regardless of their racial or ethnic affiliation) opportunities to engage in critical thinking and to develop more reflective thinking about what they are learning. Curriculum knowledge should reflect community knowledges and not only knowledge of the dominant socioeconomic group in Canada. Mainstream schools should adapt inclusive knowledge that prepares children to live and play their adult roles in a Canadian multicultural society. Proponents of Afrocentrism and Afrocentric or/and other "separatist" schools in Canada should fight against knowledge biases and misrepresentations that are taking place in mainstream schools. It is important to focus on correcting these curriculum biases and other misrepresentations and under-representations, rather than creating a parallel school system that "corrects" knowledge for some, while leaving others misinformed. Retreating from the mainstream schools is a defeatist attitude that will continue to haunt the learners through stigmatization, labelling, and ostracism. African Canadian educators and parents should focus on fighting the prejudices in the mainstream schools, and advocate for curriculum transformation and critical anti-racist epistemologies and pedagogies. The mainstream curriculum should be inclusive, and the staffing process in schools should also be inclusive. Mainstream schools must also have minority teachers who act as physical role models who bring diverse histories, value orientations, and experiences to the classroom.

REFERENCES

Allahar, A.L. 1994. "More Than an Oxymoron: Ethnicity and the Social Construction of Primordial Attachment." *Canadian Ethnic Studies* 26(3): 18–33.
– 2010 "Political Economy of 'Race' and Class in Canada's Caribbean Diaspora." *American Review of Political Economy* 8(2): 54–86.
Allman, D. 2013. "The Sociology of Social Inclusion." *Sage Open January–March* 3(1): 1–16.
Andrade, S.Z. 1990. "Rewriting History, Motherhood, and Rebellion: Naming an African Women's Literary Tradition." *Research in African Literatures* 21(1): 91–110.
Asante, M.K. 2003. *Afrocentricity*. Trenton: Africa World Press.
– 2008. *An Afrocentric Manifesto: Toward an African Renaissance*. Oxford: Polity Press.
Agyepong, R. 2010. "Black-Focused Schools in Toronto: What Do African-Canadian Parents Say?" PhD diss., University of Toronto.
Dei, G.J.S. 1994. "Afrocentricity: A Cornerstone of Pedagogy." *Anthropology and Education Quarterly* 25(1): 3–28.
– 2005. "Speaking Out with Professor George Dei: The Idea of a 'Black Focused' School Is Not New." *Ghanaian Mirror* 2(2): 12–13.
– 2006. "Black-Focused Schools: A Call for Re-visioning." *Education Canada* 46(3): 27–31.
Dei, G.J.S., J. Mazzuca, E. McIsaac, and J. Zine. 1997. *Reconstructing 'Dropout': A Critical Ethnography of the Dynamics of Black Students' Disengagement from School*. Toronto: University of Toronto Press.
Deloria, V., Jr. 1981. "Identity and Culture." *Daedalus* 11(2): 13–27.
Delpit, L. 1995. *Other People's Children: Cultural Conflict in the Classroom*. New York: The New Press.
Dragnea, C., and S. Erling. 2008. *The Effectiveness of Afrocentric (Black-Focused) Schools in Closing Student Success and Achievement Gaps: A Review of the Literature*. Etobicoke, ON: Toronto District School Board.

Du Bois, W.E.B. 1986. "Dusk of Dawn an Autobiography of a Race Concept." In *Du Bois Writings*, edited by N. Huggins, 358–547. New York: The Library of America.

Durden, T.R. 2007. "African Centered Schooling: Facilitating Holistic Excellence for Black Children." *Negro Educational Review* 58:23–34.

Flusty, S. 2004. *De-Coca-Colonization: Making the Globe from the Inside Out.* London: Routledge.

Fordham, S., and J. Ogbu. 1986. "Black Students' School Success: Coping with the 'Burden of Acting White.'" *Urban Review* 18:176–206.

Fredericks, B. 2010. "What Health Services within Rural Communities Tell Us about Aboriginal People and Aboriginal Health." *Rural Society* 20: 10–20.

Furr, G. 1996. *Fallacies of Afrocentrism.* Accessed 6 March 1996. http://msuweb .montclair.edu/~furrg /afrocent.html.

Ginwright, S.A. 2004. *Black in School: Afrocentric Reform, Urban Reform, and the Promise of Hip-Hop Culture.* Columbia, NY: Teachers College Press.

Haycock, K. 2002. "State Policy Levers: Closing the Achievement Gap." *National Association of State Boards of Education* 1:7–13.

Henry, A. 1993. "Missing: Black Self-Representations in Canadian Educational Research." *Canadian Journal of Education* 18(3): 206–22.

Hopper, T. 2011. "Africentric High School Approved for Toronto, Critics Fear Segregation." *The National Post*, 2 April. http://news.nationalpost.com /2011/11/16/africentric-high-school-approved-for-toronto-critics-fear-segregation/.

James, C.E. 2010. *Seeing Ourselves: Exploring Race, Ethnicity and Culture.* Toronto: Thompson Educational Publishing.

Joireman, S.F. 2003. *Nationalism and Political Identity.* London: Continuum.

Kambon, K.K.K. 2005. "The Cultural Misorientation Construct and the Cultural Misorientation Scale: An Africentric Measure of European Cultural Misidentification among Africans in America." In *Afrocentric Traditions*, edited by J.L. Conyers, 15–34. New Brunswick: Transaction Publishers.

Kurzban, R., and M. Leary. 2001. "Evolutionary Origins of Stigma: The Functions of Social Exclusion." *Psychological Bulletin* 127:187–208.

Leman, M. 1999. *Canadian Multiculturalism.* Ottawa: Political and Social Affairs Division, Parliament Research Branch.

Lomotey, K. 1992. "Independent Black Institutions: African-Centered Education Models." *Journal of Negro Education* 61(2): 456.

Maat, S.R.E.K., and K.K. Carroll. 2012. "African-Centered Theory and Methodology in Africana Studies: An Introduction." *The Journal of Pan African Studies* 5(4): 1–11.

Marks, J.B., and K.L. Tonso. 2006. "African Centered Education: An Approach to Schooling for Social Justice for African American Students." *Project Innovation* 126(3): 481–94.

McConnachie, K., D. Hollingsworth, and J. Pettman. 1988. *Race and Racism in Australia*. Sydney: Social Science Press.

McKenzie, K., and K. Bhui. 2007. "Institutional Racism in Mental Health Care." *British Medical Journal* 33(4): 649–50.

Mills, C. 1997. *The Racial Contract*. Ithaca, NY: Cornell University Press.

Milner, H.R. 2010. "Developing a Multicultural Curriculum in a Predominantly White Teaching Context: Lessons from an African American Teacher in a Suburban English Classroom." In *Culture, Curriculum, and Identity in Education*, edited by H.R. Milner, 37–75. New York: Palgrave Macmillan.

Moses, W. 1996. *Classical Black Nationalism: From the American Revolution to Marcus Garvey*. New York: New York University.

Mubenga, P.T. 2006. *Closing the Achievement Gap between African American Children and Their Caucasians Counterparts Using Collaboration Learning Setting*. ERIC Document Reproduction Service No. 490762.

Murrell, P.C. 2002. *African-Centered Pedagogy: Developing Schools of Achievement for African American Children*. Albany, NY: State University of New York Press.

Rivera, J. 1995. "The Politics of Invisibility." *Georgetown Journal on Fighting Poverty* 3:61–6.

Semmes, C. 1995. *Cultural Hegemony and African American Development*. Westport: Praeger.

Shannon, G.S., and P. Bylsma. 2002. *Addressing the Achievement Gap: A Challenge for Washington State Educators*. Olympia, WA: Office of Superintendent of Public Instruction.

Thompson, D., and J. Thompson. 2008. "Afrocentric Schools and the Politics of Invisibility." *The Ardent Review* 1(1): 45–9.

Toshalis, E. 2010. "The Identity-Perception Gap: Teachers Confronting the Difference between Who They (Think They) Are and How They Are Perceived by Students." In *Culture, Curriculum, and Identity in Education*, edited by H.R. Milner, 15–35. New York: Palgrave Macmillan.

Walker, C.E. 2001. *We Can't Go Home Again: An Argument about Afrocentrism*. New York: Oxford University Press.

Wiggan, G. 2010. "Afrocentricity and the Black Intellectual Tradition and Education: Carter G. Woodson, W. E. B. Du Bois, and E. Franklin Frazier." *The Journal of Pan African Studies* 3(9): 128–49.

Winks, R. 1997. *The Blacks in Canada: A History*. 2nd ed. Montreal & Kingston: McGill-Queen's University Press.

ya Azibo, D.A. 1989. "African-Centered Theses on Mental Health and a
Nosology of Black/ African Personality Disorder." *Journal of Black Psychology* 15(2): 173–214.

ya Azibo, D.A., and P. Dixon. 1998. "The Theoretical Relationship between
Materialistic Depression and Depression: Preliminary Data and Implications for the Azibo Nosology." *Journal of Black Psychology* 24(4): 211–25.

Žižek, S. 1999. *The Sublime Object of Ideology*. New York: Verso, 1999.

13

Reflections on African Canadian Education

George J. Sefa Dei
(Nana Sefa Tweneboah I)

INTRODUCTION

In this concluding chapter, similar to the purposes of Abdi (this volume), I broach some philosophical issues about black/African Canadian education while reflecting upon the terms of engagement in the dialogue on educational change in Canada. I start with an interrogation of certain aspects of Euro-Canadian schooling that is anchored in the liberalism and dictates of a capitalist modernity. Then I work with some of the ideas of "race literacy framework" as taken up by Guinier (2004) to interrogate and to make the case for African-centred schooling as a legitimate course of action for the black/African Canadian community as far as the education of our children is concerned.

My passion for the question of African Canadian youth schooling is to ensure that the school system works for all youth. Like many, I am impressed by the hard work of parents, students, and educators to ensure educational excellence for all. Usually, such work is not heralded and can be thankless. But we know that the many youth who dare to confront the future always look back with gratitude to the struggles and sacrifices of their peers, parents, school teachers, and the broader community that made it possible for them to be where they are. These youth are quick to tell you that education has been a big factor in their lives. This chapter is also a recognition of the long road ahead and the necessity of shifting gears to comprehend the complex dynamics of the challenge and possibilities of African Canadian schooling and education.

It is an understatement to point out that black/African Canadian youth education has been a major concern of educators, parents, and students in our community for years (see Cooper, this volume; Brathwaite and James 1996; Canadian Alliance of Black Educators 1992). What has so far been done with the extensive studies on black education in Canada and North America in general? Have these research studies been exercises in futility? Have we learned from the vast lessons of community activism when it comes to black education in Canada?

Not even a dozen full-sized manuscripts can document the political activism of interested bodies on this subject. There is a growing feeling that the community – in this case, black parents – can no longer wait for systemic change to happen. Friedland's and Alford's (1991) "dynamics without change" best describes the frustration. The "more things change, the more they remain the same." One can discern well-placed concerns about youth education at a variety of sites. From critiques about the pathologization of families and communities as being uninterested in youth education, to the dumbing down of parents and students, to teacher-bashing, as well as calls for the recognition of black students' agency, we see evidence of engagement in educational questions (Shizha; Nashon; Egbo; Cooper Diallo; this volume).

While schools are sites of indoctrination and reproduction of inequity, they are also sites of empowerment, resistance, and transformation. But how are we to articulate the fault-lines in these discussions?

Local communities have always been critical of the ways academic research assigns discursive authority for elite scholars to speak on behalf of others. In our supposedly scholarly engagements, there has been a failure to make a distinction between "school success" and "student success." The angry voices of parents, students, and local communities in revolt against our current educational system are usually dismissed. There is a collective realization among local communities that silence through the "culture of fear" can be detrimental to systemic change and transformation. In fact, our communities have always insisted upon an anti-colonial presence. This type of resistance emerges from the histories of struggles for educational change to empower youth to be responsible adults and to ask critical questions that challenge the status quo.

I acknowledge what may be a contradiction on my part. Here, I clearly charge that academics speak on behalf of communities, and yet it may appear I am doing this as well, even though I am pointing to the ways other scholarship has ignored community concerns. How do we get around this contradiction? Perhaps I need to make the distinction of "speaking with others" rather than "speaking for others," and also to emphasize the involvement of the academic/researcher in community and its politics as something that needs to be strived for.

Arguably, we live in a postcolonial context, which has provided, and continues to provide, an articulating tool to express the emerging conditions of the human. However, in doing so, the postcolonial exerts a particular disciplinary pressure on the colonial, while at the same time foregrounding the sense of belonging through different cultural forms and expressions. Race is one area for a critical engagement in the contemporary cultural politics of schooling (Ibrahim; Simmons; this volume). The centrality of reading race through the anti-colonial framework and the urgency to offer a counter-hegemonic reading that disrupts the production and dissemination of colonial knowledge marking the civilizing narratives of what it means to be a contemporary learner need to be interrupted. We can only succeed if we position identity (race, class, gender, sexuality, [dis]ability, and by extension, identifications) as historically constituted and laden with politics.

The practice of racism in schooling is manifested through the ontological presence of capitalist modernity. This modernity masks itself in a neo-liberal sway of fairness and justice, while a spirit of individualism, competition, and markets decide the fate of participants in the social and political economies of schooling. It is a phase of modernity that breeds a creeping survivalism in the arena of fierce market competition and a craze to provide education to the highest bidder. In this phase, questions of equity (if ever raised at all) can only be grasped in the marketplace of ideas and of which knowledge makes good business sense. One is lucky if one is able to compete. This is also the phase that embraces such buzz words as "accountability," "competence," "standards," "quality education," "individual responsibility," "choice," "freedom and individual rights." Furthermore, questions of identity as constituted through the intersections of race, class, gender, sexuality, ability, and religion come to be shaped and formed through the contours of capitalism (Thésée and Carr, this volume).

Particularly for the marginalized body in the Euro-colonial context, to have to construct one's identity by oneself is to resist this imperial and capitalist presence. In the context of a capitalist and Euro-colonial modernity, claiming identity has always been a struggle for African and black bodies. This is, in part, due to our identities being continuously constructed for us within an Euro-American ideology and hegemony. Even though we claim our identities, there are expectations as to what such claims should imply, and, at times, such claims of identity are misread as oversimplifications, and, hence, are dismissed or devalued. Even when we question the limits and the oppressive nature of the idea of "porosity of identity" – more especially, for someone who wears a black skin in a white dominated context – we are often heard as insisting on fossilized, static and bounded identities. The lived realities of our blackness (which is more than insisting on the complexities of our blackness) is always misread, misplaced, and questioned. What do the complexities of our blackness mean for anti-black racism?

This resistance is not simply a question of subverting the socioeconomic order. I am speaking about this resistance in terms of developing a critical, anti-colonial, anti-capitalist consciousness and intellectual stance. This is a huge challenge, since the imperial subject comes to know the self through relations of capital as capital forms itself within the present. We need critical anti-colonial education to help us think about the possibilities of the human condition outside the jurisdiction of the Western capitalist modernity. The anti-colonial context must help learners with counter and oppositional ways of knowing for the learner as a human being. Put another way, as we seek to understand the anti-colonial through the experience of culture, the imperial power must be challenged. We must take up the problematic of colonial relations as historically informing the human condition, and must find ways of working against the spaces of capitalist modernity.

In this context, critical education is about affirmation and resistance. In order to assist marginalized youth in affirming pride in culture, history, and collective identities, education must offer counter discourses to pathologization (of their homes, cultures, communities, and subjectivities). We must critique the seduction of the Euro-modernist framework, and ask some questions: How is such modernity constructed? What is absent and what are the limitations of modernity? How do we also implicate the modernist project in constructions of race? Is modernity itself a Eurocentric configuration? The idea of modernity is the result of colonialism. It is important to situate the idea of modernity in relation to colonial histories. Long ago, Charles Mills asked us to focus on the "racial dimension of European domination" that is manifest through liberalism's claims to a particular version of morality (Mills 1998, 98). The contemporary nation state is constructed upon racial hierarchies, and we must understand how hegemonic systems and hegemonic knowledges work to create dominance, advantage, and privilege, as well as subordination, disadvantage, and punishment for different bodies.

Very often, radical black and Indigenous educational politics that call for developing "distinctive Black or Indigenous voices" (as in demands about black self-determination, autonomy, and independence) are seen as heresy (Cooper, this volume). But for these communities, sometimes even strategic separation becomes a question of survival. In the contemporary context, when many black and Indigenous bodies are disenfranchised by the existing colonial and imperial order of schooling, a call for self-determination and community empowerment for black peoples (and, in fact, for all colonized peoples) has to be understood differently. It is a call for self- and collective preservation of black/African/Indigenous peoples, a call to take responsibility for our own problems and design our own futures. It is a call to think through solutions to the problems that confront our varied communities through a search for our voices and for an approach pursued on our terms. It is also a realization that responses to challenges we face cannot be filtered through the perspectives of the dominant and the colonizing apparatus/status quo or colonial governance.

If anything at all, what such calls speak against are oppressions in all their varied forms (not, in particular, the power and privilege of dominant bodies in formulating what is normal, valid, reasonable, neutral/objective, and acceptable). It is a call to assert our legitimate rights to valued goods and services of society as equal human bodies. Such calls have nothing to do with taking away other peoples' rights and freedoms or their access to valued goods and services of society. If our world today is about difference, then we must engage this difference. Unfortunately, we have not always done this. The celebratory approach of multiculturalism has failed, so far, to address critical issues of power and power sharing, hence the need to dialogue with critiques of multiculturalism in order to broach significant questions concerning power, equity, difference, and social responsibility, while also confronting questions of racism, sexism, homophobia, etc. It is important to acknowledge our differences and celebrate what we all bring to the table. But we must also be prepared to respond to the challenge that difference makes in our lives. In other words, difference should be an opportunity to acknowledge, validate ourselves, and to learn to share power (e.g., address key issues that afflict marginalized communities such as unemployment, housing, health, and the legal/criminal justice system). Identities (such as race, class, gender, sexuality, and disability) are real and consequential. We must affirm our identities in their complexities and wholeness, and be proud of who we are as a people.

In addressing schooling possibilities and challenges, we must look for points of synergy rather than of incongruence. A very structural-ized approach to schooling and education may not formally take on the other aspects of learning (i.e., ways of knowledge production, in-terrogation and validation, the place of embodiment in coming to know, the role of spirituality in education, etc.). Yet, these consider-ations help bring into focus a stronger first-person, experiential analysis in educational journeys. A focus on such areas still holds out a little hope for real, inclusive, antiracist, and anti-colonial change in schools.

RECLAIMING PAST, HISTORY, CULTURE, AND LANGUAGE AS CORNERSTONES FOR BLACK/AFRICAN CANADIAN EDUCATION: ACCOUNTING FOR THE INDIGENOUS

The past is always about memory and remembrance of our histories. The reference to the past is not about remaining static in that frame of mind, time, and space. The past teaches us lessons that should guide us on how we can live the present and move towards the future. The past evokes culture as central to our existence. The past is never lost. It is about power. The past is forever ingrained in the present and the fu-ture. It is the past that connects us to our histories, cultures, and In-digenous languages. Knowledge of the past is about place, location, and politics. Such knowledge works with history as a way of knowing and accounting for collective struggles, resistances, and contestations. We all came from somewhere/some place. We do not lose our past and our identities simply by becoming mobile subjects or migratory pat-terns. This is why any claims of identity must be related to land, place, culture, and memory. This means acknowledging the places we go and making connections from our connected past, histories, and cul-tures and how these continually shape identities about who and what we say we are and why. Our memories of the past help inform how we move to (new) places and come to inhabit certain spaces. To under-stand the politics of belonging to a given space, we must bring into sharp focus the intricate and dynamic connections of land, place, memory, past, and the present, as well as our psychic, spiritual, and cultural ties to knowledge and bodies. In the context of this paper, what all this points to is the powerful connections of identity (as in race, gender, class, sexuality, [dis]ability, language, religion, etc.), Indigeneity, and the struggles for decolonization.

Critical and oppositional discourses and practices in the (Western) academy are always met with charges of too much emphasis on romanticism of histories and identities, over-glorification of culture, and a fetishization of the past. But I do not see a tension in speaking about re-affirming culture, past, and history and engaging in broader systemic struggles against social oppressions such as racial, class, gender, disability, and sexual inequities. I also believe in the power of imaginary mythologies in helping us create communities that would work together collectively for systemic change.

In my own work, I have begun to rethink how a theoretical approach to anti-racism and black youth education would include an understanding of ongoing colonialisms, including the understanding of Canada as a colonial-settler state, and what this means for Indigenist, anti-colonial scholarship. As many have argued, anti-racism must also ask questions about implications and complicities. Anti-racism must centre on issues of how racialized immigrant bodies are implicated in white-settler colonial projects that oppress Indigenous peoples of Canada and on the responsibilities to resist ongoing colonizations of all forms. Rather than dismiss anti-racism as being a colonial project, I maintain that anti-racism is indispensable for those of us wanting to understand histories of racialization, colonization, and imperialisms, as well as classism, sexism, homophobia, and ableism and the way these oppressions and colonizations interconnect and affect us all (see various writings by Alfred and Corntassel 2005; Lawrence and Dua 2005; Sharma and Wright 2009; Smith 2010; Trask 1991; Waldron 2003).

I am also searching for discursive spaces that keep responsibility and complicity in the forefront. This is because ethics, responsibility, and complicity are critical for discussions about decolonized education. I have personally struggled with how we can begin by identifying educational sites when people are reclaiming spaces for decolonized education, mindful of the possible fluidity of identities (see also Egbo; James; Ibrahim; Simmons; this volume). It is possible to identify such sites or spaces without falling prey to dominant notions of what constitutes spaces of resistance and how such identifications could be implicated in the reorganization of colonization.

A major challenge of Eurocentrism as a worldview is how it continues to impose a "crisis of enunciation," particularly so (and more importantly so) within the locatedness of a self-referential analysis. Critical thinking requires that we work through this contention and seduction, and begin to interrogate the paradigms through which the ideas of "schooling and education" are produced. The normalizing gaze of schooling polices and scripts bodies, practice, and action, and any transgressions are punished accordingly. For example, there are established ways of producing, interrogating, and disseminating what is deemed valid knowledge, both within local, national, and international academies as institutions of learning and within local communities outside of "schooling." To lay claim to knowledge outside what is normal and ordinary comes with intellectual risks, especially when such knowledge is critical, oppositional, and resisting.

Reclaiming marginalized cultures, histories, and the past, including Indigenous knowledges and languages, constitutes a huge undertaking. As we know, for example, the colonist silencing of the "Native/Indigenous" languages occurred for many colonized and oppressed peoples. Language is not simply linked to culture; language actualizes a culture. Language makes a civilization and a humanity a national culture. The imposition of the colonizer's language is part of the colonial project of subjugation and the making of the colonial sub-human, as well as the coming into being of the colonized in the image of the colonizer. The colonized must be stripped of an identity, culture, and sense of self and history. Language is also a question of power, and the claiming of language as identity makes for the authenticity and power of the colonized. Language is critical to articulating one's identities and resistance. Language also presents the colonized body with another political question about colonialism and colonization. The colonized must continually engage the politics of language and address the colonial history of Europe and the continual presence of its language (English/French) of material power and cultural capital in the colonies. If Indigenous identity is also tied to language, then, for colonized and oppressed peoples, language is a battleground for collective/shared identities. Language then is about resistance.

UNDERSTANDING EDUCATIONAL SUCCESS

Elsewhere, we have outlined some of the challenges of writing and rewriting educational success (Dei et al. 2010). A major problem we are confronted with is how to subvert hegemonic conceptions and constructions of success and how it is achieved. Success must be perceived as collective rather than individual achievement. Success that is simply understood as individual is never lasting. It is lost when the individual is lost. Our collective success cannot be at the expense of the failure of others. Our definitions of success cannot be so restrictive as to leave others behind or to prevent others from identifying with them.

Schools, educators, and parents have a responsibility in exploring multiple assessment strategies in order to uncover the hidden talents and skills of our students. It is important to let students develop a sense of ownership of knowledge and of their schooling, and education is critical to ensuring success, broadly defined. Students also need support networks – in school and out of school – to succeed. Educators need to provide students with options and opportunities to display their brilliance, talents, and educational excellence. Both teachers' and parents' expectations of students and their children are critical to promoting brilliance in learners.

There is a concern that there is "too much schooling, too little education" (Shujaa 1994), that students go to school to learn skills and competencies, but such knowledge acquisition does not translate into a transformation of lives in terms of responsibilities and wider social expectations. Education is broader and may be concerned more with how students think and apply knowledge.

Schooling is also increasingly being geared towards the "best," "brightest," "smart," and "gifted," and there is a downside very inimical to youth learning in general. This prism is the counterpoint of the deficit model of education. The increasing use of tests and test scores have become the order of assessing the quality and performance of schools in a neo-liberal context. To play fair, there has been an insistence of standardizing curriculum and academic tests. But what does it mean to standardize the curriculum and the tests? What is being left behind, and what experiences, histories, and stories are being told or neglected? How are we reading these test results? Is it not a best approach to consider results over time, across regions, and among different populations to see who is or is not served by the school system? The "cult of individualism" helps create the competitive rather than the cooperative individual learner. Similarly, tests seek to sort students and create artificial boundaries and hierarchies. There is a current focus on merits/meritocracy, achievements, "standards," "quality," "accountability," "transparency," "excellence," etc., which are all fine, except there is no attempt to situate equity seriously and centrally in such discussions.

It has been asked whether exams are a true measure of our young learners' abilities. I would answer, "Not at all." Examinations only provide a
snapshot of what students have learned. They do not measure issues about
how students learned and the effects of such learning. They simply measure "what" students have learned at a particular time. They are definitely
one of the measures of abilities, for sure, but absolutely not the correct
measure of students' abilities. Students have multiple abilities, and the
"marks race" and the overemphasis on test scores can be detrimental. We
know of students who score well on tests but fail in terms of social responsibility and a connection to a community. Furthermore, there are restrictive, socio-economic conditions that stifle the abilities of children and
impinge on their learning and performance. When we focus simply on the
test, something may be missing. We also need to measure students' success
differently. Testing is one of many measurements.

Bad marks do not suggest learners are "dumb." Marks are only a partial reading of excellence. In fact, when we consider that exams are neither the true nor complete measure of childrens' abilities, then marks
in and of themselves present us with no effective measure of educational success. Bad marks may reflect a poor day for the student taking
the exams. They may reflect a student's inability to comprehend what
is on the test but not necessarily what has been learned and applied. I
would venture to argue that the issue of bad marks raises the whole
question of the curriculum. Was the syllabus or the curriculum on
which the student was examined reflective of the child's experience?
There is also the teacher's capability and effectiveness to make students
learn and excel. School failure can be reflective of the teacher's knowledge and performance, as well. If learners deserve to be in that class, is
such a bad mark not reflective of the teacher's failure to enhance success for the learner?

As already noted, the factors that may well affect students' performance include curriculum, classroom pedagogy, teacher expectations, cultural discontinuities in schooling and education, and a host
of socio-environmental and political factors. Many times, tests do not
gauge these pressures faced by young learners. This does not mean
there is no individual responsibility on the part of the learner. However, we must draw attention to a bigger picture that is often lost. Students learn differently, depending on their socio-economic and
cultural backgrounds. Language, identities, and cultures are critical
factors impinging on different and multiple learning styles of students.
For example, co-operative learning, rote learning, individual learning,

learning by example and by imitation point to differences in learning strategies, and it is incumbent upon schooling to explore the possibilities and challenges posed by each. There is a need for multiple assessment methods and evaluation strategies for students besides tests/exams. Assessments have to be age-, grade- and subject- specific. There are a host of opportunities for educators, including research projects, presentations, and hands-on, kinetic learning activities, all of which can incorporate multiple media approaches (see Duncan-Andrade and Morrell 2008).

Students who face challenges in school are often labelled and categorized. Disadvantaged youth are often tagged "at-risk." Using one term to describe a host of educational and social situations and conditions is problematic to begin with. We might start by asking what people mean. This will produce a host of results and, perhaps, might encourage us to investigate some of the assumptions that feed these misleading terms. "At-risk" is a label that does very little to help a child shine. It casts a shadow. We know that certain educational contexts produce "at-risk" youth, while others work as deterrents to students getting into trouble. We might better ask what aspects of the system are putting these children at risk. This is true of the notion of bad marks, as this ties into standardized comparisons and testing. Perhaps a better way to assess the system's success might involve looking at results over time, or in certain areas, or with certain populations. We might ask how the system is working to serve the diverse needs of a diverse student population. Which groups are consistently enabled to succeed and which are consistently unsupported?

Thus, there is a need for divestment from such nomenclature. The contested truth of the matter is that all learners are born with remarkable abilities of one form or another. There is some danger in conventional lines of questioning and designations, such as "at-risk," "successful," "smart," "bright," "high achievers," "failures," and "underachievers," etc., if the data supporting the "objective" determinations is measured by subjective educational measures. We need look no further than IQ tests, now widely recognized as culturally specific, to know that it is difficult to measure intelligence outside of a specific socio-cultural context (Nashon, this volume). Certain knowledges, abilities, and proclivities are obviously more celebrated than others in each educational context; hence, such designations seem difficult to make on purely empirical grounds, not to mention the positivist obsession that too often accompanies such claims.

As a matter of fact, students are best served by a variety of evaluation strategies. Students' learning must be assessed on a case-by-case basis which indicates that the student is learning differently. It would be worth considering which assignments have engaged the child and which have not.

COUNTER-VISIONING SCHOOLING
FOR BLACK/AFRICAN CANADIAN YOUTH

How do we re-imagine schooling and education? What are the possibilities of such new imaginings? We cannot operate as if there are no other possibilities for a new (educational and social) future. There must be new possibilities of schooling and education that will ensure success for all. For black bodies, schooling has not been "home" for us, despite pretensions to the schooling. Our educational success does not necessarily mean the "school" is a friendly environment and a cultural home. The school and the conventional educational site have been, and continue to be, alienating spaces for many of us. This is why many youth are perpetually searching for a place to belong. They are looking for spaces where they are not continually under the dominant gaze watching over them and punishing them for what may be deemed "black transgressions." This does not mean we do not want success and excellence. It is a question of asking and exploring what our existing understandings of "excellence" and "success" have come to mean and imply, and how they are achieved with differential costs for different bodies. In defining and charting an agenda for youth educational success, black leadership is key. We must consider solutions to our communities' educational challenges, problems, and possibilities.

A persistent debate in the education of black youth in Canadian and, particularly, in Ontario schools is the efficacy of the long-standing call for "focused schools" that cater to the needs of African Canadian youth. While many of us have written numerous times on the relevance of such counter schools, the persistence of ignorance about such schools also requires us to constantly keep reiterating our ideas. For one thing, it has been difficult to present a critical reading of the rationale and arguments for the school, because the terms of the debate have largely been set by the dominant/mainstream media, which has created a hysteria among the average Canadian. Unlike media preoccupation and (mis)representations, much of everyday public discussions about the school point to a search for knowledge. The seduction of media tales and sensationalism has also had a stranglehold even on many segments of the African Canadian community, who begin to interrogate the school using an Eurocentric lens that places dominant groups at the centre of their concerns. For example, what would mainstream society think of the focused school and the products of the school? What does it take by way of leadership, vision, and other pedagogic, curricular, and instructional changes to ensure the school meets its objective of redefined black excellence?

A number of African Canadian scholars, researchers, and community workers have pointed to the need to educate young African learners to resist the Europeanization of our minds, that is, to think outside the dominant norms and values of Eurocentricity. As black and minority learners and scholars, we need to search for our intellectual footing outside of the dominant paradigms. As educators, we have also been asked to ask new, critical, and not so comfortable questions. For example, why is it so difficult to try something different when we know the current school system is not working for some youth? What accounts for the resistance to finding other ways to educate the African child? How did we get to where we are at the moment in terms of beginning these discussions about creating counter spaces outside the school system for the education of black/African Canadian youth? Why are we surprised that some would argue for an African-centred school? (See also Dei 1993, 1995, 2008; Dei and Kempf 2013.)

We begin by appreciating the long history of black parental and community advocacy. The long history of community activism by the Black Education Project [BEP], The Black Liaison Committee [BLC], and the Black Heritage Association [BHA] in the 1970s, followed by the 1980's and 1990's community advocacy and educational work of such associations as the African Heritage Educators Network (AHEN), Scarborough Black Educators Organization (SBEO), Canadian Alliance of Black Educators (CABE), and the Organization of Parents of Black Children (OPBC) on behalf of black/African Education, is well documented (see Brathwaite and James 1996; CABE 1992). The questions that educators were asking in the early to mid-1900s are still with us: How do schools respond to the multiple needs, concerns, and aspirations of a diverse student body? How do we ensure that excellence is not simply accessible but also equitable to multiple bodies and partners? How do we ensure that all our students are able to develop a sense of connectedness to and identification with their schools, so they may claim that the school is for them? How do we move beyond the bland and seductive politics of inclusion to the pointed discourses of transparency and accountability (Dei 2008)?

Integration and inclusion have been very seductive and morally appealing concepts. Yet, when it comes to education of our children, what can African Canadian parents show so far for the success of integration? It seems that integration is being touted as an ideal, without critically examining what the costs are and to whom. How do we assess and measure the "success" and outcomes of "integration" and "educational inclusion"? Has integration, as we know it, been a good guarantor of success for all youth? (See also Dei and Kempf 2013.)

Separate schooling has been seen as inherently unequal rather than as an appreciation that what really makes a school "unequal" lies in our responses and reactions, as well as in the particular educational practices of the school. What does equality and equity mean in the context of a sustained history of colonialism, racism, oppression, and unequal power relations? True equity and integration do not mean one size fits all. Treating everyone the same does not necessarily mean justice and fair treatment. We have always been quick to refer to the US ruling of the mid 1950s that "ended" segregation as a reason not to encourage educational outlets that smack of opposition to "inclusion" and "integration."

Yet, as noted in Dei (2014, 25), in her insightful piece, Guinier (2004) argues that the Topeka Board of Education v. Brown case (1954) actually treated the symptoms of the disease rather than the disease. The decision gave formal credence to "formal equality" and not "substantive equality," which would entail making structural and fundamental changes to the broader economic, social, and political order. Guinier's (2004) "racial literacy framework" sheds further light on the Court's decision, pointing to the sway of the conventional "interest convergence" argument, the whole idea of how the interests of Northern white liberals converged with Southern black interests in demanding an end for segregation of schools. Such race literacy is insightful in helping us understand how race, class, and geography conflate and converge to maintain racial hierarchies, and how they also ensure that the plight of poor blacks and poor whites are ignored by larger society.

Guinier's (2004) theoretical analysis is influenced by US racial and class educational history and politics. I want to extrapolate and borrow freely from Guinier's (2004) arguments to show the relevance for the "focus school" debate in Canada. I would point to the following as failures of the Board v. Brown decision and how the reasoning of desegregation has embedded cultural logics that need proper contextualization.

First, separation is always read negatively as being about exclusion, creating an inferior space, or seeking to advantage. It has never been read as something positive (i.e., solution-oriented), an approach to self- and collective determination. In fact, there is a whole falsehood in the idea that separation generated feelings of black inferiority; that is, separation has a relation to black personality development, a stigma of self-hate. Such thinking is built on the "psychological damage imagery" (Guinier 2004). There is a "myth of Black racial inferiority." Did separation make blacks feel inferior, or did the mindset of whites about what is superior and inferior cause this? There is the failure to see the interconnectedness of black inferiority and white supremacy, or in other words, a double-sidedness which itself is a creation of the dominant and the powerful. As Fanon (1963, 1965) argues, black inferiority was not a given but a creation of white supremacy.

Second, the African-centred school is usually read as a race-based schooling approach. In conventional society, anything that reifies race or even alludes to race is seen as "creating a problem." That race speaks to an experiential reality, is about a socio-historical condition, and has a materiality is often denied, hence the idea that "colour blindness" is seen as the "beat" thing to do. The fact of the matter is that race is an integral part of the organization of North American society. In the US context, Guinier (2004) cites the Constitution as built on race hierarchies. In Canada, we see the process of colonization and racialization as connecting state, nation, and race.

Third, "separation" and "integration" are often and uncritically presented as opposite sides of the proverbial coin! As already noted and as shown in history, for blacks and racially minoritized bodies, sometimes strategic separation is a matter of survival. Such is "survival" in a search for a correct path of social integration. Such a reading emerges when we are bold to question what, when it comes to the education of our children, African Canadians have to show for integration.

Next, throughout history, black and African peoples have been at the forefront of civil and human rights struggles without necessarily benefitting from the changes. Other racialized groups, including women, have stood to gain more, and yet, black and African people may have borne the brunt of the hard work of collective struggles and sacrifices. Such developments have not been challenged or found to create any discomfort or dissonance on the part of the dominant group because of an idea that black peoples' rights are dispensable. In other words, in this case, black rights (e.g., freedom of association) can be sacrificed for the common good (e.g., the dominant group's need for an integrated society). In fact, this notion fails to accommodate how black agency comes to fruition. Through these moments of coming together, black agency emerges to either create a collective awareness and consciousness and to resist and/or to think out solutions and answers to our own problems.

In addition, there is a political agenda that conflates distinctive struggles through the belief or argument that involved parties share common interests. It is a sense of shared common interests of the different parties in struggle, a belief that there is an interest convergence here and that the question of power and social difference can be muted. So, for example, the interests of blacks for equality converges with the interests of whites. Yet, how do we explain white working-class racialism?

Furthermore, there is clear evidence that, even in a supposedly inclusive/integrated school, there are differential outcomes for different bodies defined along lines of race, ethnicity, gender, class, sexuality, and disability. In other words, desegregation cannot be seen as an end in itself. Rather, we must see desegregation and inclusion as means to an end. The end should be about how we come to share power and address inequities to create fairness of opportunity and outcomes for all groups.

Also, the overzealous focus on the ills of "Separate as Unequal" has helped create a situation over time where there has been no counter/oppositional healthy discourse on the merits of a "Different but Equal" argument. Separation was and is morally indefensible, so that's the end of the story. A critical discussion of the relative benefits of separate schooling and integrated education for black youth could, but has not, been entertained. It is seen as an immoral stance. So the main attention has been on ending separation rather than on removing the systemic and structural conditions of unequal resourcing and power. We must be bold to ask how desegregation addresses the systemic problems of racism, racial hierarchies, and class inequity.

Finally, rights discourses have the potential to influence social policy, but there are also important limits of legal discourses. This realization necessitates asking what really accounts for the failure of Brown v. Board of Education in meeting the promise of enhancing education for all youth. As Ferri and Connor (2005) long ago showed, Brown v.

Board of Education was a legal document that failed to anticipate the schools' uncanny ability to impose other forms of segregation (e.g., streaming/tracking, special education, etc.). The court's ruling also failed to recognize the fact that there are powerful vested interests bent on maintaining the status quo and that these interests would evoke their power to resist change. Today we continually witness the "hyper-segregation" in our schools (Ladson-Billings 1994).

As I have argued in other works, it will only be a partial reading to argue that public resistance and controversy with African-centred schools in Ontario and Canada are due to a lack of critical reading around such questions as separation, segregation, inclusion, and integration in schooling. Particularly in Ontario, the whole question of "focus and separate schooling" has brought to the fore the issue of funding for public schooling and other religious schools. Funding religious schools presents a marked difference between a publicly funded African-centred education and publicly funded Catholic schools. For one thing, at present and, for quite some time, one is funded while one is not! Some public resentment and anger greeted the first African-centred pilot school, which was publicly funded through the Toronto District School Board, when it opened its doors for junior kindergarten to grade 6 learners at the Sheppard Public School in September 2009.

It is important to stress that an African-centred approach to schooling is a specifically pedagogical undertaking, with approaches to history, civics, and humanities that are much more in keeping with public schools than that of Catholic schools. Catholic and religious-based schools teach a particular religious dogma to serve sacred interests. As noted, the call for, and creation of, an African-centred school are the result of a demonstrable failing and shortcoming of the current system. The school aims to create success where there is a noted and tangible lack thereof. Catholic schools support a particular philosophy, while African-centred schooling is geared to support particular, interested students. The topics (history, languages, math, science, etc.) and teachings (respect, community, accountability, critical thinking, etc.) in the African-centred school are not ideological in the same way that those of religious education are. While we have a raging current and historical debate around the separation of church and state, we do not have a public push to exclude the values and teachings extolled by African-centred education from the public discourse. We can ask, then, what each approach does to benefit our communities and our children. Who suffers in the absence of each? African-centred schooling is not about politics as much as it is about our children. It is not about ideology as much as it is about inclusivity.

Now and historically, parents, communities, and students clearly have different ideas about what they understand as the purposes and proper contents of education. Obviously, spirituality is something that many feel has a place, at some level, in education. This should not be ignored. The point is that we know the boards and ministry are capable of providing education that takes different forms, works with different ways of knowing and believing, and works with the needs and expectations of various communities. It is the enhancement of these provisions towards which we should all be working.

ACKNOWLEDGMENTS

I would like to acknowledge the anonymous contributions of the reviewers of the article for their additional insights. Special thanks to Raneem Azzam for reading, commenting on, and helping revise an earlier draft of this chapter.

REFERENCES

Alfred, T., and J. Corntassel. 2005. "Being Indigenous: Resurgences against Contemporary Colonialism." *Government and Opposition*. Accessed 2 June 2005. http://web.uvic.ca/igov/uploads/pdf/Being%20Indigenous %20GOOP.pdf.

Brathwaite, K., and C. James. 1996. *Educating African-Canadians*. Toronto: James Lorimer.

Canadian Alliance of Black Educators (CABE). 1992. *Sharing the Challenge, I, II, III: A Focus on Black High School Students*. Toronto: Canadian Alliance of Black Educators.

Dei, G.J.S. 1993. "Narrative Discourses of Black Parents and the Canadian Public School System." *Canadian Ethnic Studies* 25(3): 45–65.

– 1995. "Examining the Case for African-Centred Schools in Ontario." *McGill Journal of Education* 30(2): 179–98.

– 2008. *Racists Beware: Uncovering Racial Politics in Contemporary Society*. Rotterdam, The Netherlands: Sense Publishers.

– ed. 2010. *Learning to Succeed: The Challenges and Possibilities of Educational Development for All*. New York: Teneo Press.

– 2014. "A Prism of Educational Research and Policy: Anti-Racism and Multiplex Oppressions". In *Politics of Anti-Racism Education: In Search of Strate-*

gies for Transformative Learning, edited by G.J.S. Dei and Mairi McDermott, 15–28. New York: Springer.

Dei, G.J.S., and A. Kempf. 2013. *New Perspectives on the African-Centred Schooling in Canada.* Toronto: University of Toronto Press.

Duncan-Andrade, J.M.R., and E. Morrell. 2008. *The Art of Critical Pedagogy: Possibilities for Moving from Theory to Practice in Urban School.* New York: Peter Lang.

Fanon, F. 1963. *The Wretched of the Earth.* New York: Grove Press.

– 1967. *Black Skin, White Masks.* New York: Grove Press.

Ferri, B.A., and D.J. Connor. 2005. "Tools of Exclusion: Race, Disability, and (Re)segregated Education." *Teachers College Record* 107(3): 453–74.

Friedland, R., and R.R. Alford. 1991. "Bringing Society Back In: Symbols, Practices, and Institutional Contradictions." In *The New Institutionalism in Organizational Analysis*, edited by W.W. Powell, and P.J. DiMaggio, 232–63. Chicago: University of Chicago Press.

Guinier, L. 2004. "From Racial Liberalism to Racial Literacy: Brown v. Board of Education and the Interest-Divergence Dilemma." *The Journal of American History* 91(1): 92–118.

hooks, b. 1992. *Black Looks: Race and Representation.* Boston: South End Press.

Kerr, L. 2005. Personal communication. Department of Sociology and Equity Studies, Ontario Institute for Studies in Education of the University of Toronto. 14 July.

Kerr, M. 2009. "Just Out: Ontario's New 'Equity and Inclusive Education Strategy – April, 2009.'" Email correspondence to "Colour of Change Network." Toronto, 6 April.

King, A. 2002. *Double Cohort Study: Phase 2 Report.* http://www.edu.gov.on.ca/eng/document/reports/dcohortp2.html.

– 2003. *Double Cohort Study: Phase 3 Report.* http://www.edu.gov.on.ca/eng/document/reports/phase3/.

King, J. 2005a. *Black Education: A Transformative Research and Action Agenda for the New Century.* New Jersey: Lawrence Erlbaum.

– 2005b. "A Transformative Vision of Black Education for Human Freedom." In *Black Education: A Transformative Research and Action Agenda for the New Century*, 3–17. New Jersey: Lawrence Erlbaum.

Ladson-Billings, G. 1994. *The Dreamkeepers: Successful Teachers of African American Children.* San Francisco: Jossey-Bass.

Lawrence, B., and E. Dua. 2005. "Decolonizing Antiracism." *Social Justice* 32(4): 120–43.

Levin, B. 2004. *Students at Risk: A Review of Research Prepared for Toronto Learning Partnership.* http://www.thelearningpartnership.ca.

Levin, M.H. 2002. "A Comprehensive Framework for Evaluating Educational Vouchers." *Educational Evaluation and Policy Analysis* 24(3): 159–74.

Mills, C. 1998. *Blackness Visible: Essays on Philosophy and Race.* Ithaca: Cornell University Press.

Sharma, N., and C. Wright. 2009. "Decolonizing Resistance, Challenging Colonial States." *Social Justice* 35(3): 120–38.

Shujaa, M. 1994. *Too Much Schooling, Too Little Education: A Paradox of Black Life in White Societies.* Trenton, NJ: Africa World Press.

– 1996. *Beyond Desegregation: The Politics of Quality in African American Schooling.* Thousand Oaks, CA: Corwin Press.

Smith, A. 2010. "Indigeneity, Settler Colonialism and White Supremacy." *Global Dialogue* 12 (2): 113–24.

Trask, H. 1991. "Coalition-Building between Natives and Non-Natives." *Stanford Law Review* 43(6): 1197–213.

Valencia, R. 1997. *The Evolution of Deficit Thinking: Educational Thought and Practice.* Washington: The Falmer Press.

Waldron, J. 2003. "Indigeneity? First Peoples and Last Occupancy." *The New Zealand Journal of Public and International Law* 1:55–82.

Contributors

ALI A. ABDI is professor of education and dean of the Department of Educational Studies at the University of British Columbia. Previously he served as professor of education and co-director of the Centre for Global Citizenship Education and Research (CGCER) at the University of Alberta. His areas of research include citizenship and human rights education; social and cultural foundations of education; and postcolonial studies in education. His recent co-edited/co-authored books include *Education and the Politics of Difference*, *The Dialectics of African Education and Western Discourses*, *Decolonizing Philosophies of Education*, and *Educating for Democratic Consciousness*.

PAUL R. CARR is associate professor in the Departments of Sociology and Interdisciplinary Studies at Lakehead University in Orillia, Canada. His research is broadly focused on social justice and political sociology, with specific linkages to the areas of democracy, peace, media literacy, and transformational change in education. His publications include one single-author book, nine edited books, and a number of articles and book chapters. He is the co-founder and co-director of the Global Doing Democracy Research Project. In 2012, his research was recognized with Lakehead University's Contribution to Research Award, and his books have won several awards, including the Critic's Choice Award from the American Education Studies Association. Dr Carr speaks English, French, and Spanish, and undertakes research with colleagues in a number of countries.

AFUA COOPER is a leading historian of Black Canada, and a foremost scholar of Canadian slavery. She earned her PhD in African Canadian history and the history of the African Diaspora at the University of

Toronto. Dr Cooper has done groundbreaking research on the eighteenth- and nineteenth-century Black histories of Canada. Areas of expertise include slavery and abolition, gender, education, Black Atlantic studies, and Black literatures and culture. Publications including award-winning works such as *The Hanging of Angelique: The Untold Story of Canadian Slavery and the Burning of Montreal*, and *We're Rooted Here and They Can't Pull Us Up: Essays in African-Canadian Women's History*. In addition, Afua has done extensive public history work. Exhibits she has curated or co-curated include *The Transatlantic Slave Trade*, *Enslaved Africans in Upper Canada*, and *Black Communities in British Columbia, 1858–2008*. Afua has also published in the areas of fiction and creative non-fiction. She is the James Robinson Johnston Chair in Black Canadian Studies at Dalhousie University. Dr Cooper's papers are housed at the Thomas Fisher Rare Book Library, University of Toronto.

HABIBA COOPER DIALLO is a youth author and women's health advocate. She graduated from high school in the spring of 2014. A recurring problem she faced in her high school education is the negative portrayal of Africans and the impact this has on the bodies of African Canadian students. She addresses these issues through writing and awareness building. "High School and the Black Body" is her first contribution to an academic anthology.

GEORGE J. SEFA DEI is professor of humanities, social sciences, and social justice education at the Ontario Institute for Studies in Education of the University of Toronto (OISE/UT). His teaching and research interests are in the areas of anti-racism, minority schooling, international development, anti-colonial thought and Indigenous knowledges systems. He has published extensively on African youth education, anti-racism, Indigenous knowledges and anti-colonial thought. In June of 2007, Professor Dei was installed as a traditional chief in Ghana, specifically, as the Adumakwaahene of the town of Asokore, in the New Juaben Traditional Area of Ghana. His stool name is Nana Sefa Atweneboah I.

BENEDICTA EGBO is a professor of education at the University of Windsor. Her research interests are interdisciplinary, and include minority education, social justice and equity issues, multiculturalism and multicultural education, teacher education, and education policy. She has published widely in these areas. She is the author of *Teaching for Diversity in Canadian Schools* (Pearson Education, 2009).

AWAD IBRAHIM is a professor in the Faculty of Education, University of Ottawa. He is a curriculum theorist with special interest in cultural studies, hip-hop, youth and black popular culture, social foundations (i.e., philosophy, history, and sociology of education), social justice and community service learning, diasporic and continental African identities, ethnography, and applied linguistics. He has researched and published widely in these areas. Among his books are *The Rhizome of Blackness: A Critical Ethnography of Hip-Hop Culture, Language, Identity and the Politics of Becoming* (Peter Lang, 2014); *Critical Youth Studies: A Reader* (Peter Lang, 2014, with Shirley Steinberg); *Provoking Curriculum Studies: Strong Poetry and the Arts of the Possible* (Routledge, 2016, with Nicholas Ng-A-Fook and Giuliano Reis); *Global Linguistic Flows: Hip-Hop Cultures, Youth Identities and the Politics of Language* (Routledge, 2009, with Samy Alim and Alastair Pennycook).

CARL E. JAMES teaches in the Faculty of Education and in the graduate program in sociology at York University, where he is currently the director of the York Centre for Education and Community (YCEC). He teaches courses on adolescents and schooling, and urban education; his research interests include educational equity for marginalized youth and the complementary and contradictory nature of sports in the schooling and educational trajectory of racialized students. His most recent publications include *Life at the Intersection: Community, Class and Schooling* (2012).

SAMSON MADERA NASHON is professor of science education, Department of Curriculum and Pedagogy, at the University of British Columbia. He researches ways of teaching and learning generally and, in particular, students' alternative understandings that have roots in cultural backgrounds and curricula. His research uses and elaborates primarily contemporary theories of constructivism.

CHARMAINE A. NELSON is an associate professor of art history at McGill University, Montreal. Her research interests include postcolonial and black feminist scholarship, race and representation, and the visual culture of slavery. She has published five books including *The Color of Stone: Sculpting the Black Female Subject in Nineteenth-Century America* (University of Minnesota Press, 2007), *Representing the Black Female Subject in Western Art* (Routledge, 2010), and *Ebony Roots, Northern Soil: Perspectives on Blackness in Canada* (Cambridge Scholars Press, 2010).

EDWARD SHIZHA is an associate professor at Wilfrid Laurier University in Brantford, Canada. He has published widely in refereed journals and contributed a number of book chapters in the areas of education and globalization, education and development, and indigenous knowledges in Africa. He has edited *Restoring the Education Dream: Rethinking Educational Transformation in Zimbabwe* (African Institute of South Africa, 2013) and was co-editor of *Indigenous Discourses on Knowledge and Development in Africa* (Routledge, 2013, with Ali Abdi) and *Indigenous Knowledge and Learning in Asia/Pacific and Africa Perspectives on Development, Education, and Culture* (Palgrave Macmillan, 2010, with Dip Kapoor). He has co-authored *Education and Development in Zimbabwe: A Social, Political and Economic Analysis* (Sense Publishers, 2011, with Michael Kariwo) and *Citizenship Educational and Social Development in Zambia* (Information Age Publishing Inc., 2010, with Ali Abdi and Lee Ellis).

MARLON SIMMONS is assistant professor at the Werklund School of Education, University of Calgary. His research interests include culture and leadership, intergenerational knowledge, and governance of the self. Marlon's research is grounded within the Diaspora and communicative network practices of youth.

GINA THÉSÉE is associate professor in the Department of Education and Pedagogy at Université du Québec à Montréal (UQAM) in Canada. Her research interests include the socio-educative issues related to Afro-descendants/heritage, anticolonialism, gender, inter/multiculturalism, race, epistemology, and critical pedagogy. She is co-editor for the French-language editions of the *International Journal of Critical Pedagogy* and the *Canadian and International Education Journal*. Dr Thésée speaks French, English, and Créole, and is involved in research networks throughout the francophonie. She is a co-investigator along with Paul R. Carr on a SSHRC-funded research project entitled "Democracy, Political Literacy and Transformative Education."

Index